Dictionary of Catholic Devotions

DICTIONARY *of* CATHOLIC DEVOTIONS

Michael Walsh

HarperSanFrancisco
A Division of HarperCollins*Publishers*

CONTENTS

For

Alexandra, Clare and Kate

to remind them

of what it once was like

INTRODUCTION

The idea for this book was born in the Senior Common Room of Heythrop College, University of London. A group of what can only be called religious professionals, mainly, though not only, priests and nuns, were talking about the curious folklore which surrounds those statues of the Christ-Child in the guise known as the Infant of Prague. It quickly became clear that none of us knew why there was such a statue: this volume is designed to answer that and similar questions about the devotional life of Christains.

What is meant by "devotion" is explained in this book in the entry under that heading. In essence I have taken it to mean, for the purpose of this *Dictionary*, the private pieties of individuals, and not those religious practices which are enjoined upon Christians at large by the requirements of the Catholic Church. Though individual religious orders are frequently mentioned, there is, for example, no entry for Jesuit or Dominican, for I take such bodies to be part of the formal structure of the Church. There are entries, on the other hand, for many of the numerous confraternities through which people, lay people mainly but to some extent clerics also, may express their own particular religious commitment. There is nothing on the mass as such, or on the divine office, for these, too, are part of the official daily life of the Church. I have, however, included many of the "feast days" and other solemnities drawn from the Church's calendar because I take it they have reached the calendar as a result of the devotional life of Christians.

When writing about the Church's calendar I became aware for the first time of how greatly it had changed because of recent reforms. Nowhere have I seen compared in detail the calendar as it was, say, in the early 1950s and that contained in the *Missale Romanum* for

7

1970. The differences between the two are enormous. In an appendix I have laid the two calendars out side by side, so that the differences can be clearly seen.

There have had to be some other omissions. The Church has officially recognized saints because, at least in theory, of the devotion which people have shown toward the men and women who have been canonized. There are, however, many excellent books which record the lives of saints, and to repeat those lives here would, I think, have been inappropriate. A few are listed for particular reasons, and a number of the historically more important patronages of saints have also been included. Again, as will be obvious if one reads the entry for "shrines", to have listed all the shrines, even in Europe, and to have said something about each of them would have turned this book into a gazetteer. A large number of the more popular ones have been included, but I am conscious of how many have had to be left out in order to achieve some sort of balance among the types of entry.

Compiling this volume would have been impossible without the resources of the Heythrop Library and, in particular, without the aid of a group of dictionaries, mainly in French, and mainly begun in the early part of this century but not yet finished. They are listed in the bibliography, and I would like to pay tribute to those who conceived them and to those who, over decades, have had the courage to continue their work. But time and again I found myself turning for help to the *Catholic Encyclopedia*, completed before the First World War, and discovering that I was reading an article written by the English Jesuit, Herbert Thurston. Reference to later sources rarely added much to, or corrected, what Fr Thurston wrote almost a hundred years ago. A collection of his pieces, for the *Catholic Encyclopedia* or for the Jesuit journal *The Month*, would almost have constituted a *Dictionary of Catholic Devotions* on its own.

Michael Walsh
Heythrop College

Dictionary of Catholic Devotions

Note to the Reader

References from within one entry to another are indicated in **bold** type. There are no other cross-references within the body of the book, but readers are advised to use the index to get full benefit from this *Dictionary*.

A

Aachen, the capital city of the Emperor Charlemagne, whose cathedral was originally the palace chapel. It now houses the **relics** of the Emperor, in a splendid gold **shrine**, and other notable relics which at one time made this one of the great **pilgrimage** centres of Europe. These relics include the **crown of thorns**, the loin cloth of Christ and his swaddling clothes, the dress of Mary and the dress of John the Baptist, all of them at one time displayed every seven years.

Absam, a **shrine** of the **Virgin Mary**, situated some six miles east of Innsbruck, Austria. On 17 January 1797 eighteen-year old Rosina Buecher believed she saw a face in the window of her house while she was sewing late in the afternoon. The face was serene, but with a tear on the cheek, and the head was covered by a veil. Rosina and her mother were convinced this was an **apparition** of the Virgin, particularly so when, the following morning, the face was still to be seen: it was witnessed by all the villagers. Pilgrimages began almost immediately, and miracles were reported. Just a month later, however, the Bishop of Innsbruck, believing the image to have been painted on the glass, ordered the pane to be taken out of the window. All attempts to remove the face failed, and on 27 March the glass was returned. On 24 June the image was enshrined on a side altar of the church of St Michael where it remains, in a glass cylinder 7" x 5" (18 x 13 cm), as an object of regular **devotion**. The room where the image first appeared is unused, and retained as a memorial.

abstinence, a word which in general means moderation, particularly in food, but in the Roman Catholic Church came to be identified with not eating meat on Fridays and on certain other days in the Church's **calendar** as a form of **penance**. In the early Church the laws of abstinence were severe, and included not just meat itself but other meat-related items such as milk products and even eggs. These were the provisions of the Council of Laodicea in the fourth century and of the Council in Trullo at the end of the seventh: in the Western Church such severity did not survive the Middle Ages, although for a time fish was certainly included under the law of abstinence and from the thirteenth century there was a ban on eating both fish and meat at the same meal during **Lent**. In the ninth century there was even a ban on clerics drinking wine on certain days, though this did not long survive. The days on which abstinence was imposed were Wednesdays, Fridays and, later and only in the West, Saturdays. These were days on which **fasting** was also imposed, and, as with fasting, the Saturday obligation was abandoned first - in the ninth century - and the Wednesday obligation in the eleventh. The rules governing abstinence have been steadily modified. According to the 1983 Code of Canon Law, fasting and abstinence are to be observed on **Ash Wednesday** and **Good Friday**. It is now left to local conferences of bishops to determine other days of fasting and abstinence. The Friday abstinence is no longer of obligation either in the United Kingdom or the United States.

acathistus, a word which in Greek means "standing" or, more literally, "not sitting", and is applied to a particular **hymn** of the Greek liturgy which is always sung standing up. The author of the hymn, which is in honour of the **Virgin Mary**, is uncertain. It is variously attributed to the Patriarch Sergius, to George Pisides the sacristan of Santa Sophia whose known works are similar in style to the hymn, and to the Patriarch Germanus. Modern scholarship tends to favour Germanus, and to accept the explanation that he wrote it to celebrate the defeat of the Moslem armies before Constantinople in 717-718. The hymn is extremely long, each of the twenty-four stanzas beginning with a letter of the alphabet, and it is sung by the Greeks on the **Saturday** of the fifth week of **Lent**. Its importance in the East has been likened to the role of the **Te Deum** in the West as a song of thanksgiving. It claims for Mary powers which, theologically speaking, belong only to God.

accountancy, the evangelist St Matthew has been cast in the role of **patron saint** of this profession since the Middle Ages because of his profession as a tax gatherer for the Roman administration in Palestine. For the same reason he has been formally recognized as the patron of tax collectors, as well as of customs officers.

acting, there are two **saints** who have traditionally been regarded as the **patron** saints of this profession, both of them thought to be early (c. 300?) martyrs but of whom little or nothing is known. St Genesius the Comedian is said to have been suddenly converted to Christianity in the middle of an anti-Christian burlesque performed in front of the Emperor Diocletian. St Vitus' association with the profession is even more obscure, though it appears to have arisen because of his **patronage** of a group of nervous diseases, of leprosy, rabies and Sydenham's Chorea - "St Vitus' Dance", a link for which it is also impossible to give any clear explanation. The connection with acting may be through the use of the word "dance", though it is a very remote possibility.

ad limina apostolorum (= "To the thresholds of the apostles"), an expression used in the early Church to signify a **pilgrimage** to the tombs of the apostles Peter and Paul in Rome. In modern times, however, it has come to be used of the requirement placed upon bishops to visit **Rome** to report on their dioceses. A Synod of Rome in 743 enjoined this obligation upon all bishops of the Roman province. Pope Gregory VII extended this requirement to all metropolitans of the Western Church, and it was imposed upon all bishops in the thirteenth century. Pope Sixtus V in 1584 said bishops near to Rome had to come every three years, those furthest away every ten, and in 1909 the time span was settled at five years. This remains in force in the latest Code of Canon Law (1983).

Adeste fideles (= "O come, all ye faithful"), a **hymn** now thought to have been written, and the music composed, by John Francis Wade (1711-86) who for a time taught Latin and Church music at Douai. It has been argued that the date of composition must be pre-1744. The best-known of the forty or so translations into English is by Frederick Oakley (1820-80).

adoration, strictly speaking the form of worship which is owed to God (in which sense it translates the Greek "latreia"), but is often used more widely of the veneration given to creatures. During the **iconoclast** controversy a distinction was made between "latreia" and "douleia", the latter being used of the veneration due to creatures, and this distinction was carried over into the West. "Douleia", or "dulia" as it is more commonly spelt, is again divided into dulia which may be paid to the **saints** and "hyperdulia" which can be paid only to the **Virgin Mary**.

Adoration of Catholic Peoples in Reparation, Pious Union of, an association founded in the church of St Joachim, in Rome, in 1883. This **confraternity** is under the spiritual guidance of the Redemptorists, who have charge of the church of St Joachim. Its purpose is to pray for the Church beset by so many evils, and to placate God's anger at the suffering of his Church by prayers. Members of the confraternity who live in Rome are expected to attend the **Forty Hours** devotion at least once a week to spend half an hour in prayer. Those outside Rome equally are expected to spend half an hour in prayer before the tabernacle on the day assigned - a different day of the week being assigned to members of different countries. On Sundays, for example, members in Italy, France, Spain, Portugal and Belgium carry out the **devotion**, while the remaining countries of Europe do so on Monday, North and Central Americans on Thursday, South Americans on Friday and so on.

Adoro te devote (= "Devoutly I adore you"), a **hymn** which used to be recommended in the Roman Missal to priests as part of their prayers of thanksgiving after saying mass, though no longer so in the new missal of Pope Paul VI. It is frequently attributed to St Thomas Aquinas, including in the old missal, but on no firm grounds. The earliest manuscripts which contain the hymn are no older than the fourteenth century, and the first biographers of Thomas do not claim it for his authorship. Some students of the Saint's writings also argue that the eucharistic theology is not Thomas's, though the matter is debated. There is some indirect evidence, on the other hand, that if it was not by Thomas himself, it must have been written about his time, for a work of Jacopone da Todi's seems to depend upon it.

Advent, the season of the liturgical year immediately before **Christmas**. In its earliest form it appears to have begun in Spain, with a **fast** to mark the approach not so much to Christmas as to the **Epiphany** as the day on which baptisms took place. But it appears also that this period of fasting coincided with the pagan holidays to mark the end of the year, and the first day laid down in the Council of Saragossa in 380 for the beginning of the fast was the festival of the Saturnalia. But as baptisms were not universally conferred at the Epiphany, an alternative explanation has to be found for the wide-spread practice of the pre-Christmas fast. At Tours in 567 such a fast was put as an obligation upon monks, and it was extended to the laity at Mâcon in 581. It seems likely that this fast was considered to be a pre-Christmas equivalent of the **Lent** fast: it was, indeed, called St Martin's Lent. Advent did not reach Rome until the second half of the sixth century, although long before there had been a celebration marked with a fast to solemnize the end of the agricultural year. This was a festival taken over from pagan Rome, and it was associated not with the nativity of Christ as such so much as the last fortnight in December.

Aeterna Christi munera (= "Let us sing of the eternal gifts of Christ"), the oldest known **hymn** for the **feasts** of martyrs. It is generally attributed to St Ambrose, and though some scholars put it in the fifth century rather than the fourth, the manuscript evidence and the language of the hymn correspond to what would be expected if Ambrose were to be the author. It was divided up, possibly in the tenth century, to provide hymns for other feast days, some lines being used at Matins for the feast of Apostles outside the **Easter** season, and others at Matins for the feasts of martyrs.

agnus dei, best known as a formula recited three times over in the Roman liturgy, but as a **devotional** practice it is a disc of wax on which there is the figure of a lamb - the words mean "Lamb of God"-

which is blessed by the pope. These discs may be derived from pagan amulets, but if so they were a long time in the development, for the earliest unambiguous reference to their existence is not until the early ninth century when they were being fashioned from the wax of the previous year's paschal candle. In earlier centuries fragments of the paschal candle had been used as charms against tempests and blight, so there may be in this a link with pagan charms. In the ninth century the wax was mixed with chrism, and the agnus deis were distributed the Saturday after **Easter** by the Archdeacon. Later the pope took over both blessing and distribution. The practice developed of popes blessing the wax discs only in the first year of the pontificate, and then every seventh year. In the prayers which accompany the blessings, mention is made of the agnus deis as protection against storms, disease, fire and flood, and as protection for women in childbirth. In Elizabethan times the import of agnus deis into England was expressly prohibited. One quite distinct form of agnus dei is a wax disc in which has been mixed dust from the tombs of martyrs, kept as **relics**.

Agonizing Heart of Jesus and of the Compassionate Heart of Mary, for the Salvation of the Dying, Archconfraternity of the, an association founded by a Jesuit priest, Jean Lyonnard, and formally established at Jerusalem in June 1864, being raised to the rank of an Archconfraternity five years later. Members of this **confraternity** cultivate a particular **devotion** to the **Sacred Heart** of Christ in Gethsemane, and to the heart of the **Blessed Virgin**, afflicted by the sufferings of her son. They also pray for the salvation of the souls of those on the point of death. They do so by fulfilling the requirement of spending at least half an hour in prayer each month for the intentions of the confraternity and for the dying, and by providing for masses for the dying.

Agua Santa de Baños, a **shrine** in Ecuador where a statue of the **Virgin Mary** has been venerated since the early seventeenth century.

Aigu, Our Lady of Mount, a **shrine** of the Virgin in Belgium and a centre of **pilgrimage** since the twelfth century when a statue of the

Virgin was set in the bough of a tree. There was an increase in the number of pilgrims from the fifteenth century, and the church which now houses the statue was built in the first quarter of the seventeenth century.

All Saints, the commemoration now celebrated on 1 November of all who have died with a reputation for holiness of life ("All Hallows"). The origins of this **feast** are obscure, though in some form (the commemoration of all **martyrs**) it may be as old as the middle of the fourth century, where it seems to have been kept at Edessa on 13 May. The precise day varied as the feast came to be observed elsewhere in the Church: the first **Sunday** after **Pentecost** being a preferred date both in the East and in the West. Nonetheless, when Pope Benedict IV was given the Roman Pantheon at the beginning of the seventh century to serve as a church, dedicated to the **Virgin Mary** and the martyrs, he chose 13 May for the occasion for the ceremony. The day was subsequently observed as a feast day, but whether it was chosen because 13 May was already the appropriate day in the **calendar** in 609 or 610, or whether it became the official feast thereafter is unclear. There is also a suggestion that it was chosen to replace the pagan festival of *Lemuria*, the placating of the gods, which was held in **Rome** on 9, 11 and 13 May. The 1 November date appears first in England in the middle of the eighth century, and there is a distant possibility that the dedication of a chapel to all saints in the **basilica** of St Peter's occurred on this date under Pope Gregory III (731-41). For whatever reason, the celebration of All Saints' Day on 1 November became the common usage, and the alternative 13 May date had entirely disappeared by the twelfth century. There is a completely different account of the origins of the feast on 1 November, however, which argues that it comes from Ireland to Northumbria and thence to the continent of Europe. The Celtic Winter began on 1 November, and the first of each month was reserved in the calendars for particularly important feasts so, it is suggested, the November date was chosen as one of particular solemnity. The feast was marked by a **vigil** (**Hallowe'en** or "All Hallows' Eve") very early on, but it was suppressed as a liturgical practice in 1955.

All Souls Confraternity, an association founded c. 1450 for Germans living in **Rome** by Johannes Golderer, an Augustinian. The statutes of the confraternity were approved in 1461 and in 1519 it was raised to the rank of an Archconfraternity. It is now known (in Italian) as the "Archconfraternity of Our Lady of the Pietà of the Germans and Flemings", and its members are devoted particularly to praying for souls in **purgatory**: the **feast** of **All Souls** is their major feast day.

All Souls Day, a **"feast"** commemorating all those who have died, in order to pray for their release from **purgatory** and passage to heaven. It is kept in the Western Church on 2 November, the day immediately following the celebration of the feast of **All Saints**, and on a variety of different days in the Eastern Churches. The 2 November date is thought to be the result of a decree by St Odilo (c. 962-1049) as abbot of Cluny, when he instructed that it should be observed as a day of prayer throughout the Cluniac foundations. He chose this date precisely as the day following All Saints, and his instructions were to pray for deceased monks, but the practice became generally extended. At the time of St Isidore of Seville (c. 560-636) the Monday after **Pentecost** was kept as a day of prayer for the dead, at least in Spain. The practice of each priest offering three requiem masses on 2 November seems to have begun among Spanish Dominicans in the fifteenth century, and, after papal approval of the custom in 1748 to have been extended to countries under Spanish or Portuguese influence. Its extension to the whole world came as a result of the First World War: one mass has to be said for a particular person or group, one for all those who have died, and the third for the intentions of the pope. The **toties-quoties indulgence** can be obtained on this day. Some of the superstitions surrounding this day have been transferred to **Hallowe'en**.

Alleluia, a Hebrew expression meaning "praise God", which was taken over, apparently from the Greek to judge by the spelling of the word, into the worship of the earliest Christian communities - its usage as a form of praise is evident from the text of the New Testament. At the end of the second century it was being employed as an acclamation, and under Pope Damasus (368-84), influenced possibly by St Jerome and by the practice of the church of **Jerusalem**, it had entered the mass. It was used only at **Easter**, but by the fifth century it was employed in the whole Easter season, and under St Gregory the Great's pontificate (590-604) it was used throughout the year except in penitential seasons such as **Lent**. It is now used as a form of **antiphon** to a verse of a psalm, but it is not clear when this custom began.

alms and almsgiving, a devotional practice of Christians from the earliest days of the Church, and witnessed to, in quite practical ways, both in the Pauline letters and in the Acts of the Apostles. By the end of the first century Clement of Rome was writing to the Church at Corinth that almsgiving was better than either **fasting** or prayer as a penance for sin. Justin Martyr records in the middle of the second century that gifts were brought to the Sunday worship and given to the bishop for the benefit of the poor. The task of distributing these gifts was then handed over to deacons and deaconesses, under the supervision of the bishop. There were categories for whom special arrangements were made, widows and orphans, and those Christians held captive or sent to work in the mines. Although it was the task of the deacons to visit prisoners, all individuals were encouraged to do so, and efforts were frequently made to ransom them. The sick were also visited, and the dead were buried—those who had died in poverty were interred at the expense of the community.

Because Christianity was from the beginning a "catholic" faith, one which gradually took root throughout the Empire, members of one community travelled to another: hospitality to travellers was one of the early features of Christianity, as was the acceptance of one community of a member of another although the danger of abuse led to the introduction of a form of Christian "passport". As Christianity became more socially acceptable, and attracted wealthier converts during the fourth century, so the level of private benefaction to the poor seems to have increased. But so did the wealth which the Church itself had at its disposal for the benefit of the needy. It was able to construct houses for the homeless and hospices for the sick and for travellers. All this, however, reflects a basically urban Church. As the conversion of those who lived in rural areas progressed, authority had to be delegated to parishes, and this included responsibility for the community's charitable activity. Charitable giving, and the charitable institutions supported by the almsgiving of both clergy and laity, had varying fortunes in the Middle Ages, and were affected both by changing political situations and by the attempt of the nobility to dominate the Church. At the same time, however, the rise of monasteries for whom care of the needy was part of their way of life, according to the Rule of St Benedict, provided an additional source of support for the poor. The monasteries also provided guest houses, and not infrequently hospices for the sick, the aged, and beggars. In the high Middle Ages there were also various kinds of "hospitallers" founded as religious orders, for whom care of the sick and needy was part of their way of life. These were formal religious orders, but there were other **confraternities** of lay people often encouraged by such orders, particularly by the Franciscans and Dominicans, which undertook similar activities as works of **devotion**. Mention should perhaps be especially made of the pawnshops, the *Montes pietatis*, which were established to help the needy, and were associated in particular with the Franciscans.

The seizure of Church lands and the closing of monasteries, associated in some countries with the Reformation and in others with the climate of secularisation in the eighteenth century and most particularly with the French Revolution, put at risk the charitable works of the Church, though not of course of individual Christians. In the nineteenth century there was a great revival of religious congregations dedicated to charitable works as part of their way of life, caring for the aged, educating the poor and so on, but perhaps most important of all for the devotional life of individual Catholics was the establishment of the **St Vincent de Paul Society** which is now only one, albeit on a world scale easily the best known, of many organizations soliciting alms from members of the Church to support the needy, both in their own countries and in the developing world.

Alphonsus Rodríguez, Pious Union of St, a society founded in Palma, Majorca, to foster **devotion** to St Alphonsus Rodríguez, the Jesuit lay-brother who is **patron** of the island.

altar, the table at which the mass is said. In English-speaking countries since the Reformation it has been the practice to have the tabernacle on the altar for the reservation of the sacrament, but that was not the custom everywhere, or even in the English-speaking countries in the Middle Ages and down to the present day in cathedrals. The host was frequently hung above the altar in a pyx, or kept in a special "sacrament-house". The altar then became an object of **devotion** in its own right and used in a variety of ways. Oaths were taken by laying hands on the altar; contracts were exchanged or property conveyed by laying the document or some symbol of the exchange on the table; the sick tried to spend a night under, or on, it; knights-to-be laid their swords upon it the evening before they were dubbed; letters asking favours from God were often laid upon the altar - and some letters from him were alleged to be found there. Such practices were common in the Middle Ages: that of kissing the altar survived down to modern times, at least for the priest for whom, up to the reform of the liturgy after the Second Vatican council, eight kissings were prescribed in the rubrics. When they were allowed to approach it, the laity also kissed the altar and, dating from at least the end of the eighth century, monks and others living in monasteries would go round the altars kissing them, or at least the sanctuary or the pedestals of **statues**, before retiring for the night.

altar, privileged, an **altar** to which is attached a plenary **indulgence** whenever a requiem mass is said thereon, the indulgence to be applied to the deceased person for whom the mass is offered. If for any liturgical reason the mass cannot be that of requiem, the indulgence may be gained by whatever mass is permissible. In normal circumstances this privilege is, as the name suggests, attached to a permanent altar, but the privilege can also be attached to a priest, so that any altar at which mass is said becomes *ipso facto* privileged. On the commemoration of **All Souls** all altars are privileged in this manner.

Alttöting, a **shrine** of the Virgin in Bavaria. The wooden statue dates from the fourteenth century, but **devotion** to it began rather later, said to be 1489, when a small boy who had been drowned was miraculously raised to life through his mother's pleas before the statue. The shrine is particularly linked to the Wittelsbach family, the ruling family of Bavaria.

Amen, a word frequently used in Scripture to mean "so it is", or "it is ratified". Thus when Christ uses Amen to introduce a statement it means "this is certain" or "on divine authority". It was used in the synagogues to acknowledge a prayer said by the rabbi, and this usage was taken over into Christianity, first of all as a response of the hearers to a prayer, but only slightly later (by the middle of the second century), it would seem, used by the person praying. By the end of the fourth century, it would seem, in the liturgy it was the priest who used the term more frequently than the congregation. The congregation, however, had two very particular occasions when it responded with an Amen: at the end of the eucharistic prayer (the canon of the mass), which was not broken at the saying of the words of institution "This is my body ... This is my blood", but continued through to the **doxology**. The other occasion was, and is, on receiving communion. These practices, likewise, are very ancient, dating at least from the second century in the case of the Amen at the doxology, and from the third in the other instance.

Amiens, a city in northern France which was renowned in the Middle Ages for the **relic** of the head of St John the Baptist, transported there from Constantinople in 1206. It is traditionally the place where St Martin of Tours (c. 316-97), while a soldier serving in the Roman army, divided his cloak with a beggar. A chapel marked the spot which, in 1073, became the Abbey of St Martin aux Jumeaux.

anchor, a symbol used in earliest Christianity to signify hope: it is to be found in the Epistle to the Hebrews 6:19 where it clearly indicates security. It was frequently used in the catacombs, sometimes associated with the other common symbol of fish. The **cross** was not used in early Christian art, but the cross-piece and shaft of the anchor were sometimes drawn in such a way as to suggest a cross. Use of the symbol died out in the fourth century.

anchorite. a word which etymologically means one who has withdrawn from the world, and therefore is no different from "hermit". As time went on, however, usage has divided the two meanings so that a hermit is someone who withdraws physically to some distance from habitation, while an anchorite lives with close links to a community. In the Middle Ages anchorites sometimes lived in cells built against the sides of churches.

Andacollo, a **shrine** of the **Virgin Mary** in the Chilean Andes. Its origins are obscure, though **devotion** to Our Lady of the **Rosary** is attested there as early as 1575. The present cedar-wood statue, some three feet tall, seems to have arrived there in the latter part of the seventeenth century, after 1668.

angels, intermediate beings of a wholly spiritual nature between God and humankind. As such they are to be found in many religions and appear frequently in both the Old Testament and the New in a variety of roles, coming to a high point in the Book of Revelation. Though there is no doubt that the early Christians believed in their existence, little was written about them, apart from the *Celestial Hierarchy* of the Pseudo-Dionysius (c. 500). This work, drawing on references to the names of the angelic "choirs" to be found in the Old Testament and in St Paul, fixed the order of nobility of the angels as, in descending order: Seraphim, Cherubim and Thrones; Dominations, Virtues and Powers; and Principalities, Archangels and Angels. Only the last two groups had direct contact with people.

The nature of angels was much debated by the medieval theologians, but there was general agreement that they were created at the same time as the creation of the world, and that they were put to a test, which some of them (the devils) failed. In the early Church **devotion** to the angels was problematic. St Paul was eager to demonstrate Christ's superiority to angels, and the notion that there were spiritual intermediaries through whom it was necessary to pass before reaching God was a belief which the Fathers of the Church had to combat. But the opposite was also true: it was necessary to acknowledge belief in angels lest the Christians appear to be atheists. There were a number of roles assigned to them in apocryphal writings, almost always concerned with death. Thus angels help the soul to escape peacefully from the body; they watch over the dead; they accompany the soul; they "weigh" the soul, and they sometimes fight over borderline cases with the devil.

The first angel to have had a chapel and a mass dedicated to him was St Michael, and it may have been this mass which inspired Alcuin (c. 735-804) to compose a "mass to obtain the prayers of angels", which he ascribed for use in his Sacramentary to Tuesdays. Other similar masses began to appear in similar collections of liturgical formularies, and by the middle of the ninth century there was a straightforward "mass of the angels" (*missa de angelis*). Among the angels St Michael has always kept the most prominent place, but a mass of St Gabriel appears at Paris in the thirteenth century, and by the fifteenth a day had been fixed for the celebration of his **feast**, variously 18 March and 3 December. St Raphael emerged only slightly later, his feasts being kept on 8 July and 6 and 13 October. The cult of the angels underwent considerable development in the sixteenth century and in 1561 Pope Pius IV consecrated Michelangelo's church in the Baths of Diocletian to Mary and the Seven Archangels. Gabriel's feast was eventually fixed for the day before the **Annunciation**, and Raphael's to 24 October. St Michael had two feasts: on 8 May was celebrated his appearance on Monte Gargano, and on 29 September the **dedication** of his church in Rome.

Angels, Our Lady of the, a small chapel dedicated to St Mary of the Angels is enclosed within the **basilica** near Assisi - it is one to which, according to tradition, St Francis had great **devotion**. As a consequence the Franciscans celebrated a **feast** of Our Lady of the Angels on 2 August. It was on 2 August in 1636 that an Indian in what is now Costa Rica found a stone statue of the **Virgin Mary** carrying the child. Every time he tried to move it from the place of its discovery near the city of Cartago it moved back again. A **shrine** was eventually built on the spot, and Mary under this title - chosen because of the day it was found - became the **patron** of Costa Rica.

Angelus, a prayer which traditionally has been repeated three times a day, at morning, noon, and evening, at the ringing of a **bell**. It takes its name from the opening word of the prayer in Latin: *Angelus Domini nuntiavit Mariae*, "The angel of the Lord declared unto Mary". It continues, "And she conceived by the Holy Spirit ... And the Word was made flesh and dwelt among us". A **Hail Mary** is recited after each of these three verses. It is in the triple recitation of the Hail Mary that the origin of this **devotion** would appear to lie, though there is just a possibility that it was linked to the sounding of the curfew bell: Pope Gregory IX (1227-49) is thought to have instructed people to pray for the success of the Crusades at the ringing of the town bell for curfew. By 1269, however, the Franciscans were being exhorted by St Bonaventure to encourage lay people to say the three Hail Marys when the bell was rung for Compline: there was a popular belief that the **Annunciation** took place at about the time Compline was celebrated. It may be that these three Hail Marys were regarded as a lay equivalent of a series of three prayers which monks were accustomed to say after Compline, before Matins and at Prime, sometimes at least, it would seem, to the sound of a triple peel on a bell. The practice of saying these prayers in the evening had become widespread in Europe by the fourteenth century, and as early as 1318 there is evidence in the city of Parma of a bell being rung in the morning (i.e., around the time of Prime), citizens being encouraged on hearing it to say three Hail Marys for peace. This may well have been in imitation of the evening prayer. The midday prayer seems to have had a rather different history. When it first appears at the Synod of Prague in 1386 the bell was rung, and the prayers said, only on Fridays, and quite clearly in commemoration of the Passion (sixteenth-century prayer books which print the Angelus occasionally recommend an alternative form, associated with the Passion, for the midday Angelus). It spread gradually to other days of the week (Pope Callistus III asked for prayers throughout the world in this manner for victory over the Turks in 1456) and eventually lost its distinctiveness. Though the form of the three verses and the Hail Marys first appeared in the mid-sixteenth century, the version as it is now recited does not appear before the second decade of the seventeenth. At about that time the substitution of the *Regina Caeli* for the Angelus at **Easter** time was recommended, and finally became the rule.

Anima Christi, a **prayer**, commonly, though inaccurately, attributed to St Ignatius Loyola. The Saint quotes and recommends it in his *Spiritual Exercises*, but it was certainly in existence long before his time: the earliest indisputable reference appears to be from Germany in the mid-fourteenth century, though the prayer itself must be older and is possibly from a Dominican source. Even the earliest versions are remarkably like the formulation which we have today, though in the exact words in which it was known to St Ignatius it dates from the very beginning of the sixteenth century. In modern times it has become very popular as the **hymn** which begins, "Soul of my Saviour...".

Annunciation, the celebration on 25 March commemorating the announcement to the **Virgin Mary** that she was to be the Mother of Jesus, as recounted in Luke 1:26-38. The existence of this **feast** cannot be established before the Council of Toledo of 656, when it pointed out the problem of celebrating the feast on a date which occurs within **Lent**: St Ildephonsus of Toledo, who died a dozen years after the Council, wrote a mass for the Annunciation which was to be celebrated on 18 December. At the Council in Trullo in 692 it was declared that the feast could be marked on 25 March, despite its falling into the season of Lent. At just about the same time there occurs the first evidence, in the account in the *Liber Pontificalis* of Pope Sergius (687-701), that the feast was celebrated in Rome. It is clear from the Acts of the Council of Toledo that by the middle of the seventh century the feast was already being celebrated elsewhere than Spain, but where it began, and at what date, is uncertain. It is not impossible, however, that the feast goes back to the fourth century, and was celebrated in Bethlehem at the basilica which marked the place where the Annunciation was believed to have taken place. If that is so, it has to be explained why there is no mention of the Annunciation as a liturgical feast until the seventh century, despite the not infrequent mention of the Annunciation as an event. By the eighth century the feast was widely celebrated, though in some places the date of 18 December remained for a time. While it seems that the date of 25 March was settled by the date of **Christmas** - being nine months before - so simple an explanation is misleading because 25 March was long believed to be the date of Christ's death on the **cross**, and it seems that his birth and his death were marked on the same day in some ancient calendars. On this principle, the date of Christmas was in practice fixed by the date of Christ's birth, after it was decided to separate his birth and death, and not the other way round. The Annunciation was originally a feast in honour of Christ - of his conception - rather than of Mary: when it was established in Rome it was called "the Annunciation of the Lord". It was, however, observed as a Marian festival for over a thousand years until restored to its Christological orientation by the reform of the **calendar** in 1969.

Annunciation, Archconfraternity of the, a society or **confraternity** established in Rome in 1406 to provide dowries for poor girls. It afterwards became associated with the Dominican church of Santa Maria Minerva, where a chapel of the **Annunciation** was built, and where the dowries were distributed on the **Feast** of the Annunciation, sometimes by the pope himself.

Anthony of Padua, Pious Union of St, a society founded in the church of St Anthony, near the **Lateran** basilica in **Rome** in 1894, and under the spiritual guidance of the Franciscans, whose Minister General is its head. It exists to give thanks for the many gifts of St Anthony and to pray to him for all who are seeking the kingdom of God and who are in need, whether of body or spirit. Members of the **confraternity** pray particularly for the conversion of unbelievers and for sinners, for those in need and those who have suffered. As well as praying for them, members are required to give alms to the poor.

antiphon, literally, from the Greek, "sounding against", but generally used of one or more verses from a psalm which have been selected to draw attention to the meaning of the psalm or canticle, and sung before it. Though its earliest meaning appears to have indicated groups singing verses of psalms alternately, it had by the sixth century come to have the sense of a refrain. "Antiphonaries" were books containing such chants, and other melodies as well. The "Marian antiphons" are not antiphons at all, though they were originally sung in connection with psalms. Since 1239, by order of Pope Gregory IX, they have been sung as independent chants at the end of the Divine Office. They are the *Alma Redemptoris Mater, Salve Regina, Ave Regina Caelorum* and the *Regina Caeli*.

Aparecida (= "she who has appeared"), a title under which the **Virgin Mary** is revered in Brazil. This small, black wooden statue was found by a group of fishermen on the shore of the river Paráiba, at the port of Itaguaçu, Brazil, in 1717. The **shrine** built for the statue, not far from Sao Paulo, became a major centre of **devotion** and, under this title, Mary is the **patron** of the country. The **feast** of Our Lady Aparecida is celebrated on 11 May.

Apostleship of Prayer, Pious Union of, an association begun by Fr Xavier Gautrelet S.J. in the Jesuit scholasticate at Wals in the diocese of Le Puy, France, in 1844, but which quickly spread throughout the world. It exists to promote the glory of God and the salvation of souls through a programme of constant prayer, particularly to the **Sacred Heart**. It remains under the spiritual direction of the Jesuits, whose Superior General is its head, though it is organized on a diocesan basis. Its publication, *The Messenger of the Sacred Heart*, was at one time very widely distributed in a range of languages and formats. It listed the intentions for which members of this **confraternity** were expected to pray. There are different levels of membership. The first obliges individuals to make a daily "oblation" or offering of their "prayers, works, sufferings and joys" as one formula puts it, though no particular formula is prescribed. Together with the offering, they pray for the intentions of the pope, as listed in *The Messenger* or other publications. The next grade of membership is expected to add, at least once a month, attendance at Mass and Communion to the offering. The third grade undertake to say at least one decade of the **Rosary** each day. Above these are members who are called "zelators" whose task it is to promote the Apostleship of Prayer and **devotion** to, above all, the Sacred Heart. As this confraternity is concerned wholly with private devotion, members are encouraged to join more active organizations within the Church.

Apostleship of the Sea, an association founded in Glasgow in 1920 to look after the spiritual needs of sailors, and which received a papal letter of approval two years later, thanks to the good offices of the Archbishop of Glasgow. Centres for sailors were established, or designated, all over the world - by 1927 there were two hundred of them. The Vatican took over the supervision of chaplains in 1942, and ten years later a General Secretariat was set up in Rome.

Apostolate of the Sick, Pious Union of the, a society which seeks to unite Catholics who are sick with the person of Christ carrying his cross, so that they may learn to suffer with Christ, and that their suffering may be to the glory of God and the salvation of souls. It was founded in the diocese of Haarlem, Holland, in 1925, but quickly spread throughout the Church, in particular to North America. The regulations vary slightly from place to place, but all sick may be members.

apostolic blessing, a form of **blessing** given by the pope on solemn occasions, such as the *Urbi et Orbi* (= "to the City [Rome] and the World") blessing from the balcony of St Peter's after his election or on **Easter Sunday**. All bishops may give such a blessing on occasion, and all priests may administer one to the dying. To it is attached a plenary **indulgence**.

Apostolic Crusade of the Blind, a society founded by a Jesuit priest, Fr Mallat, in Lodi, Italy, in 1955, both for the spiritual guidance of those who are blind, and for the production of religious works in braille for their benefit. Members are linked to the **Apostleship of Prayer,** and are expected to pray for those "intentions" which are laid down for members of that association, and to offer their own affliction likewise. There is a membership fee, which is spent on producing books for the Crusade.

Apostolic Union of Diocesan Clergy, an association founded by Canon Victor Lebeurier of the diocese of Orléans in 1862, though it was inspired by the work of Bartholomew Holtzhauser who had formed an "Institute of diocesan clergy living in community" in Bavaria in 1640, an organization which lasted until 1804. Pope St Pius X, who had himself been a member, made the pope patron of this union in 1903, and it has since received many commendations from the Holy See. The purpose of this society is to bring together diocesan clergy under a freely-elected head, to pursue a common manner of life, and to lend each other mutual support and encouragement in their priestly ministry. The ideal is to have an association in each diocese, though in some instances one association has to cover a wider area. The obligations placed upon members include saying Matins and Lauds of the Office before they celebrate mass, and devoting time to meditation and spiritual and theological reading. They are also expected to spend a day each month in quiet reflection.

Apostolic Work of Jesus Christ the Worker, Pious Union of the, a society founded in the parish of St Clotilde in Geneva in 1916 by Abbot Julius Schuh to foster the conversion and sanctification of workers through the merits and example of daily work that was left by Christ during his hidden life in Nazareth. It is open to both men and women who are prepared to give their colleagues in the workplace an example of the Christian way of life, in honour of Jesus Christ the worker. There are three distinct forms of the organisation. Groups can be formed in a parish, or at a place of work such as a factory, or can bring together workers who share a particular trade or profession. In addition to pious practices, members are expected to be involved in Catholic action in some form, and to study and teach the social doctrine of the Church. Though the association began in Geneva it grew so rapidly that its headquarters were moved to Rome in 1928, and committed to the supervision of the Master General of the Dominicans.

apparition, in a religious context, the appearance of some holy figure, more often than not the **Virgin Mary,** to an individual or to a group of visionaries, accompanied by the communication of a private revelation, frequently of an apocalyptic nature, warning of disasters to come if some pious act is not performed or the world do penance. A number of such apparitions are recounted elsewhere in this book, but it would be quite impracticable to record them all. It has been calculated that there have been over sixty well-reported cases this century, two-thirds of them in Europe, and that there may be as many as an average of five such events reported annually, most of which do not give rise to any significant form of **devotion.**

Archconfraternities see **confraternities;** individual Archconfraternities are listed under their distinctive title, for example the Archconfraternity of the Blessed Sacrament is to be found under **Sacrament, Archconfraternity of the Blessed.**

Archsodalities see **confraternities;** individual Archsodalities are listed under their distinctive title, for example the Archsodality of Saint Joseph is to be found under **Joseph, Archsodality of Saint.**

Ars, a small town some twenty miles north of Lyons in France, and the parish of St John Vianney. John Vianney was born at Dardilly, near Lyons, on 8 May 1786 and spent a remarkably pious childhood and youth. After a period in hiding to avoid conscription into Napoleon's armies, he received the tonsure in 1811 and was ordained priest four years later. Two years after that he had become parish priest of Ars. As parish priest he set out on a campaign to raise the moral standards of his town, attacking blasphemous speech, drunkenness and dancing. He fed the poor and saw to the education of the young. He established a **shrine** to saint **Philomena,** but he himself, and his reputation as a confessor, attracted great crowds of pilgrims to the town even during his own lifetime. He was renowned for working miracles, but these he attributed to the intercession of Philomena. He found his work as priest of Ars stressful, and several times attempted to escape from the place, but died there on 4 August 1859. He was **canonized** in 1925, and made **patron saint** of diocesan clergy in 1929. His **feast** is celebrated on 4 August.

Ascension, the celebration of Christ's rising into heaven, forty days after the **feast** of **Easter.** The earliest evidence of its becoming part of the calendar seems to be at the beginning of the fourth century, when the Synod of Elvira rejected the attempt to resume the practice of **fasting** after the fortieth day of **Pentecost,** proponents of the resumption of fasting apparently arguing that at that time "the bridegroom had been taken away". The marking of the fortieth day as the feast of the Ascension is clearly mentioned in the *Apostolic Constitution,* but the exact date of that document is not certain: it is probably about the end of the fourth century. There are also mentions of it in sermons of around the same period by St John Chrysostom and others.

Ash Wednesday, the day on which **Lent** begins. The **fast** which marked the celebration of Lent was moved back at the beginning of the sixth century so that it would consist of forty days actual fasting, so it began on the Wednesday four days before the first **Sunday** of Lent. Certainly by the eighth century the Christian community in Rome was accustomed to make its way in **procession** to the first mass of Lent, singing an **antiphon** which contained the words "Let us put on sackcloth and ashes": the practice of penitents covering their

31

heads with ashes being well represented in the Old Testament. In Rome at this time there was, apparently, no distribution of ashes as such: this practice seems to have begun in the Rhineland, and the earliest evidence is from a liturgical book written in Mainz in 960. By the beginning of the eleventh century it was customary at least in England for everyone to receive ashes, and at the end of the century Pope Urban II made the practice universal. It did not become part of the papal ritual itself, however, until the thirteenth century. The words which accompanied the imposition of ashes in the form of a **cross** on the forehead (those with tonsures traditionally received them on the crown of the head) were "Remember that you are dust, and shall return to dust", but since 1970 the minister may say instead "Turn from sin and obey the Gospel".

ashes, as used in the liturgy, is a practice taken over from Jewish ritual: ashes and dust (very similar words in Hebrew) are taken to represent mortality and therefore mourning and penitence. Christian use in the same sense dates from at least the end of the second century. In the Middle Ages those dying were sometimes laid upon the ground and ashes sprinkled on them. The custom of sprinkling ashes on the head on **Ash Wednesday** is recorded in England in the tenth century, and was universal in the Church after the Synod of Benevento in 1091. They were also, of course, used for all those undergoing public penance. Ashes are used in Gregorian **Water**.

Asperges, the sprinkling of a congregation with holy **water** which used to be done before the main **Sunday** mass, and on other solemn occasions: the chant which accompanied this ritual is taken from Psalm 51:7, "Purify me with hyssop till I am clean, wash me till I am whiter than snow". Hyssop was a plant referred to in the Bible as being used for sprinkling water, and the original means of sprinkling in the Christian Church was likewise with a plant or leafy branch. The first mention of a special "aspersorium" does not occur until almost the end of the eleventh century, though the practice of sprinkling congregations in this way is mentioned by Hincmar of Rheims (c. 806-82). During the **Easter** season the "Asperges" chant was replaced by the "Vidi Aquam" (= "I saw water"), an antiphon constructed out of Ezekiel 47, with the first verse from Psalm 118.

Assumption, a **feast** of the **Virgin Mary**, now celebrated on 15 August, which commemorates her being taken up bodily into heaven. Evidence for this belief, which became a dogma of the Roman Catholic faith only in 1950 with Pope Pius XII's Apostolic Constitution *Munificentissimus Deus*, is traced back to a very slight hint in St Epiphanius, Bishop of Salamis (c. 350-403). The major development of this feast, however, came in the wake of stories of the **Dormition** of the Virgin dating from the late fourth or fifth centuries, which recount the finding of her empty tomb by the apostles who had been present at her deathbed. Jerusalem celebrated a feast of Mary the Mother of God on 15 August originally on the spot at which, by tradition, Mary had rested on her way to Bethlehem. However, towards the end of the fifth century the celebration was transferred to the **basilica** at Gethsemane where it was believed the tomb of Mary had been located. Epiphanius was from Palestine, and it is from that region that possibly the earliest firm assertion of the assumption comes, sometime between 550 and 650, in a sermon by Bishop Theoteknos of Livias, in which it is directly related to the apocryphal stories of Mary's death. In the West Gregory of Tours (c. 540-94) certainly believed in the assumption of Mary though other theologians of the time clearly did not. The feast of 15 August itself was introduced into **Rome** possibly by Pope Theodore between the years 642-9: it seems certain that it was the Assumption as it is now known which was being celebrated, although until the Gregorian Sacramentary of the 770s the name remained that of the Dormition.

As with the commemoration of other **saints**, it is the date of their death that is important, and on which they are remembered; likewise with Mary: the Dormition/Assumption becomes the most significant, and most popular, feast in the Marian **calendar** because it recalls the day of her death. Pope Sergius I (687-701) instituted a **procession** in Rome, celebrated by the light of torches, during which an image of Christ was taken from the **Lateran** and carried first to the Forum and then to Santa **Maria Maggiore**, where it was greeted by an image of Mary as *Salus populi Romani* (= "Salvation of the People of Rome"). (The procession survived a thousand years, being suppressed only towards the end of the sixteenth century by Pope Pius V.) Ambrose Autpert, a monk from Provence who ended his days - in 784 - as abbot of a monastery in Southern Italy, argued in defence of the feast exactly along those lines: if we celebrate the deaths of martyrs, how much more so ought we to celebrate the feast of the Queen of Martyrs. But this does not commit Autpert to a belief, which indeed he seems to repudiate, in the bodily assumption of Mary, only in the assumption of her soul. Though there was discussion of the appropriateness of the assumption of the body - because Christ's body, formed from Mary's, was already in heaven so it was fitting hers should be also - in so far as the basis for the doctrine of the bodily assumption remained the apocryphal stories which could not easily be reconciled with scripture, there remained doubt. At the beginning of the twelfth century, however, an anonymous treatise argued that since Christ could save his mother from the corruption of the tomb it was fitting that he would do so. Abelard (1079-1142) even went so far as to suggest, contradicting the apocryphal stories, that, although Christ lay in the tomb three days, he honoured his mother by taking her immediately to paradise. There were still some theologians in the West, fewer in the East, who were hesitant in asserting the bodily assumption, but belief in it became much more widespread, culminating in the declaration of the dogma, as noted above. Even so, Pope Pius XII was careful in what was asserted: the Constitution does not enter into the question of whether or not Mary died, or, if she did die, how long after her death the assumption took place.

Augustinian Friars, Third Order of, an association or **confraternity** of lay people living a life dedicated to achieving Christian perfection under the guidance of the Augustinian Friars. The Order to which they are linked claims a tradition going back to St Augustine of Hippo, but was created in 1256 out of several groupings of Italian hermits and given the Rule of St Augustine. The historical development of a **Third Order** of the friars is uncertain. It has been suggested that a chapter of the friars held in May 1300 refers to the existence of tertiaries: the first clear reference to them in a papal document occurs only in 1470. They have a particular **devotion** to Our Lady of **Consolation**.

Auxiliary Catechetical Work, Pious Union of, a society founded in Rome in the early 1950s specifically to bring young women and widows to the assistance of those teaching Christian doctrine to women, in order to release the clergy for work with men. Its members receive training both in the art of teaching Christian doctrine but also in the spiritual life.

Ave maris stella (= "Hail **star of the sea**"), a **hymn** used at Vespers on **feasts** of the **Virgin Mary**, though it seems it was first intended for the feast of the **Annunciation**. It is one of the greatest Marian hymns, and, unlike most of the early hymns of the breviary, it has remained in its original form. Who wrote it remains doubtful. St Bernard had been suggested, but as it appears in a ninth-century manuscript that attribution is now known to be impossible. A more likely candidate is the learned Paul the Deacon (c. 720-800), a monk of Monte Cassino. In its best-known English version the opening line is "Hail Queen of Heaven, the ocean's star".

Avioth, a town in north-east France which has long been a centre of **pilgrimage**, possibly as early as the eleventh century, and certainly during the Middle Ages. A wooden statue of the **Virgin Mary** in majesty is venerated in a church which dates from the fourteenth to sixteenth centuries. According to the legend, the statue was found by villagers who tried to take it to their own parish church, but it mysteriously returned to the place where it was discovered, thus indicating the particular spot where Mary wished the **shrine** to be built. A hexagonal lamp was built at the entrance to the cemetery, to provide light for celebrations which had to be held out of doors because of the number of the pilgrims. It is known as the "Receveresse", and freed prisoners were accustomed to leave their chains beside it. The shrine was regarded as particularly helpful to the insane and the possessed. During the eighteenth century the number of pilgrims declined considerably, but in the middle of the nineteenth it was re-established, taking place on the **feast** of Our Lady of **Mount Carmel**, 16 July.

B

bakers and associated professions such as cake-makers and millers have as their **patron saint** Honoratus, Bishop of Amiens, who is thought to have died c. 600 A.D. His **feast** is kept on 16 May.

Banneux, a **shrine** of the Virgin in Belgium dating from 1933. On Sunday 15 January that year, the twelve-year-old Mariette Beco claimed to have seen Mary while looking through the window of her parents' house. On the first occasion Mariette's mother prevented her child from going out of the house, but on the following Wednesday the apparition, having first prayed with the child, told her to plunge her hand into a spring and announced she was the Virgin of the Poor. The apparition was seen by Mariette a total of eight times, the last on 2 March, when she called herself "Mother of the Redeemer" and "Mother of God". The Bishop of Liège permitted **devotion** to Our Lady of Banneux in 1943, though without conceding that the Virgin had appeared to Mariette. This he did, however, in 1949, and the number of pilgrims thereafter considerably increased.

Baptism of Christ, a **feast** now celebrated liturgically on the **Sunday** following the **Epiphany**, although originally it seems, at least in some places (most of the Eastern churches), to have been identified with the Epiphany and observed in addition both as the feast of the nativity and as the beginning of the new liturgical year. Because of the theme of baptism, **holy water** was drawn - in Egypt from the River Nile - blessed (at least by the fifth century), and carried home by Christians in containers they had brought for that purpose. There is evidence that people thought of water blessed on the Epiphany as symbolizing the presence of the Holy Spirit in a similar manner to that of Christ in the eucharistic bread.

Barangay Sang Birhen, Pious Union of, a society founded in the diocese of Bacolod in the Philippines which exists to foster the spiritual life of its members, to bring people together for their mutual self-help, and to assist the poor. Members are encouraged to engage in Catholic action through joining other societies, and to say the **rosary** in family groups.

basilica, technically a form of building which was, until the sixth century, the standard type of Christian church. In Roman architecture it was a simple, though generally large, structure which might be used as an audience hall or law court, or even to hold markets. It was typically long and high, with a central area and aisles on either side divided from the centre by pillars. The end of the basilica opposite the main door terminated in an apse, in which there might be a tribune or dais. In modern terminology, however, the word "basilica" is applied to a number of churches of particular importance: the title can only be bestowed by the Holy See. **Rome** has a number of "major" basilicas, four of them traditionally entitled "patriarchal" because they are in theory the seats in the city of certain patriarchs: the **Lateran** (the patriarch of the West, the pope); the Vatican (the patriarch of Constantinople); St Paul's Outside the Walls (the patriarch of Alexandria) and Santa **Maria Maggiore** (the patriarch of Antioch). St Lawrence Outside the Walls was also assigned to a patriarchate - that of **Jerusalem** - though it did not become a "major" basilica. To these five patriarchal basilicas two more were later added so that there might be seven basilicas in Rome for a pilgrim to visit, and thereby gain a special plenary **indulgence,** instituted by Pope Pius IX (1792-1878, pope from 1846), provided the visits were made between the evening of one day and the evening of the next. These Roman basilicas are in charge of a cardinal, and their "college of penitentiaries" have especial authority to forgive sins. They can also grant indulgences by tapping a penitent on the shoulder with a long pole, which stands before the confessionals. Each of them has a particular door which is kept locked except during the **Holy Year.** To these major basilicas, Pope Benedict XIV (1675-1758, pope from 1740) added the church of the Franciscans at Assisi. In addition there are a number of "minor basilicas", a title granted to important churches as a mark of respect, and which grants them, or their clergy, some privileges, particularly in terms of precedence. There are eleven such minor basilicas in Rome, and a large number elsewhere in the Catholic world.

baths, cold, a form of mortification much employed as a remedy against temptations against chastity by Celtic monks, though not only by them. Lives of the Irish **saints** make frequent mention of their standing in cold ponds or even in tubs of water at night. Bathing in the waters of the lake around St **Patrick's Purgatory** was part of the ritual endured by **pilgrims** up to the seventeenth century, but this was eventually reduced simply to standing in the water on the edge of the lake. Records of saintly people undertaking such immersions continue on down to recent times, if not to the extent that the Irish monks appear to have done so. These were voluntarily-embraced penitential practices, but it seems that cold baths could also be imposed as penances for serious offences, though the evidence for this is slight.

Beauraing, a **shrine** of the Virgin Mary in Belgium. Albert Voisin, a 12-year-old walking with some companions to his sister's school, claimed to see Mary dressed in white and walking above a railway bridge on 29 November 1932. On 3 January the apparition identified herself to Albert's sixteen-year-old sister Fernande as "the **Immaculate Conception**, the Mother of God, the **Queen of Heaven**". The five children who had the visions described them in detail, and a statue was created following the descriptions and set up in 1946, though formal approval was given by the Bishop of Namur only three years later, after a number of cures at the shrine had been accepted as miraculous. The figure always appeared dressed in a long white robe, sometimes with golden rays around the head and, in the last apparitions, with a golden heart emitting rays at the breast.

Beguines, a spiritual movement for women (their less numerous male counterparts were called "Beghards") which began at Liège in Belgium c. 1170. The origin of the term is uncertain, though it has been suggested that it is derived from Lambert le Bègue ("the Stammerer") who may have been the inspiration for women to gather together in a form of devout religious life, without taking permanent vows, renouncing their property, or establishing formal religious orders, which in any case was at the time disapproved of. First formal approval of this new manner of life was obtained in 1216. Although at first Beguines appeared to have lived at home, or alone, convents began to develop, and by the middle of the thirteenth century it was more common to live in a community than outside it. Between 1250 and 1350 a hundred beguinages were founded in Cologne alone, which would have held up to a thousand members. They developed a mystical theology which, together with their relative independence of ecclesiastical structures, made people suspicious of them and contributed to their condemnation at the Council of Vienne in 1311. They survived in the Low Countries - and do so in small numbers to this day.

bells were obviously well known in pre-Christian times, but there is not much evidence of them in a Christian context until the sixth century. They were used to call people to church services, by missionaries to summon crowds, to rouse monks for the saying of the **Office** and other duties, such as attendance at the bedside of one of their brethren on the point of death. This last usage became particularly prominent and was extended to lay people, the "passing bell" being sounded while a person was dying and then again after death to encourage prayers for his or her soul. In the Celtic tradition they appear to have been treated with particular reverence, and after the death of their saintly owner were venerated as **relics**. By the eighth century they were regarded as indispensable items of church furniture. Bell towers began to be built to house them and blessings were instituted for them. Bells were pealed in medieval times for the **Angelus**, a practice which may have arisen out of the sounding of the curfew in towns, though the connection is unclear. It seems very likely, however, that church bells were often used to mark the curfew. The ringing of the bell at the elevation of the host during mass seems to have begun when the elevation became part of the ritual in the early thirteenth century. It was the big bell of the church which was used for this purpose in most places, though not exclusively: in England it is quite likely that a small hand bell was rung rather than the great bell of the church, though it is unclear whether this is the origin of the current practice of ringing a handbell at the elevation.

Benediction, a word which in origin simply means **blessing**, but came to be applied in particular to a **devotional** service, held most commonly on a **Sunday** afternoon or early evening, during which the Blessed Sacrament was placed in a monstrance, prayers said before it, a hymn sung (the *Tantum Ergo*, the final two verses of the *Pange Lingua*, being prescribed), and then the blessing being given with the monstrance. The prayers most commonly said were, somewhat incongruously, prayers to the **Virgin Mary**, either the **rosary** or the **Litany of Loreto**. This appears to reflect a twofold ancestry to the service. The elevation of the host at mass at the beginning of the thirteenth century encouraged a desire on the part of the people to see the host, and ceremonies began which accommodated this wish outside the context of the mass. The most common form of this ceremonial was the **Corpus Christi procession**, indeed so common had such **processions** become by the fifteenth century that legislation was required to limit them. In all probability the eucharistic element of the service derives from the **exposition** of the host at various stops on the route of the processions. The prayers have a quite distinct origin. Parallel with **devotion** to the host there arose the practice of **confraternities** gathering in the evening in front of a statue of Mary in order to sing hymns (*Laudes* or "praises"), to such an extent that, at least in Italy, special confraternities of *Laudesi* were established. In France, where the service of Benediction is still known as the *Salut*, by 1250 there had grown up a popular devotion of singing the *Salve Regina* as a form of evening prayer for lay people. The *Laudes*, *Salve Regina* or the Rosary were in a sense all alternatives for the laity to the singing of Vespers or Compline by monks and nuns. The coming together of exposition of the sacrament and the service to Mary seems to have occurred in the sixteenth century. The blessing with the sacrament, which forms the high point of the service with, traditionally, the ringing of **bells** and the use of **incense**, seems to have been added simply because there was a practice that the laity made the sign of the **cross** whenever the eucharist passed by.

Bermont, Our Lady of, a **shrine** of the **Virgin Mary** located a mile and a half from the birthplace of Joan of Arc, and to which the **saint** is known to have had a **devotion**. Its origins are unclear, though it is likely the chapel was originally founded at the end of the eleventh or - more likely - during the twelfth century not as a sanctuary for the Virgin but in honour of St Thiébaut of Provins. There is a spring, said to be miraculous, at the foot of the hill on which the chapel stands. The cult of the Virgin may possibly have begun when responsibility for the chapel was transferred from the Benedictine abbey of Bourgueil to the priests of the hospital of Gerbonvaux, dedicated to Mary. The statue of the Virgin, dating at least from the time of Joan of Arc, is of oak, and shows her crowned, with a sceptre in her right hand and the child Jesus on her left arm. The figure of the child is stroking a dove.

Blachernai, a **basilica** of the **Virgin Mary** located in the north-west corner of Constantinople, where there was a spring of water ("blachernai" indicates a place with a spring). It was the most famous of the Marian churches of the city, said to have been built c. 450 by the Empress Pulcheria. Leo I (c. 400-74, emperor from 457) is said to have deposited there the robe of the Virgin: a feast was kept in Constantinople in memory of this event on 2 July. Although the church was originally outside the city limits, after its survival, regarded as miraculous, during a siege by the Avars in 626, the walls were extended to encompass it. The church was twice destroyed by fire, in 1070 and 1434. The bathhouse which encloses the spring is now part of a modern church.

black madonna, images found in many of the **shrines** of the **Virgin Mary** which portray her as black - some one hundred and sixty-seven in Europe alone do so, according to one reckoning, including at such important centres of **pilgrimage** as **Montserrat, Loreto, Altötting** and **Rocamadour.** There is much dispute about the significance of this fact. In some instances it is certainly true that the present state of the image is accidental - due to age, or soot. In at least one case it would seem that the colour is a result of the oxidisation of silver with which the image was originally covered; in many cases the colour is simply the colour of the wood from which the statue has been made. As black is associated, at least in Europe, with the occult, and as images of one of the most famous goddesses of antiquity - Diana of Ephesus, from whom the cult of Mary is often said to spring - was regularly depicted as black, it has been alleged that Mary was either shown to be black, or that black images of her were given particular reverence, because in this way she was supposed to be more potent as a worker of miracles. Such a hypothesis is difficult to establish. There is little evidence that the colour of a particular image was the reason why it became a centre of pilgrimage: it has been pointed out that early accounts of the black madonna of Montserrat rarely refer to its colour, and copies were frequently produced in lighter tones. On the other hand, dark figures appear proportionately more than light ones, and appear to be in locations which have a pre-Christian history as holy places.

blacksmiths and other metal-workers and associated trades such as jewellers have as their **patron** St Eligius or Eloi who was Bishop of Noyon. He was born c. 588 and died on 1 December 660. His father was an artisan, and he himself, before becoming a priest, was a highly-esteemed goldsmith.

Blessed Sacrament, Adorers of, a pious union or association which was founded in 1887 by the founder of the Handmaids of the Sacred Heart of Jesus, and was subsequently established in every house of that Order. From 1944 girls who had made their **First Communion** and up to their fifteenth year were admitted as "Little Adorers". The purpose of the **confraternity** is to offer consolation to the **Sacred Heart** for insults offered to Christ by heretics and others; to amend for sins committed by those who take the name of God in vain; to pray for the safety of the pope and the Church; and to ensure that the Heart of Christ be better known. Members are required to spend an hour at least twice a month before the exposed Blessed Sacrament, and to undertake other **devotions** in honour of the Sacred Heart including, on the Feast of **Christ the King**, to take part in the solemn consecration of the world to the Sacred Heart.

Blessed Sacrament and the Sacred Heart, Pious Union of, an association originally founded as the **Confraternity** of the Blessed Sacrament in Nantes in January 1462. Membership was at first restricted to clerics, but after 1468 it could accept members of either sex and any status. Its seat remained located at the church of the Holy Cross until 1758, when it was transferred to the church of St Saturninus.

The confraternity of the **Sacred Heart** was joined to that of the Blessed Sacrament in July 1806. Members are required to insist upon the true presence of Christ in the Sacrament, go frequently to Mass, regularly to visit churches to pray before the tabernacle, to take part in eucharistic processions and in particular in the **Forty Hours** devotion, and to meet together to say certain prayers.

Blessed Sacrament, Archconfraternity of, an association under the spiritual guidance of the Dominicans, one of whom, Fr Thomas Stella, Prior of the Roman house of Dominicans attached to Santa Maria sopra Minerva, is generally credited with founding the **confraternity** at the church. However that may be, the Franciscans had promoted societies named after the Most Holy Body of Christ at the end of the previous century, and a confraternity of the same name and purpose was set up at San Laurentio in Damaso in 1501. When Pope Paul III came to issue his Bull on 30 November 1539 approving the Santa Maria sopra Minerva confraternity, he said that all other societies with the same purpose might enjoy equal privileges, providing they linked themselves to that of the Dominican church. A later Roman decree expressed the wish that there be a Blessed Sacrament Confraternity in every parish, a desire which found its way into the 1917 Code of Canon Law, and one which was very largely achieved. The purpose of the Blessed Sacrament Confraternity is to promote public **devotion** to the Holy Eucharist, regular visits to churches for private prayer before the tabernacle, and frequent reception of the sacraments.

Blessed Sacrament, Archsodality of Perpetual Adoration of, and of Work for Poor Churches, an association founded as an association in Brussels in 1848 by Anna de Meeus, and instituted as an "Archassociation" five years later. As a **confraternity** it seemed unlikely that its members could maintain the perpetual adoration to which they were pledged, and consequently a religious order was also founded, with Anna de Meeus at its head. The association moved its seat to Rome in 1879, and by a decree of 1895 other similar associations were able to establish links with it, under its title of an Archsodality. Its purpose is to promote **devotion** to the Sacrament, to make reparation for offences and injuries done to the Sacrament, and to support poor churches by providing all that is necessary for the mass. Members are required to attend **exposition** of the Sacrament, and to spend an hour each day before the tabernacle.

Blessed Sacrament, Confraternity for the Nocturnal Adoration of, an association or **confraternity** which began in Rome in February 1809, when a priest of Santa Maria in Via found that he did not have enough people to watch overnight before the tabernacle during the celebration of the **Forty Hours**. He therefore persuaded a small number of his lay friends to move from church to church as required to maintain constant vigil. The group grew in size, and formed a pious union among themselves. Among the intentions for which they prayed during their watch before the Sacrament was the return to Rome of Pope Pius VII, who had been taken to France as a prisoner of Napoleon. On his eventual return in 1814 Pius thanked the members of the pious union for their prayers, and granted them a number of **indulgences**, and it was the following year raised to the status of an Archconfraternity. The Vicar General of the pope is head of this confraternity, and it has three levels of membership: (1) those men, clerical or lay, of at least 22 years of age, who both attend the Forty Hours overnight and support it by donations; (2) those who only attend the **devotion** and do not give donations; (3) and those, with no limitation on age or sex, who support it only by giving donations.

Blessed Sacrament, Pious Union of, an association or **confraternity** under the spiritual guidance of the Fathers of the Blessed Sacrament, to promote adoration to Christ in the Sacrament. It was formally established by Bishop de Mazenod in Marseille on 17 November 1859, though almost a year earlier Pope Pius IX had granted indulgences to the association then existing in Paris. A youth section was begun, also in Marseille, in 1861. It became an Archsodality, to which others might be linked, by a Brief of Pope Leo XIII, dated 8 May 1897. There are three levels of membership. Members of the first undertake to spend an hour a month in prayer before the exposed Sacrament; those of the second are required to devote a week every three months to making visits to churches to pray before the Sacrament and to help towards the cost of preparing altars for **exposition** of the

Blessed Sacrament. The third group are required to attend mass and receive the Sacrament, to spend time before the Sacrament or, if that is not possible, an equivalent time in meditation, to engage in spiritual reading and, where possible, in the recitation of the **Office** of the Blessed Sacrament, and in the study of eucharistic theology and **devotion.**

Blessed Sacrament, Pious Union of Daily and Universal Adoration of, an association or **confraternity** which began in Turin in 1870, under the inspiration of two sisters, both members of the **Third Order** of St Francis, Teresa and Josephina Camoglio. It was formally established in Turin in 1892, received papal recognition in 1894, and allowed to extend beyond the bounds of Italy in 1909. Its purpose, which its members achieve through daily visits to pray before the tabernacle, is both adoration of the Blessed Sacrament, and reparation for neglect of **devotion** to the sacrament.

Blessed Virgin Mary Assumed into Heaven for the Assistance of the Souls in Purgatory, Archsodality of, a society founded in December 1840 in the church of Santa Maria in Monterone in Rome, a church in the charge of the Redemptorist Fathers. It was elevated to the rank of an Archsodality the following year. Its members undertake, by prayers and attending - or saying, in the case of priests - mass for the benefit of those suffering in **purgatory**. Members are required to pray first for those who have asked the support of the **confraternity**, then those who need greatest help, or have no one else to pray for them.

Blessed Virgin Mary Immaculate and St Aloysius Gonzaga, Pious Union of, a society founded by the Jesuit priest Vincent Basile and approved by Pope Pius IX in 1865. Basile was a missionary among the Southern Slavs, and was very disturbed by their indecent jokes and their frequent use of cursing and oaths. Members of this society - it was never technically a **confraternity** and could therefore be created by any priest wherever it was felt to be needed - undertake not to use either indecencies of language or blasphemies, nor to allow others to use them in their presence. Members wear a **medal** of the **Immaculate Conception** around their necks to remind them of their promises.

45

blessing, a calling down of God's power on a person, place or thing, usually through a prayer and often by means of the sign of the **cross**. The origins of the Christian tradition of blessing is usually thought to be the Jewish *berakah*, a prayer of praise and thanksgiving to God for his goodness, and to petition for his help. The aspects of thanksgiving and praise are particularly evident in the earliest Christian blessings, but that of protection from evil in the form of exorcism, or the driving away of evil, soon develops. Protection against the devil, however, was sought more through the prayers of a holy individual, a holy man or hermit or bishop, than through the prayers themselves. Later that protection came to be mediated through the **relics** of a holy person or saint, or indeed through any object upon which, by a prayer of blessing, the saint's power had been invoked. Simple things were frequently blessed, such as **water**, the presence of which in a household was believed to guard against illness or other evil. By the sixth century this had already developed into the requirement that all items intended for the cult should be blessed, which meant not only a driving out of the power of the devil from that object but also its setting aside for, or "consecration" to, a sacred purpose. This divided the world into sacred and profane areas which the earliest Christian, and the Jewish, prayers of blessing had never intended. In medieval times anything could be blessed, either to call down God's favour upon it, or to drive out Satan's power. This lasted down to modern times, though in practice blessings were more frequently applied to quasi-sacred objects such as **rosary** beads, **scapulars** or **medals**. Consonant with this sacred / profane division, blessings came to be restricted to the clergy. In the latest *Rituale Romanum* (1985), the notion that parents might bless their children, for example, has been revived, and it has been suggested that lay people might preside over certain blessings. The idea that anything might be blessed has been restricted slightly in the *Rituale* to those objects or occasions which might be expected to promote, rather than hinder, human and Christian growth: weapons of war are not seen as appropriate objects for blessing.

blood miracles, a collective name for a number of discrete happenings mainly in the region of Naples, though not entirely so, in the course of which a substance in a reliquary, claimed to be a saint's blood, appears to liquefy. The best-known example is the blood of St Januarius, preserved in the cathedral of Naples. Januarius (Gennaro) was bishop of Benevento and was martyred possibly about the year 305, according to fifth-century sources. The **relics** of the **saint** were brought to Naples in the early fifth century, but the earliest recorded occasion of liquefaction was not until 1389. The translation of the relics is celebrated for an **octave** beginning on the first Saturday in May; the **feast** proper on 19 September is also celebrated with an octave; and the proclamation of the saint as **patron** of the city is remembered on 16 December. On all of these occasions the relic is venerated, and is expected to liquefy. Of all the many similar instances recorded in the Naples area, none is as old as that of St Januarius, and most would seem to date from the sixteenth or seventeenth centuries. With the exception of two in addition to Januarius, all appear to have ceased liquefying. The two that continue to do so are St Pantaleone's blood at Ravello, from 26 July to 11 September, and St Patricia's, actually in Naples itself, at the church of San Gregorio Armeno, which liquefies every Tuesday. Pantaleone is said to have been a bishop, martyred at a similar date to Januarius, while Patricia is claimed as a niece of the Emperor Constantine, who fled to Naples to preserve her virginity when a marriage was arranged for her, and who died there a natural death: the blood came when a relic-seeker attempted to remove a tooth from her skull.

Blue Army, a lay organisation committed to prayer for the conversion of Russia, as requested by Our Lady of **Fatima**. It was founded in 1947 by an American priest, Harold Colgan, in fulfilment of a promise that he would make Fatima better known were he cured of the disease from which he was then suffering. It was called the "blue" army in contrast to Russia's Red Army, and because blue is the colour associated with the **Virgin Mary**. A million people had signed pledges to pray for Russia's conversion by 1950, and the organisation now claims a membership of many millions more. An International Headquarters was established at Fatima in 1956, and a statue of Our Lady of Fatima is taken from place to place each year to propagate the message of repentance, devotion to the **rosary**, and prayer for Russia.

Boldo, Our Lady of, a **shrine** of the **Virgin Mary** in the town of Concepción, 300 miles south of the Chilean capital of Santiago. Veneration goes back to the end of the sixteenth century, when it begin in thanksgiving for deliverance from the earthquake of 8 February 1570. Twenty-eight years later, when the town was attacked by Indians, it was saved, according to tradition, by the appearance of a young woman who held up the assault. This vision was held to be that of the Virgin of Boldo.

Boulogne, Our Lady of, a **shrine** of the **Virgin Mary** in this seaport of northern France. In 636 a ship, guided by angels, arrived at Boulogne from Antioch in Syria, carrying this statue and nothing - and no-one - else. Sailors of Boulogne carried the statue on their shoulders to the upper town where it was put first into a wooden chapel, and then into a succession of cathedrals built for it. The statue, sometimes also known as "Our Lady of the Ship", holds the Child Jesus, Saviour of the World, in its arms: it was much venerated throughout the Middle Ages and into modern times. During World War II it was carried around France and returned to Boulogne only after the Liberation. It therefore became known as "Our Lady of the Great Return".

Bourguillon, Our Lady of, a **shrine** to the **Virgin Mary** in Fribourg, Switzerland, located in what is said originally to have been a leprosarium just outside the city boundaries. The statue, which is life-size, is called locally "Guardian of the Faith" because the fact that Fribourg remained Roman Catholic is attributed to Our Lady of Bourguillon by the city's inhabitants.

boy bishop, a practice of electing a boy on the **feast** of St Nicholas to preside over a diocese or parish until the feast of the Holy Innocents (28 December). He was elected from the monastic or the choir school where one existed, and was dressed in pontifical robes. This custom seems to have been particularly prevalent in England and was abolished in the sixteenth century. On the continent of Europe it was abolished much earlier, at the Council of Basel in 1431, but was occasionally revived.

brandea, pieces of paper or, more commonly perhaps, cloth, such as handkerchiefs, which were lowered into the tombs of those who had gained a reputation for holiness, and allowed to touch their bodies, thus becoming a personal **relic**. Brandea could however also be a piece of the tomb itself, or even dust from around it, anything, indeed, which might have gained virtue by its proximity to the body of the saint.

bread, used in the liturgy of the Church is either leavened or unleavened, the former being used in the Eastern Churches, the latter in the Western: it is unclear which of the two Christ would have used at the Last Supper and it is agreed that there is no doctrinal issue involved in the use of one kind for consecration rather than the other. In the early Church a piece of consecrated bread, the *fermentum*, was sent by the bishop of Rome to the priests of the major churches of the city as a sign of unity, and from a bishop of any diocese to his clergy for the same purpose. The practice did not last long because of the danger of abuse of the consecrated host, but it was replaced by the sending of blessed bread to those who did not communicate at the mass. This bread, called *eulogia*, a word which simply means "blessing", was brought up to the altar at the offertory of the mass and blessed at that point, but set aside and not consecrated. It was then distributed at the end of the service. This was a fairly universal practice, but survives now only in Eastern liturgies. In the West, however, at least in some countries, bread was also blessed and distributed down to modern times, but with a separate blessing from that of the offertory prayer itself. The blessing used, and the point of the mass at which it is given, varies from place to place. In some monastic communities there was the custom of distributing bread blessed at mass in the refectory after the service.

Bread, St Anthony's, a pious custom of giving money to the poor under the patronage of the Franciscan friar, St Anthony of Padua (1195-1231) who was renowned for his service to the poor, and for his sermons against avarice and usury. "St Anthony's Bread" began in the middle of the nineteenth century, and in some places survives to the present day.

Bread, St Nicholas's, pieces of **bread** given to the sick, to pregnant women, and even to animals, and swallowed with water. It was claimed for St Nicholas of Tolentino (1245-1305) that he healed people by giving them pieces of bread over which he had invoked the **blessing** of the **Virgin Mary**. He is consequently frequently depicted with a basket of bread beside him. His **feast** day is 10 September.

Brezje, Our Lady of, a **shrine** of the **Virgin Mary** in Slovenia, where the first church dedicated to Mary was built only in 1800. At the time of the Napoleonic wars a painter, Leopold Layer, was imprisoned for forging money. He took an oath that, should he be released, he would paint a picture for the new church. He was released, and fulfilled his promise. By the mid century miracles were being reported, and the church became a place of **pilgrimage**. A new church was consecrated in 1900.

bricklayers, and all those engaged in the building trades, have had as their **patron** since medieval times St Stephen, whose death by stoning is recorded in the Acts of the Apostles. His **feast** is celebrated on 26 December.

bridges are under the **patronage** of St John Nepomucen (c. 1345-93), who was assassinated for withstanding the King of Bohemia, Wenceslaus. He was murdered by being thrown into a river from a bridge. St John's **feast** is kept on 16 May.

bridge-builders, associations or **confraternities** of which existed in the Middle Ages, particularly during the twelfth and thirteenth centuries. Even where none of these societies had formally been created, it was common for bishops to grant **indulgences** or other spiritual benefits to anyone who contributed to the building of bridges in any way. The bridges were obviously of assistance to travellers in general, but more particularly they helped those on **pilgrimage**, and some of the bridge-building confraternities seem also to have offered hospitality and collected alms for pilgrims.

Bromholm, a **shrine** of the True **Cross** which was located in the Cluniac priory of Bromholm on the northern coast of Norfolk. The

relic of the cross, itself fashioned into a small cross, was brought to the priory by an East Anglian priest who had served as chaplain and keeper of relics to Count Baldwin of Flanders who had, in the course of the Fourth Crusade, briefly become Emperor of the East. After Baldwin's defeat the priest returned to England with the cross and other relics (including two fingers of St Margaret), and the cross he eventually sold to the monks at Bromholm. Almost immediately the priory became a **pilgrimage** centre of considerable importance: King Henry III visited it in 1226, granting the right to hold fairs at the **feasts** of the **Exaltation of the Cross** and on St Andrew's day, which events substantially added to the income of the monks. There were many stories of miracles, and mention was made of the shrine both in *Piers Plowman* and in the *Canterbury Tales*. At the dissolution of the priory in 1537 the relic was removed, and disappeared.

brown scapular is the **scapular** worn by members of the **Confraternity** of **Our Lady of Mount Carmel**, and is the oldest such form of **devotion** dating back, as far as its use by the laity is concerned, at least until the fifteenth century, though tradition claims that the scapula was handed by the **Virgin Mary** to St Simon Stock, the English Prior General of the Carmelites in 1251. There is a promise to the wearer of the scapular, according to the story of the **apparition**, that he or she will undoubtedly be saved.

Bruges, an important and attractive town in Belgium much famed in the Middle Ages for its **relic** of the **Precious Blood**. This relic was brought to the city by Duke Thierry of Alsace on 7 April 1150. The solemn **procession** of the Precious Blood did not, however, begin until 1303. It was instituted to celebrate the deliverance of the city from the French, and still takes place on the Monday after the first **Sunday** in May.

burial customs among the earliest Christians appear not to have differed significantly from those of the peoples among whom they lived, though as early as the beginning of the third century there is reference to a priest saying prayers. Somewhat later it would appear that **hymns** were sung and - possibly slightly later still, by the end of the fourth century - mass was being said. Towards the end of the eighth century corpses were being anointed with oil and, for a time, the Eucharist was placed on the tongue of the deceased, though this custom was soon forbidden. The custom of holding a "wake", still common in Ireland, at the house of the one who has died, is also very ancient and is not specifically Christian. In monastic communities it was usual to pray in relays for the soul of the deceased, which was no doubt the theory elsewhere, though such gatherings sometimes degenerated into excuses for eating and drinking.

C

Caacupé, a **shrine** of the **Virgin Mary** in Paraguay, between the rivers Acaroisa and Ortega. According to tradition the wooden statue venerated there was carved by a newly converted Indian, in thanksgiving for his safety after an attack by pagan tribesmen. This event took place at the beginning of the seventeenth century, but it was not until 1750 that the sanctuary began to be built: it was finally dedicated on 4 April 1770.

Cælestis urbs Jerusalem (= "Jerusalem, heavenly city"), a **hymn** used for the **feast** of the **Dedication of a Church** and of unknown authorship. It is thought to date from the sixth, seventh or eighth centuries, though since that time it has been reworked in a new metre, and the words revised.

calendar, the organization of the **feasts** of the Christian week and year, the individual elements of which are discussed elsewhere in this book. The basic structure was set by the weekly memorial of Christ's resurrection on **Sunday** - though the first mention of it is not until Justin Martyr early in the second century - and the annual commemoration of Christ's passion, death and resurrection at **Easter**, the date of which was determined by reference to the Jewish passover. The date of the passover in any given year, however, was not itself determinative, for it was taken for granted that Easter would be celebrated on a Sunday, whatever its date. It was thought by Tertullian (c.160-c.220) that the date of Christ's death could be calculated as having occurred on 25 March, and this belief affected the structure of the Church's year. It might have been expected that Easter would have become an observance fixed for that particular day as **Christmas** came to be for 25 December, but the lunar months of the Jewish calendar proved to be the more influential. Christmas was being observed in Rome by 354, the date possibly determined by the earlier conviction that Christ had died on 25 March, a date to which the feast of the **Annunciation** was therefore assigned on the grounds that Christ had been conceived and died on the same day of the year. Meanwhile the day on which martyrs had died was being celebrated, at least it would seem from the middle of the second century, as the *dies natalis*, or birthday into heaven. These memorials were at first confined to the locality in which the **saint** had died, but as **relics** were more widely distributed so was the region in which the festival was kept. It was not long before the names of eminent bishops and of some who had suffered for their faith but had not been put to death ("confessors" as they have come to be called) were added to the lists of those commemorated in a particular church. Indeed, that is strictly what a "calendar" now is: it is the chronological list of the fixed feasts of the liturgical year observed by a local church. In this it is distinguished from the "martyrology", which is a chronological arrangement of the feasts of the year as celebrated throughout the whole Church, including therefore some feasts of the **Virgin Mary** or of saints which might be celebrated in, say, the United States but not in dioceses in the United Kingdom, and vice versa. Despite that, modern calendars do not display vast differences.

It was not so in the Middle Ages when, in the seventh, eighth and ninth centuries particularly, the number of saints' days vastly increased. Local calendars then showed marked divergences, representing the devotional life of the local church. When **canonization** became a formal procedure these divergences tended somewhat to decrease so that, for instance, the fame of a saint such as Thomas Becket came to be widely known with his feast appearing on calendars across Europe. There was, nonetheless, a considerable degree of confusion, a situation the Council of Trent tried to remedy. A new Breviary appeared by Trent's authority in 1568, and a missal two years later, both of which sought to impose a new and uniform calendar on the Church, while allowing for some local variation, and for the feasts peculiar to particular religious orders. The calendar was still very crowded with saints' festivals, and more were added over the centuries, as well as further feasts of Mary and some, such as **Christ the King**, of Christ himself. The computation of which feast would take precedence when two coincided became a complex undertaking. Feasts were given ranks: Doubles of the First Class; Doubles of the Second Class; Greater Doubles; Doubles and Simples (listed here in descending order of dignity). Where in this context the word "Double" arises is not clear. It may originally have meant that a feast was so important that part at least of the Divine Office for that feast had to be read in addition to the office for the day. When the Tridentine Breviary was produced there were less than two hundred feasts of saints: in the next four hundred years nearly another hundred and fifty were added.

On 14 February 1969 a major reform of the calendar was promulgated which restored to prominence the seasons of the Church's year, and reduced to less than one hundred and eighty the saints who were listed in the calendar. In all cases, feasts of saints were, where necessary, transferred to the date of their deaths (the *dies natalis*), except for a small number of important saints whose commemoration would otherwise fall within **Lent** (Saints Benedict, Gregory the Great and Thomas Aquinas). Most of the saints who remained in the Roman Calendar were given only "optional memorials", and the whole complicated arrangement of Doubles and Simples has disappeared, as has all mention of **octaves**, except in the case of Christmas and Easter. The current arrangement allows for greater freedom to celebrate the memory of saints to whom there may be a local **devotion**.

candles, lighted tapers which came into use very early in the Christian Church, and not simply to provide illumination but apparently to add dignity to the service. In this they clearly took over a role they had played in pagan times. It is known that they were used at funerals by the middle of the third century, and at the beginning of the fourth the burning of candles in cemeteries in broad daylight was condemned by the Synod of Elvira as superstitious. As **devotional** objects, however, they were, and are, burned before statues and at **shrines** to obtain some favour. At the end of the sixth century, the practice developed, lasting well into the Middle Ages particularly in England and northern France, of burning candles of the height of the individual seeking the intercession of the **saint** before whom they were placed, a custom known as "measuring to the saint".

canonization, the formal process by which holy men and women are declared to be **saints**, and may therefore be granted public honour. The "canon" in this sense is a list of those whose patronage was invoked, in the first instance by a particular local church. The written lives of saints (hagiography) played an important part in this process: they gave testimony to an individual's reputation for holiness and, more importantly perhaps, his or her reputation as the worker of miracles. It was natural that bishops should seek to control the addition of new names to the local **calendar**, and that the calendars of different churches should be exchanged, leading to the wider acknowledgement of particular men or women of especial fame. Fame was an essential part of this process: people became recognized as saints precisely because there was already a **devotion** to them.

That at least was the theory, though it is evident from the study of those who became saints that the process could be manipulated to serve political ends. The first recorded canonization by a pope - that of Ulrich of Augsburg by Pope John XV in 993 - was probably arranged for just such a reason. Ulrich, of a noble family, had appointed a relative to succeed him. Though Ulrich was undoubtedly a man of exemplary holiness, his successor, in seeking to have that sanctity formally recognised by the highest ecclesiastical authority, was in a sense also securing his own position, and to some extent that of his family. In 1170 Pope Alexander III decreed that papal authorization was required before anyone could be given even local veneration. That decree was ineffective in itself: it became more effective when in 1234 it was republished as part of the *Decretals* of Pope Gregory IX, and thereby became part of the *Corpus Iuris Canonici*, the Church's body of law. Formal processes were developed, though slowly, which required detailed accounts of the lives of candidates for canonization, and, wherever possible, the testimonies of eye-witnesses. These processes came to be thought of as a court-case in which it was a person's reputation for sanctity that was on trial, with one official to argue the case for canonization, and another (the "devil's advocate", though the official title was "Promoter of the Faith") to argue against. It was all very slow.

Many cults of saints flourished without waiting upon the outcome of such investigations. A distinction was therefore drawn between saints proper, formally canonized, and the "beati" or "blessed", whose cults flourished purely locally, or within the confines of a particular religious order. The latter, however, were far more numerous than the former, and represented a real devotion on the part of the people, which was missing from many, if not from most, of those formally declared saint by popes in the later Middle Ages. In the wake of the Council of Trent (1545-63), which reasserted against the Reformers the value of devotion to saints, came a restructuring of the papal curia (government) and in 1588 the establishment of the Congregation of Rites with responsibility for canonization. There were further reforms under Pope Urban VIII (1623-44), which laid down the procedures both for beatification (recognition of someone as a "blessed", a step on the way to canonization) and for canonization itself. He also permitted any cult which had existed from time immemorial, i.e., was more than a century old, to be continued, thereby providing another route to sainthood which has lasted down to the present day, that of "equipollent" (= equivalent) canonization. No account of the history of this process, however brief, can ignore the major work on the subject published in five massive volumes between 1734 and 1738, *On the Beatification of Servants of God, and the Canonization of the Blesseds*. Its author, Prospero Lambertini, had worked in the Congregation of Rites, and knew the system thoroughly. He went on to become that most genial of popes, Benedict XIV.

What the system entailed, down to 1982, was proof that the candidate was either a martyr, or had displayed "heroic" virtue throughout his or her life; that miracles had been worked after prayers had been directed to him or her (two for beatification and a further two for canonization - it became increasingly difficult to verify that cures were miraculous as medical knowledge increased); and there was nothing in any writings by the candidate that could be judged unorthodox. There were other criteria, but these were the main ones. Although the above account stresses the role of the papal curia in the making of saints, a good deal of the preparatory work was done at diocesan level, where the individual lived and died. Evidence that there existed a devotion to the person had to be produced, his or her writings gathered together, witnesses examined, and so on.

This process remains, but from the beginning of 1983 the Roman system changed dramatically with the abandonment of the quasi-adversarial procedure (and therefore the abandonment of a role for the "Devil's Advocate"). In its place has come a more history-oriented procedure, which fundamentally consists of the writing of a life (a *positio*) of the person under consideration, based at least in part on the evidence gathered in the diocesan process. It is the diocese, rather than the curia, which now makes a judgment about orthodoxy. Miracles are still judged independently, but the number has been halved: only one is now required for beatification (none if the person is a martyr) and one more for canonization. One problem about this system is that the goal is beatification: once that has happened there is nothing to hold up a canonization except the requirement of another miracle. It seems not unlikely, therefore, that the distinction between the two stages will be dropped.

Canterbury, a cathedral city in the south-east of England, and the site where, in 597, Saint Augustine began the work of converting the Anglo-Saxons to Christianity. For that reason it became, and remains, the premier see in England of the Church of England, though it had been originally intended that the premier see should be in London. The first cathedral on the spot was, in all probability, a Roman basilica converted into a Christian church. Whatever remained of that building was destroyed by the Danes in 1067, and rebuilt immediately, to be consecrated in 1130. It was in this church, shortly afterwards burnt down, that Thomas Becket was murdered on 29 December 1170. The chief fame of Canterbury, and its position as one of Europe's major places of **pilgrimage**, dates from that event. Thomas was born in London in 1118 and educated at Merton Priory and in Paris. He entered the service of Archbishop Theobald of Canterbury, who sent him to study law in Bologna and Auxerre, before making him Archdeacon in 1154. The following year he was appointed Chancellor of England by the young King Henry II, and, despite Thomas's protests, Archbishop of Canterbury in 1162. Becket soon resigned his post as Chancellor, and dedicated himself to regaining lands lost to the Church as well as preserving its independence from the Crown. The outcome was a clash with the King, and Thomas fled to France. He returned in November 1170 with the conflict unresolved. At that time Henry was himself in France, and on hearing - wrongly - that Thomas was turning public opinion against him, exclaimed "Who will rid me of this turbulent priest?" Four knights took him at his word, journeyed to England, and late in the afternoon killed Thomas in his cathedral. The King did penance, travelling on horseback to St Dunstan's Church on the road into the city, and from there, in monk's dress, walking to the cathedral and to Thomas's tomb. Thomas was first buried in the crypt, but after the fire of 1174 his remains were moved first to a new chapel, and then, in 1220, to a **shrine** behind the high altar. From his death onwards numerous miracles were recorded at the shrine, and Thomas was **canonized** by Pope Alexander III on 21 February 1173. The shrine became one of the most popular pilgrimage centres, and its rich decoration of gold plates and precious stones (including, it is said, one of the rubies now in the crown jewels of England) was a source of astonishment to visitors. Henry VIII and the Emperor Charles V made the pilgrimage in 1520: in 1538 the shrine was destroyed on Henry's command.

Carmelites, Third Order of, an association or **confraternity** of lay people which derives its particular character from Carmelite spiritual direction and governance. It was clearly in existence in an informal way by the Constitutions of the London Chapter of 1281 which talked of lay people being received into the Order, and a number of societies appear to have been established about that time, following Carmelite spirituality and attached to Carmelite houses. It had no proper juridical existence, however, until a bull of Pope Nicholas V in 1452 extended to the Carmelite **Third Order** the privileges enjoyed by the Third Orders of St **Francis** and St **Dominic**. The right of Carmelite superiors to receive lay people of either sex into their Order and to grant them the **habit** was conceded by Sixtus IV in 1476. At this time a formal rule was drawn up, but when the Order itself split into Carmelites of the Old Observance and the Discalced Carmelites, so did the Third Order. As with the Carmelites themselves, members of the Third Order cultivate **devotion** to Our Lady of **Mount Carmel**, and promote the good of the Church through an apostolate of prayer and penance, and works of mercy. They are also bound by the vows of obedience and chastity, though these are understood according to the member's own state of life.

Cecilia, Pious Union of St, a society founded by Francis Xavier Witt, a German priest, who in 1860 petitioned Pope Pius IX that he establish such an association to foster church music. This the Pope approved in 1869, though the statutes were only finally drawn up in 1876. The purpose of this loosely-linked federation of associations is to promote church music according to the rules laid down by the Holy See. Anyone interested in liturgical music can be a member, though rules vary from place to place. It takes its name from the **patron saint** of music.

Chapelet des Enfants, Pious Union of, an association set up in July 1933 in Paris, and placed under the general direction of the archbishop of that city, to encourage the saying of the **Rosary** by children. The young members are asked to say in a group, and daily, one decade of the Rosary, asking for the **Virgin Mary's** protection for themselves, their families, and their country, and for the spiritual renewal of their diocese. If they cannot attend the group Rosary, they are encouraged to say their decade at home with their families.

Chapi, Our Lady of, a small **shrine** lying in a valley south-east of Arequipa in Peru. The cult of the **Virgin Mary** at this spot dates only from the end of the nineteenth century, particularly after a spring had been discovered beside the sanctuary which was credited with miraculous powers.

Charity of Cobre, National Association of Our Lady of, an association founded in the **shrine** of **Cobre** in Cuba in 1919 by the then Archbishop of Santiago de Cuba to promote **devotion** to the **Virgin Mary** under the title of Our Lady of Charity of Cobre, and for the sanctification of its members. It was created an Archsodality in 1921. Members, who must be more than seven years old, have to make a personal application, and are then elected to this **confraternity** after a short probation. They receive a **medal** and the diploma of the society. The medal has the image of the Virgin of Cobre on one side, and that of the **Sacred Heart** on the other. It hangs from the neck on a red, white and blue cord.

Charity of El Cobre, Our Lady of, a **shrine** of the **Virgin Mary** in Cuba. According to tradition one of the *conquistadores*, Alonso de

Ojeda, was wrecked on the island in 1508 and took a vow to the statue of the Virgin he was carrying that, should he be rescued, then he would give the image to the first village to which he came - which he did. El Cobre ("The Copper" - the area was renowned for its copper mines) is some ten miles west of Santiago. The statue is small, and carries the infant on its left arm: the figure of Christ holds a globe of the world. The shrine developed into a popular place of **pilgrimage** and Virgin Mary under the title of the Blessed Virgin Mary of Charity of Cobre became the **patron** of Cuba after the war of independence at the end of the nineteenth century. The **feast** is held on the **Nativity of the Blessed Virgin Mary**, 8 September.

Charity towards the Departed, Pious Sodality of, a society founded in Rome in 1844 which, in 1873 was raised to the rank of an Archconfraternity, to pray for the speedy release from **purgatory** of the souls detained there. There is a secondary purpose to the **confraternity**, which is to foster among its members **devotion** to the **Sacred Heart** of Christ, and toward the **Virgin Mary**, under the title of **Mother of Mercy**. There are three levels of membership: contributing members give money, participate fully in the **indulgences** attached to membership, have prayers offered for them after their deaths, and have the right to be buried in cemeteries owned by the association; simple "adherents" receive the prayers and indulgences, but not the right of burial; while honorary members, chosen to bring distinction to the society, receive only the prayers. Membership is open to both men and women.

Chartres, our Lady of, a **shrine** of the Virgin in France which owes its prominence to the possession of an undergarment, worn, it was claimed, by Mary while carrying the Child Jesus in her womb. The statue in the crypt of "the Virgin-about-to-give-birth", was traditionally attributed to pre-Christian times, but the original (the present one is a copy) seems to have dated from the fourteenth century, and may have been modelled on the miracle-working statue of **Conques**.

Chèvremont, Our Lady of, a **shrine** of the Virgin near Liège in Belgium, originally established by the English Jesuits as a chapel for their "villa" or holiday house, after they had opened their College at

Liège in 1614. It afterwards passed to the Carmelite fathers, and became a popular centre of **pilgrimage**.

childbirth, patron saint of, is, traditionally, St Margaret of Antioch, sometimes known as St Marina. There is no evidence whatsoever to justify **devotion** to her: the account of her life is clearly fictional and was recognized as such as early as the fifth century. Nonetheless she enjoyed enormous popularity in the Middle Ages. Hers was one of the voices which spoke to St Joan of Arc, and she was numbered among the **Fourteen Holy Helpers**. In the legend which passes for a life, she is swallowed by a dragon whose belly then splits open to allow her to emerge unscathed. According to some versions of the story she promised that pregnant women who prayed to her would have safe deliveries. Either of these reasons could account for her undoubted popularity as the **patron saint** of childbirth, though other **saints** were also invoked. One other such patron was St Raymond Nonnatus (1204-40) who was given his name (*non-natus* or "not born") because he was taken from his mother's womb after her death during labour. Leonard of Noblac was also regarded as the patron of childbirth and pregnant women because, according to a life written c. 1025, the wife of Clovis I was safely delivered of child through his prayers when she was suddenly brought to childbirth while out hunting with her husband near the saint's hermitage. This story would place St Leonard in the sixth century, but nothing is known of him before the eleventh. Likewise nothing except legend is known of St Erasmus or Elmo, said to be a Syrian bishop, though his death is ascribed to the persecution of Diocletian, and therefore c. 300. He comes to be patron of childbirth apparently through a misunderstanding. He was first patron of **sailors**, and was depicted with a windlass. Later it was believed that the windlass was the method of his martyrdom, his intestines being dragged out by this means. Hence he became the patron of all suffering abdominal pains, including those of childbirth. The **feast** of Margaret of Antioch is celebrated in the East on 13 July. It was abolished in the West with the revised **calendar** of 1969, but had been 20 July. The feast of St Raymond is 31 August, of St Leonard 6 November and of St Erasmus 2 June.

Children of Mary Auxiliatrix, Pious Union of, a society founded by the Salesian priest Michael Rua in Turin in 1895 for the spiritual formation of girls through **devotion** to the **Virgin Mary**, according to the spiritual teaching of St John Bosco. Members of the **confraternity** are elected after a probationary period of at least six months. They must be twelve years old, or above, be prepared to attend regular meetings, and wear the insignia of the association. A number of pious exercises are expected of them, as well as an exemplary style of life, but their specific devotion is to Our Lady **Help** ("Auxiliatrix") **of Christians**. On public occasions they wear their **medal** hanging by a blue ribbon round their necks, and they have a banner which shows Mary Help of Christians on one side, and the **Eucharistic Heart of Jesus** on the other.

Children of Mary Immaculate, Archconfraternity of, a society founded in Barcelona in 1849, and raised to the rank of an Archconfraternity in 1861. The seat of the **confraternity** was later transferred to the Roman basilica of St Agnes.

Children of Mary, Pious Union of, a society which has a variety of different roots, one of them stretching back to the foundation of a **confraternity** of this name by Blessed Peter de Honestis in the thirteenth century - though it does not seem to have survived the founder's death. That which is historically the most significant, however, was begun in 1864 by a Canon Regular of the Lateran, Orestes Passeri, in the Roman church of St Agnes. Membership is restricted to girls, who must undergo a period of probation of at least three months before admission. The purpose of the society is to foster **devotion** to the **Virgin Mary**, and to prepare young girls for adult life. Members are expected to carry out a number of pious practices and to attend regular meetings. They wear a **medal** of the virgin on a blue ribbon.

children, patron saint of, is a title usually ascribed to St Nicholas of Bari, Bishop of Myra, who is believed to have lived during the first decades of the fourth century. According to legend he raised to life again three children who had been drowned in tubs by a butcher, hence the patronage. His **feast** is celebrated on 6 December, on which day it was customary in the Low Countries to give presents to children. This custom was transferred to America by Dutch settlers, and in time St Nicholas became Santa Claus, and the bearer of gifts at **Christmas** rather than on his proper feast - though that practice continues in some countries.

Chiquinquirá, Our Lady of, a **shrine** of the **Virgin Mary**, located in a village some ninety miles north of Bogotá in Colombia. Venerated there is a picture of Our Lady of the **Rosary**, painted by Alfonso de Narváez, which in the sixteenth century was the property of Antonio de Santana. Because the picture had deteriorated so much it had been withdrawn from public view, but a cousin of de Santana's, Maria Ramos, undertook to have it repaired. On 26 December 1586, while Maria Ramos was praying before it, the canvas was miraculously repaired: there was a bright light, and a new image of Mary was left upon it. During Colombia's first Marian congress in 1919 Our Lady of Chiquinquirá was declared Queen of the country. The **feast** is celebrated on 18 November.

Christ Child Society, a pious association or **confraternity**, established by Mary Virginia Merrick in the District of Columbia in 1887, though it spread rapidly throughout the United States of America. Its purpose is to promote the spiritual life of its own members especially through work for poor children. To this end, it has supported settlement houses, clubs and summer camps in the USA, as well as teaching catechism to the young. It has also supported convalescent homes and health clinics, as well as providing clothing for the newly-born. Members, who may be of either sex, are expected to attend mass on the twenty-fifth of each month.

Christ of Orense, Confraternity of the Most Holy, an association to foster **devotion** to a particular **crucifix** which has been preserved in the main church of Orense, Spain, at least since the thirteenth century, though the **confraternity** itself dates from a century later and was formally approved by a Bull of Pope Innocent VIII in 1487. Because of the seizure of ecclesiastical property in the middle of the nineteenth century the confraternity, which had been extremely wealthy, lost all its riches, and was on the point of extinction, but was revived at the beginning of the twentieth century. Membership is through co-option by existing members, and the payment of the required dues. Members must be male, and include the bishop of Orense and the canons of the chapter, and others who fulfil the necessary acts of piety and of alms-giving. Through these acts and alms they promote devotion to the crucifix and act as a guard of honour. They wear a black **habit** with a medal of the effigy of Christ around their necks, and carry a black flag with the effigy on one side and on the other that of Our Lady of **Sorrows**. Days of especial celebration for this confraternity are 3 May, the **feast** of **Corpus Christi**, and **Good Friday**.

Christ, relics of, clearly present a problem because the body of Christ, according to the New Testament was taken up physically into heaven. Nonetheless, during the Middle Ages a number of physical relics of Christ were venerated, in particular those which had been separated from the person of Christ during his lifetime. Thus there were relics of the foreskin of Christ, removed at the Circumcision, venerated in the **Lateran basilica**, Rome, in the monasteries of **Conques**, Charroux and Coulombs in France (the last was sent to England in 1421), and in Boulogne and Antwerp - the latter dating only from around the beginning of the fifteenth century. The Lateran had in addition Christ's umbilical cord, while phials of his blood were discovered at Mantua (twice, once in the early ninth century and the second time in the mid eleventh century), at Fécamp in Normandy and at **Bruges**. The seamless robe, or **tunic**, which he wore on the way to his crucifixion, is venerated at Trier in Germany. There is another at Argenteuil in France. In the treasury of the cathedral in Valencia there is a chalice claimed to be the one used by Christ at the Last Supper. See also **cross; relics of the passion**.

Christ the King, a **feast** celebrated in the Roman Catholic Church on the **Sunday** before the feast of **All Saints**. It was created as recently as 1925, even though the notion of Christ's triumphal sovereignty can be found in several other liturgical observances from the **procession** on **Palm Sunday** to the **Ascension**. Agitation for the observance of such a feast had begun in the 1880s led by those who were opposed to the gradual secularization of the state during the nineteenth century, and Pius XI was presented with a petition for its establishment from sixty-nine cardinals on the occasion of the 1922 **Eucharistic Congress** in Rome. This request was repeated with still greater numbers of signatories the following year. The encyclical which acceded to the request explicitly linked the new feast with an annual **consecration** of humankind to the **Sacred Heart**. The differences between the text of the mass as originally included in the missal in 1925 and that of the revised version of 1970 are very striking. The former, which stresses subservience to authority, is clearly imbued with the notion, not to be found in the 1970, that it should be possible to re-establish "Christendom", a society ruled in all its aspects by religion. In 1970 not only had this disappeared, but the emphasis is on liberty rather than obedience, and a liberty which includes the freedom to acknowledge Christ.

Christ the King, Society of, an association founded by Bishop Giovanni Oberti of Saluzzo, Italy, in the church of St Nicholas in February 1934, for the sanctification of its members and of others through them, so that the Kingdom of Christ might be more widely known. To this end members of the **confraternity** make an especial act of consecration, which they are expected to renew every day. They are also required to be active members of Catholic Action.

Christian Doctrine, Confraternity of, a society which began in the first half of the sixteenth century, under the inspiration of Marco de Sadis-Cusani. He came to Rome from Milan and, gathering around him a number of devout men, began teaching the faith to both children and adults. His work so impressed Pope Paul IV that he granted them the church of St Apollinaris from which to work. In time, however, the group grew so large that it divided into those who decided to undertake a form of religious life by living together in a community - they became known as the Fathers of Christian Doctrine - and those who remained lay people, thus forming the **Confraternity** of Christian Doctrine. In time popes granted them other churches: Santa Agatha in Trastevere, and the church of St Martin. In 1571 Pope Pius V decreed that the society should be established in every Catholic diocese, and in 1607 Pope Paul V raised it to the rank of an Archsodality. Pope St Pius X instructed that every parish should have a branch of this confraternity.

Christian Mothers, Archsodality of, an association founded in Pittsburgh, Pa., in the church of the Capuchin friars, to combat the dangers that were then perceived to attack the Christian family. It was created an Archsodality in January 1881, and its purpose is to foster Catholic family life, especially through the intercession of the **Virgin Mary** Mother of **Sorrows**. Widows may join, but it is required that they be mothers. Apart from the prayer proper to the **confraternity**, members are expected each month to attend a special homily and then to pray for families, and twice a year to come together as a group to attend Mass and to receive communion.

Christian Teachers, Pious Union of, a society created in Rome in 1956 to foster among Christian teachers a proper sense of the dignity of their profession, and a **devotion** to St John Baptist de la Salle as their **patron**. It was indeed the declaration of the Saint as patron of teachers made by Pope Pius XII in May 1956 that inspired the founding of this society. The Brothers of the Christian Schools (sometimes known as the de la Salle Brothers) organized a day of prayer for teachers on the **feast** day of their founder in a large number of dioceses, and it was the success of this initiative that encouraged them to begin the association. In addition to practising and promoting devotion to their patron, members are expected to spend at least a quarter of an hour in meditation each day, and to say a special prayer before school begins.

Christmas, the **feast** in the Christian **calendar** which marks the birth of Christ and is celebrated on 25 December. The earliest evidence for that particular date comes from a Roman calendar which must have been drawn up in 336. This lists 25 December not only as the day of Christ's nativity but also as the beginning of the liturgical year. The Roman list of dates naturally records current practice, so presumably the feast was marked before 336 at least in Rome, but just how long before it is impossible to say. An inference drawn from a sermon by St Augustine of Hippo at the beginning of the fourth century seems to suggest that the establishment of Christmas preceded the Donatist schism of 311, but this would cause difficulties for the commonly-held view that the date of Christmas was fixed to coincide with the pagan Roman feast of the *Sol invictus*, held at the Winter solstice. This latter feast had been established only in 274, and it is unlikely that before the Emperor Constantine demonstrated his tolerance of, and support for, Christianity, the Church would have wanted to take over a pagan festival for its own purposes. After Constantine came to power, on the other hand, such a move was quite understandable, especially so because Constantine before his "conversion" had him-self harboured a **devotion** to the *Sol invictus*. Christians also had their own reasons for regarding 25 December as the day of Christ's birth. He was already for them the "sun of righteousness" prophesied by Malachi, so the solstice was an appropriate day on which to mark the nativity. But it was also nine months after what we now celebrate as the **Annunciation**, the day on which Christ was conceived. The date of that feast appears to have been fixed because it was a tradition, taken over from Jewish traditions about the Patriarchs, that Christ had died on the same date in the year on which he had been conceived, and it was thought that he had died on 25 March. After the date had been settled in the West it had to travel Eastward. For many years it seems that the feast which celebrated the **Baptism of Christ** also marked his nativity, but Constantinople from around 380 and Antioch from a little later took the 25 December date from Rome. From these cities it passed to others, though Jerusalem and Alexandria held out against its introduction for a century or so.

Christmas masses, the unusual celebration of three masses, one at midnight, one in the very early morning, and one later in the morning, to mark the **feast** of **Christmas**. This practice in origin seems to have been a papal custom, in use at **Rome** by the end of the sixth century. In the fifth century there had been only one, said by the Bishop of Rome in the basilica of St Peter's, but in the sixth century a replica of the **crib** of Bethlehem was built in Santa **Maria Maggiore**, and the Bethlehem custom of having a mass at night before the crib was adopted. The second (dawn) mass was simply the commemoration of the martyr St Anastasia, and was said in her basilica: in time the Saint was replaced, apart from a commemoration, by a Christmas mass. The third mass was the original mass of Christmas said in St Peter's, though that was eventually transferred back to the **shrine** of the crib in Santa Maria Maggiore. The widespread adoption of what was a papal practice came in the eighth century when Roman liturgical books came to be used elsewhere. It should be noted that, though a "midnight" mass has become the custom, the liturgy prescribes only a service at night.

Christopher, Pious Union of St, a society founded at Baldwin on Long Island, in the diocese of Brooklyn, N.Y., in 1934. Its purpose is to foster **devotion** to St Christopher among **travellers**, but particularly among riders of motorbicycles, and to pray that they may be saved from danger of death. Members are expected not only to pray to St Christopher daily, but to carry a properly blessed **medal** of St Christopher on their machines.

Circumcision, feast of, a celebration formerly held on 1 January, the **octave** day of **Christmas** - it remained known in the Roman missal as the octave, but was originally in Rome the most solemn of the **feasts** of the **Virgin Mary,** acknowledged as mother of God. In 1969 it reverted to the title of the **Solemnity of Mary**. The name "Circumcision" follows naturally from the New Testament account of the birth of Christ (Luke 2:21ff.), but seems first to have been used for a liturgical commemoration about the seventh century, in Spain and France. It entered **Rome** much later. Because of its origins as a Marian feast it was allotted a **stational** church with, it is thought, a Marian dedication, though it is unclear which one. Pope Callistus II (1119-24) transferred it to Santa Maria in Trastevere. The Marian connotations were lost partly, it is assumed, because there was from very early times a penitential aspect to the liturgy of 1 January as Christians, who were themselves not averse to joining in the pagan new year festivities, were urged to make **reparation** for the excesses of the festival. The same passage of St Luke associates the circumcision with the bestowal of the **Holy Name of Jesus**.

Clergy, Pious Union for the, an association founded in Venice in April 1930 and formally established in the church of St Joachim of that city in 1942. It brings together women (only) who seek to assist priests by their spiritual works: they are required to pray regularly, for example, that the clergy will flourish both spiritually and materially and to help needy members of the clergy, especially the sick. They are also encouraged to foster respect for priestly dignity, and to assist the mothers and sisters of the clergy by their prayers.

Clermont, Our Lady of the Gate at, a **shrine** of the **Virgin Mary** in which was venerated one of the oldest statues of Mary. She is shown seated on a throne in majesty. with the Child on her knee. It is of wood but encased in gold, and dates at least from the mid-tenth century when the cathedral at Clermont was rebuilt.

Cocharcas, Our Lady of, a **shrine** of the **Virgin Mary** in the Apurimac district of Peru, and one of the oldest in Latin America. The statue, which is a replica of that at **Copacabana**, was brought there by Sebastiano Quimichi in September 1598. Quimichi was seriously ill, and determined to make the long journey to Copacabana to seek for a cure. On the way he was healed, but continued the **pilgrimage** nonetheless. At Copacabana he bought the image, which he brought back in triumph and established a sanctuary at Cocharcas, inaugurated in August 1623.

Column of the Scourging, a small column to which, it is claimed, Christ was bound during the scourging he received before his crucifixion. The column is preserved in Rome in the church of St Praxedes, and lacks a plinth. It is less than two and a half feet high, and there are signs at the top that there was once an iron ring attached to it. The column was brought to Rome by Cardinal Colonna in 1223.

Comforter of the Afflicted, a title under which the **Virgin Mary** is honoured - in 1666 Our Lady, Comforter of the Afflicted, was proclaimed **patron** of the city of Luxembourg, and a dozen years later of the whole of the Duchy. She is represented by a medieval statue which shows a crescent at her feet. The **devotion** appears to owe its origins to the Jesuits, who opened a school in Luxembourg in 1603. From 1639 onwards the statue, which normally was housed in a chapel just outside the walls of the town, was brought from the chapel to the college. The **"octave"** associated with this cult, celebrated from the third to the fifth Sunday after Easter, is marked by processions from the parishes of the Duchy to the **shrine** in the city.

communion of reparation, a pious practice, approved in 1898 and propagated by Sister Dolores Inglese of the Congregation of the Servants of Mary Reparatrix, of receiving communion on a **Saturday** and making some act of **reparation** for the dishonour shown to the **Virgin Mary**. In return, at least from 1912, a plenary **indulgence** might be gained which could be applied to those in **purgatory**. The establishment of this **devotion** gave added impetus to the older practice of keeping the **First Saturdays** in honour of Mary.

Communion of Reparation, Pious Union of, an association founded by a Jesuit priest, Fr Drevon, in 1854 and formally established in the Convent of the Visitation at **Paray-le-Monial** in 1865. The purpose of this **confraternity** is to make reparation for offences committed against Christ, particularly in the Blessed Sacrament. To this end, members undertake to receive Communion each week on their statutory day, so that, wherever it has been established, at least one member receives communion each day of the week to pray, among other things, for the Church and the pope, and for the expansion of the Catholic Church, particularly in one's own country. In order to join, one has already to be a member of the Archconfraternity of the **Sacred Heart** of Jesus.

Conference of Our Lady of Refuge, Pious Union of, a society founded in the church of St Sebastian in Guadalajara, Mexico, in 1870, and which was raised to the rank of an Archsodality for the whole of Mexico by Pope Pius XI in February 1937. Members, who must be over fourteen years of age, have to undergo a probationary period of three months before being allowed to join the **confraternity** and have to undertake to donate money for the society's purposes, as well as supporting its poorer members. Each evening a picture of the **Virgin Mary** under the title of **Refuge of Sinners** is moved to the house of a member of the society to be shown particular reverence. Associated with the "Conference" are two additional obligations in the forms of leagues against drinking alcohol, and against prostitution.

confiteor, a public confession (*confiteor* = "I confess") of sin. From the twelfth century it was said at the beginning of mass in the Roman Catholic Church, and was frequently used elsewhere. The confession is typically made to God, to the **Virgin Mary**, to a number of **saints**, and then to others present. The list of saints has varied, reflecting local traditions, or, within the **liturgies** proper to some of the older religious orders, the saints of that order. Mention of saints in this **prayer** dates back at least to the eighth century. The phrase by which the prayer is commonly remembered - "through my fault, through my fault, through my most grievous fault" (*mea culpa, mea culpa, mea maxima culpa*) while striking the breast three times - is rather later. A single *mea culpa* occurs by the middle of the eleventh century; a triple *mea culpa* begins to appear by the early twelfth century; the insertion of *maxima* by the fourteenth. On its own the *mea culpa* was a regularly used phrase within monastic communities, probably accompanied by a beating of the breast, at least as early as the beginning of the ninth century. In later medieval times it became a common form of expressing regret for a wrong done even within the secular sphere.

confraternities, known variously as third orders, sodalities, guilds, leagues, pious associations or unions and so on, are defined in the current Code of Canon Law as associations of "Christ's faithful, whether clerics or laity, or clerics and laity together [which] strive with a common effort to foster a more perfect life, or to promote public worship or Christian teaching. They may also devote themselves to other works of the apostolate, such as initiatives for evangelization, works of piety or charity, and those which animate the temporal order with the Christian spirit" (canon 298 1). The Code then distinguishes between associations which are private, and those which are public. Only the latter must necessarily receive approval from ecclesiastical authority; the former may be formed simply by agreement among their members without reference to bishops or other ecclesiastical superiors provided that they have not been set up "to impart Christian teaching in the name of the Church, or to promote public worship, or which are directed to other ends whose pursuit is of its nature reserved to the same ecclesiastical authority" (canon 301 1). The competent authority to set up or to approve public associations is the Holy See for world-wide associations; episcopal conferences for those within its territory; or the local bishop for those restricted to his diocese (Canon 312 1). Private as well as public associations, however, are subject to ecclesiastical supervision in so far as it is necessary "to ensure that integrity of faith and morals is maintained in them and that abuses in ecclesiastical discipline do not creep in" (Canon 305 1). Both in the earlier (1917) edition of the Code, and the current one, confraternities whether public or private are tightly regulated.

Christian societies charged with the task of burying the dead existed from the earliest days of the Church. In the second half of the third century others had emerged to promote the devotional or ascetical life of their members, and by the time of the Theodosian Code (418 AD) there was an organization in Alexandria for the care of the sick. From the sixth century onwards there were "colleges" or confraternities whose members undertook to support each other during their lives, and to pray, and offer mass, for them after their deaths - and such organizations continued to flourish throughout the Middle Ages. Members of one such clerical fraternity created in Rome in the tenth century were obliged to offer forty masses a year for deceased brethren. In the Carolingian period societies were established - first known as *Geldoniae* or *Confraterniae* - and later as *Gildae* or Guilds - dedicated to works of charity, and to the construction or embellishment of churches, bridges or other public buildings: these frequently brought together workers of particular trades. The first society known to have been established in honour of the **Virgin Mary** was set up in **Cologne** in 1060. The first society to be both approved by the Holy See and to be endowed with **indulgences** for its members was also a confraternity in honour of Mary, set up in the Dominican church in Padua in 1258, in the church of the Dominicans in Piacenza the following year, and in the Dominican church in Milan the year after that. "Third Orders" as recognizable entities began with St Francis of Assisi in 1221: it was "third" because it was made up not of priests and brothers (the "first order", as founded by Francis), nor of nuns (the "second order" as founded by St Clare), but of lay people who followed in a modified manner the spiritual practices of the Order to which they were attached, and shared in its special spiritual privileges (see **Francis, Third Order of Saint**). "Pious associations" seem to have begun in the fifteenth century, possibly with the establishment by the Dominicans of the Confraternity of the Holy **Rosary** at Cologne in 1475. Just over a century later, in 1584, the Jesuits established the Marian Congregations or Sodalities of Our Lady. Confraternities of all kinds enjoyed an enormous vogue in the later Middle Ages. It has been calculated, for example, that at the end of the fifteenth century in the diocese of Rouen in France there were 1220 of them. No less than 131 of these were located in Rouen itself, a town which at that time had only 40,000 inhabitants and thirty-six parishes.

The distinctive titles - sodalities, pious unions, leagues and so on - now have little significance. The present Code of Canon Law, apart from distinguishing between private and public associations, declares that "Associations whose members live in the world but share in the spirit of some religious institute, under the overall direction of the same institute, and who lead an apostolic life and strive for Christian perfection, are known as third orders, or are called by some other suitable title" (Canon 303). It also denominates some associations as "clerical when they are under the direction of clerics, presuppose the exercise of sacred orders, and are acknowledged as such by the competent authority" (canon 302). Otherwise it makes no distinction of title, calling all such groups "associations". Earlier legislation, however, recognized three main divisions: third orders, understood as in the present Code; confraternities, which exist to promote divine worship in some form or other, and pious unions, which exist to encourage works of piety or of charity (Canon 700 of the 1917 Code). Sodalities are similar in purpose to pious unions, their distinctive feature being their organic structure rather than the pious union's looser association of members. There also exist "Archconfraternities" or "Archsodalities". These originally were titles bestowed by the Holy See on the sodalities or confraternities to which other ones of the same kind were linked, and through which some of the spiritual privileges that had been conferred were communicated to less important associations. In time, however, they were simply bestowed as titles of honour and have little real significance.

Individual confraternities, pious unions and other associations discussed in these pages are listed under the distinguishing part of their title rather than under "Confraternity of ... ", for example, the Confraternity of Our Lady of Victories is to be found under **Victories, Confraternity of Our Lady of**, and for the Confraternity of the Seven Sorrows of Our Lady see **Seven Sorrows, Confraternity of Our Lady of**. See also **Secular Institutes**.

Conques, a small French village on the pilgrim route to Santiago which houses the **shrine** of St Foy (Faith). Foy was a martyr of the third century. She is recorded as having died at Agen, whence her bones were stolen by the monks of Conques in the first half of the tenth century. In the middle of the century a **reliquary**, which still survives, was commissioned to contain her remains. It is an outstanding work of art, showing the saint seated, holding out her arms which presumably held the gridiron on which she was believed to have been put to death. The shrine had a particular reputation for healing blindness - attributed by one commentator to the statue's jewelled eyes - but was also credited with releasing prisoners. So great was the popularity of St Foy that the monastery had to be rebuilt to cope with the huge crowds: the community itself is said to have numbered 900 at its height. Other relics at Conques include an arm of St **George** and one of the several foreskins of **Christ**.

Consolation, Archconfraternity of Our Lady of, an association which is under the spiritual direction of the Augustinian Friars. It began as the **Confraternity** of the Cincture, or "girdle": there was a tradition that St Monica, the mother of St Augustine, had seen an **apparition** of the **Virgin Mary** who had held out to Monica her girdle and told her to foster **devotion** to it. The earliest formal establishment of the Confraternity of the Cincture dates from a permission to erect such societies granted by Pope Eugenius IV in August 1439, and the first one consequently founded was in the church of St James in Bologna the same year. In 1495 the title of Our Lady of Consolation was added. The society was raised to the rank of an Archconfraternity by Pope Gregory XIII in 1576. The seat of the society remained in Bologna until 1921, when it was transferred to the church of St Augustine, in Rome. Members are invested with the black leather girdle or belt, blessed by a member of the Augustinians or another priest deputed to do so, according to a special ritual. They also say a particular form of the **Rosary**, the Rosary of Our Lady of Consolation, which consists of saying thirteen times (one for each of the Apostles, and once for Christ) the **Lord's Prayer** followed by the **Hail Mary**. They then say the **Hail Holy Queen** in honour of Our Lady of Consolation - all the while counting on the special pair of beads, which has also to be blessed by an Augustinian.

Consolation, Our Lady of, an **icon** of the **Virgin Mary** under this title - "La Consolata" - has been venerated at Turin at least since the eleventh century. A church was built especially to hold it in 1682. Permission to celebrate this **feast** was granted to the Augustinians (see previous entry) in 1838. This title is identical with "Comforter of the Afflicted", by which name a medieval statue of Mary has been venerated in Luxembourg since the early seventeenth century. This **devotion** was encouraged by the Jesuits, and at the suppression of the Jesuits in 1773 it was moved from outside the walls of the city of Luxembourg into the former Jesuit church. In 1870 it was moved into the cathedral of the city of which, since 1666, it has been the **patron** (of the whole duchy since 1678).

Copacabana, Our Lady of, a **shrine** of the **Virgin Mary** on an isthmus of land on Lake Titicaca in the Bolivian Andes where is venerated a wooden statue of Mary in the form of an Inca princess, said to have been carved by an Indian, Francisco Tito Yupanqui, shortly after the conversion of the country to Christianity.

Cor, arca legem continens (= "Heart that holds the law"), a **hymn** sung at Lauds on the **feast** of the **Sacred Heart**. Its eighteenth-century author is unknown, but he wrote all three hymns for the feast, of which this is the best known.

Coromoto, Our Lady of, a **shrine** of the **Virgin Mary** near the town of Guanare in the west of Venezuela. According to the traditional story, the Virgin appeared to an Indian chief, or *cacique*, of the Cospes tribe which was considering converting to Christianity, to urge him to do so: the village of Coromoto was founded for Indians who wished to receive baptism. The chieftain himself, however, put off his reception into the Church and returned to his old ways. On 8 September 1652 the Virgin, who had appeared to him several times before, came again at night, seen not only by the *cacique* but also by two other Indians and a child. Thinking that the **apparition** was about to chide him, the *cacique* lost his temper and leapt up, trying to strangle the figure before him. As his hands closed around her neck the apparition disappeared, and the chief was left holding a **statue** of the Virgin. This image is now the object of much veneration in the parish church at Guanare, and Our Lady of Coromoto is the national **patron** of Venezuela. The **feast** is celebrated on 11 September.

Corpus Christi, literally "the Body of Christ", and a **feast** of the Church instituted to commemorate the sacrament of the Eucharist. It has no fixed date in the **calendar**, but falls on the Thursday after **Trinity Sunday**. It owes its beginnings chiefly to a vision or dream by Juliana of Liège (c. 1193-1258), who worked in a leper hospital attached to a house of Praemonstratensian canons. In the dream she saw a full moon, with a small piece of the sphere darkened. This darkened part, she was told in another vision, represented the one feast - that of Corpus Christi - which was still lacking in the cycle of feasts of the Church. She reported these visions to her confessor, John of Lausanne, and it was he, rather than Juliana herself, who made them more widely known, some twenty years after they had first occurred. There was an enthusiastic response from the laity of Liège, where, as in Northern France and the Low Countries in general, there was already a strong devotion to the presence of Christ in the Eucharist. When Robert of Turotte was elected Bishop of Liège in 1240 he came into contact with Juliana and heard reports of her visions. Shortly before his death in 1246 he ordered that the feast be observed throughout his diocese. Though his successor repealed the order to celebrate Corpus Christi, it continued to be observed by the Dominicans in the city and when Jacques Pantaleon, who had been archdeacon of Campines in the diocese of Liège, was elected to the papacy in 1261 as Urban IV he instructed that it should be included in the universal calendar of the Church, the first time that a universal feast was instituted by a pope. The instructions were given in a Bull, *Transiturus*, issued on several occasions in slightly different forms in

August and September 1264. Urban died in October, however, and dissemination of the Bull appears to have been halted, and celebration of the feast day spread piecemeal throughout Europe. In November 1317 Pope John XXII issued the *Clementines*, a new collection of canon law which had been drawn up by his predecessor Clement V - hence its title. The *Clementines* included the text of *Transiturus*, thereby making the feast of Corpus Christi known throughout the Western Church. The **liturgy** of the **mass** and of the **divine office** appears to have been the work of St Thomas Aquinas, presumably set to the task by Pope Urban. Though there is no certain proof of this traditional view, St Thomas was among the scholars surrounding Pope Urban, and the liturgy, particularly the sequence of the mass *Lauda, Sion*, and the hymns of the office such as the *Pange, lingua* and the *Verbum supernum prodiens*, reflect the Saint's doctrinal approach to the feast, rather than the devotional approach more common at the time.

Court of Mary, Pious Union of the, a society founded in the archdiocese of Santo Angelo, Brazil, in August 1913 to foster **devotion** to the **Virgin Mary** by visiting altars dedicated to her or statues of her, and to pray for a **happy death**. A group consists of thirty-one members, each of whom has the task of cultivating devotion to the Virgin under one or other of her titles, and visiting such **shrines** of her with that title in the neighbourhood, preferably on a monthly basis. Members of the **confraternity** are also expected annually to give it financial support.

crib, a representation of the manger, set sometimes in a stable, at other times in a cave, in which Christ was laid after his birth, according to the Gospel of St Luke. The tradition that it was a cave is very early, and by the third century a cave was being pointed out in Bethlehem in which Christ was born: a basilica was built around it in the fourth century which still survives. There was a crib in **Rome**, in the basilica of Santa **Maria Maggiore** from the sixth century onwards which was, certainly by the twelfth century, believed to be the one from Bethlehem. Just as the burial of Christ on **Good Friday** was acted out in churches around an **Easter** sepulchre, so, though slightly later, there was a similar development at **Christmas** which involved the building of some sort of representation of the cave or stable, to which the various people in the Christmas story came to act out the events narrated in St Luke. The evolution of the modern crib is sometimes ascribed to an initiative of Marie de Oignies (1177-1213), one of the first of the **Beguines**. More commonly, however, Francis of Assisi is credited with having thought up the idea of having a living crib at Greccio during the Christmas of 1223. He filled a manger with straw, and brought in an ox and an ass (not mentioned, incidentally, in the Gospel narratives). The Franciscans from then on became active in promoting the erection of cribs in churches, though it is clear that in general terms cribs existed before St Francis.

Croagh Patrick or St **Patrick**'s Mountain is a **pilgrimage** centre near the town of Westport in County Mayo, Ireland. It is the spot where, according to tradition, the saint spent the 40 days of **Lent** in the year 441 after he had been accused of being unfit to hold the office of bishop. The pilgrimage consists of walking up to the chapel at the top of the mountain, a journey which should take some two hours. The modern pilgrimage cycle began in 1904, and the major one takes place, with a climb up at dawn, on the last Sunday in July, though the full pilgrimage "season" lasts from June to September. In addition to the climb itself there are three penitential "stations". At the first, Leacht Benain, the pilgrim walks seven times round saying **the Lord's Prayer** and the **Hail Mary** seven times each, and then the creed. At the summit, near "St Patrick's Bed", the same prayers are said kneeling, followed by another fifteen of the Lord's Prayer and Hail Mary, and one of the creed while walking around the summit. Finally, some way down the mountain, seven each of the two prayers and the creed are repeated several times while circling the Carrdha Mor.

cross. According to accounts dating back no further than St Ambrose's *Oration on the Death of Theodosius* of 395, the cross upon which Christ was put to death was found by St Helena (c. 250-330), the mother of the Emperor Constantine, during her visit to the Holy Land. Alternatively it may be that the discovery was made while excavations were under way to build the Church of the Holy Sepulchre in 335: St Cyril of Jerusalem, the first person known to have recorded the fact, makes no mention of St Helena when he wrote about it in 346. In St Ambrose's version, which has since become the traditional one, St Helena found not only Christ's cross but the two others upon which the two thieves of the Gospel story had been crucified. In order to distinguish between them, all three were taken to a house where someone lay dying (in some versions a widow called Libania, in others a young man), and the true cross was revealed when it, unlike the others, occasioned a miraculous restoration to health. In the narrative of a pilgrimage to the Holy Land written by the Spanish (probably) abbess Etheria or Egeria towards the end of the fourth century and discovered only in 1884, she recounts how, on **Good Friday** in Jerusalem a **relic** of the cross was brought to the **altar** in its silver-gilt casket, laid in front of the bishop, and then kissed by all members of the congregation. This practice spread throughout the Church, the congregation "creeping" to a cross on their knees, or with a triple genuflection, usually, but not only, on Good Friday in the Western Church and on Holy Cross Day (14 September) in the Eastern Church. In the West the **feast** celebrated on 14 September, the Exaltation of the Cross, officially commemorates the restoration of the cross to Jerusalem in 629 by the Emperor Heraclius after his defeat of the Persian armies on the banks of the Danube, after it had been removed in 614 by the Persian King Chosroës II. The addition of this celebration to the Roman **Calendar** is generally attributed to Pope St Sergius I (687-701). The return of the cross to Jerusalem, however, took place in the Spring: the date of 14 September was originally the commemoration of the **dedication** in 335 of the basilica built by Constantine over the Holy Sepulchre, a date possibly chosen because it was thought to have been the date of the dedication of Solomon's temple. The Finding (or "Invention" from the Latin *invenire*, "to find") of the Holy Cross used to be celebrated on 3 May in the Western Church, but was removed from the Calendar in 1969.

cross, relics of. St Cyril of Jerusalem remarked in 346 that **relics** of the **cross** on which Christ had been crucified had already begun to be taken to different parts of the world: St Helena is said to have taken a large relic with her to Nicomedia in 328. Part of this was placed in the Basilica of Santa Croce in Gerusalemme, built alongside what is now the Lateran, and which, as the Sessorian Palace, had been

Helena's Roman residence, while part of it was put by Constantine inside a statue of himself in his newly-built city of Constantinople. Other portions of the cross were sent, after its return under Heraclius in 629, to different parts of the Empire for safe keeping. The Roman relic was subsequently many times sub-divided and distributed throughout the Church, leading to the accusation, attributed to Mark Twain, that there were enough relics of the cross to build a battleship. Such investigation as there has been, however, suggests the jibe is ill-founded, though this does not of course of itself substantiate the claims to authenticity of all these relics.

cross, sign of the, a gesture made by Christians, most frequently at the beginning and end of **prayers** or of the public **liturgy**. While saying "In the name of the Father, and of the Son, and of the Holy Spirit" (or, commonly until the 1960s, "Holy Ghost"), it is the practice to raise the right hand to the forehead, then to the breast, then from the left shoulder to the right. Eastern-rite Christians take the hand from the right to the left. The custom of marking oneself with this symbol of Christ's passion goes back to the very early years of Christianity, though in those first centuries the mark was made by the thumb upon the forehead rather than completely across the body. The first explicit reference comes from Tertullian, writing about the year 202: "At every step and movement, whenever we come in or go out, in dressing or in putting on our shoes, at the bath, at table, at the lighting of the lamps, in going to rest, in sitting down, whatever employment occupies us, we mark our foreheads with the sign of the cross" (quoted from Thurston, *Familiar Prayers*, p. 2). For the gesture to have been so universal, it would seem even at the time of Tertullian's treatise to have been a long-established custom. By the end of the fourth century the habit of crossing oneself on the forehead and on the breast had begun, as had the practice of making the sign of the cross on the forehead, lips and heart, but it is not clear at what date the forehead to breast movement became common, or when it was accompanied by a movement from left shoulder to right. In Spain in the thirteenth century, for example, the gesture appears to have been made across the face only, the direction of the movement across the face still being at the individual's choice. By the fourteenth century the large cross right across the body was certainly in use, but it remained the practice to make the crossing movement with three fingers rather than with the whole hand. Diverse customs still co-exist. Though the apparent earliest practice of using just one finger for the gesture has disappeared, in the East it is still usual to use not the open hand but three joined fingers, while in some countries of the West the thumb is used to make signs of the cross on forehead, lips and breast before going on to the larger cross over the upper part of the body. Frequently the fingers are then kissed. At first sight this action seems like kissing one's thumb, but what is really honoured in this way is the cross itself, symbolically represented by the thumb crossed by the first finger of the right hand.

crown of thorns, the, according to all the evangelists except Luke, was plaited by soldiers and pressed on Christ's head before the crucifixion. A tradition going back to the fifth century claims that it was preserved at Jerusalem, and St Helena, the mother of the Emperor Constantine, is credited with having sent two thorns to the Roman church of Santa Croce, where they are still venerated. In 800 the then patriarch of Jerusalem sent part of it to Charlemagne, who in turn gave it to the Abbey of St Denis. Another part was sent to him by the Empress Irene, and these went to his basilica at **Aachen**. Sometime in the middle of the eleventh century the crown was moved to Constantinople where, in 1092, it was listed among the **relics** housed in that city. In the thirteenth century it came into the possession of St Louis of France in payment of a debt. On its way across Italy some of the thorns were left at Pisa and when the King met the relic at Sens, he gave a thorn to Sens itself, another to the Bishop of Barcelona, and more to the King of Aragon. Louis then carried the remains of the crown to Paris where it was installed in the royal chapel on 19 August 1239, sending it on three years later to the Abbey of St Denis while the Sainte-Chapelle was being constructed. It was solemnly moved there on 25 March 1248. Other relics housed there were the point of the holy **lance** and a large piece of the **cross**. During the French Revolution the relics of the crown of thorns and of the cross were moved for safe keeping to the cathedral of Notre Dame, where they remain. There are several hundred examples of thorn-relics, claiming to be from the crown of thorns.

Crucified One, The Confraternity of the Most Holy, an association founded in Bertinoro, Italy, in 1832 to foster **devotion** to Christ crucified. Its members take care of the chapel of the crucifixion in the town's main church, and support the celebration of their **feast** on the second **Sunday** of October both by giving alms for the celebration and by preparing for it the eight days before with a series of spiritual homilies. Any money left over after fulfilling the obligations is given by the **confraternity** to needy members.

Crusade of the Pope, Pious Union of, a society founded at Brion-près-Thouet, in the diocese of Poitiers, France, in response to an encyclical letter of Pope Pius XI of December 1922 in which he asked that people should join him in prayers for the coming of the peace of Christ in the kingdom of Christ. Members are required to say a prayer for the pope ("Oh divine heart of Jesus, by the Immaculate Heart of Mary, bless our holy father the Pope; help him powerfully to establish throughout the world your kingdom of love and peace") frequently. Those of the higher membership are also required to offer prayers for the pope at least one day a week.

cup, or chalice, from which Christ and the apostles drank at the Last Supper. One such was preserved in Jerusalem, though early descriptions of it differ. By 1101 the crusaders seized a cup, which was said to be the Last Supper chalice, in Caesarea and it was taken to Genoa, where in was installed in the church of St Lawrence. When Napoleon invaded Italy, the *relic* was taken to Paris. The reliquary was opened, and the object inside proved to be a dish, rather than a cup, just over a foot in diameter and made of green glass. It was returned to Genoa in 1816, but was broken in the process. Valencia also claims to have the cup used at the Last Supper.

Czestochowa, Our Lady of, a **shrine** of the **Virgin Mary** in southern Poland, where is venerated a Byzantine **icon** of the Madonna. Traditionally it is said to be have been painted by St Luke on the wooden table-top of Mary's house at Nazareth, hidden by early Christians during the persecutions, found by St Helena, the mother of the Emperor Constantine, and taken to Constantinople. According to the same tradition, the picture was removed from Constantinople during the iconoclast controversy and taken first to Romania and then, in 1382, to Czestochowa where it was housed in the fortified monastery of Jasna Gora (= Mountain of Light). The Hussites attacked the monastery in 1430 and slashed the icon with swords. In November 1655 Carl Gustav X of Sweden, who had conquered most of Poland, launched an attack on Jasna Gora from Krakow. Though it looked for a time as if the monastery was bound to fall - it was garrisoned by less than two hundred soldiers and sixty-eight monks - the Swedish commander called off the siege on 26 December, a turning point in Polish efforts to free their country from Swedish domination. After his return to Poland the King, John Casimir, in a ceremony in the cathedral at Lvov, dedicated the country to the black Madonna of Czestochowa, whom he declared to be the Queen of Poland. The icon has since stood as a symbol of Polish unity. It was not until 1710, however, that **pilgrimages** to Czestochowa became a part of Polish life. In that year a plague in Warsaw ceased after its citizens had prayed to Our Lady, promising to walk to Jasna Gora from Warsaw should their prayers be answered.

D

Daily and Perpetual Adoration of the Most Holy Sacrament of the Eucharist, Pious Union of, an association founded in May 1950 by Cardinal Gilroy, Archbishop of Sydney, Australia, to foster **devotion** to the Eucharist among the clergy. It was placed by the Cardinal under the patronage of the **Immaculate Heart of Mary**. Members of the society inform the local moderator of the hour they have chosen for their period of adoration before the tabernacle: this they perform daily. There are no other obligations, though there are suggestions as to how the hour of adoration might be spent.

Dawn Gate, Our Lady of the, a **devotion** to the Virgin in Vilnius, Lithuania. The Dawn Gate is so called because it stands to the east of the city, and is the setting for an image of Our Lady, first placed there when the walls around the city were completed in 1503.

De profundis (= "Out of the depths") is Psalm 129 in the Vulgate but 130 in other versions of the Bible. It is one of the penitential psalms, and was included in the Office for the Dead from the tenth century, but along with others. That it should have become so prominent is difficult to explain: Herbert Thurston, S.J. has suggested that it may simply be a chance occurrence. The psalm's position in the office was such that, if the Office for the Dead had to be shortened for any reason, the *De profundis* would be left as the one to be said, thereby making it better known. Certainly by the middle of the thirteenth century it seems it was familiar to the laity as a prayer for the repose of the souls of the dead.

dedication of churches, a service by which a building is **blessed** or **consecrated** for use as a place of worship. The earliest known example of dedication of a Christian church is that of the cathedral at Tyre in 314, but the Jewish **feast** of dedication, Hanukkah, sometimes called the feast of lights, was instituted by Judas Maccabaeus in 165 BCE as a memorial to the purification of the Temple after it had been defiled by Antiochus Epiphanes: it was to be observed on 25 Chislev, and to continue for eight days. In Christian usage, the feast of dedication is an annual celebration of the dedication of each church, observed by the individual church, and of the cathedral, observed throughout the diocese. The dedications of two **basilicas** in Jerusalem, the Martyrium and the Anastasis, were commemorated jointly in the city on 13 September in the fourth century, and basilicas built in **Rome** in the fifth century, Santa **Maria Maggiore** (on 5 August), St Peter in Chains (on 1 August), St Michael (on 29 September) and St Lawrence outside the Walls (on 2 November). The mass which begins *Terribilis est locus iste* (= "This is a fearsome place") used for the dedication of a church was composed for the dedication of the Pantheon about the year 610. The dedication of the **Lateran basilica**, observed on 9 November, does not appear to have been kept in Rome before the eleventh century.

Descent, Our Lady of the, a **devotion** to the **Virgin Mary** in Cuzco, Peru. In May 1536, after eight months of battle for the Inca capital, the Spanish forces were besieged in a building which had a thatched roof. The Indian army determined to put it to the torch and were about to do so on 23 May (or 21 according to some sources) when they saw an **apparition** of Mary with the Child Jesus in her arms coming down on the house - known as Suntur-Huasi in the local language - where the Spaniards were taking refuge. When the Indians continued to set fire to the roof, the figure of Mary put out the flames. The Inca army retreated. Suntur Huasi became a chapel, serving for a time as the city's cathedral. The image of the Virgin is also known as Our Lady of the Triumph.

devotio moderna, a form of piety which emerged in the late fourteenth century largely through the teaching of Geert Groote (1340-84), though best known perhaps for its encapsulation in the *Imitation of Christ* by Thomas à Kempis (1380-1471). The "new **devotion**" was not a break with the past but a renewal and reform of the old monastic tradition, with considerable stress on meditation and spiritual reading. The central theme was precisely that of imitating Christ, conforming to the model of Christ, particularly in his passion. Christ is above all a model of humility, requiring from those who followed him self-mortification and contempt for the world. Although essentially a monastic spirituality, one to be lived out in a community, it was formulated in such a way that it was possible to follow the teachings of writers such as à Kempis inside the cloister or out.

devotion, a word which has two distinct, though closely related, meanings. The first, and more widely used, application of the term is to describe the quality of being dedicated to a task, possibly to the exclusion of all things else. It implies a sense of commitment or consecration to the matter in hand, and is often, though not exclusively, applied to dedication to a religious purpose. This gives rise to the second meaning. The religious purpose or object to which this dedicated attention is given is commonly, at least in Catholic use, called "a devotion". Devotions in this sense have to be sharply distinguished from the Church's liturgical forms of worship, the mass and the divine office. These are public acts of worship, and as such are not only authorized by the Church but required by the Church of its members or, in the case of the office, of some of its members. Devotions usually have to be authorized by the Church to some degree, at least if they are to be used outside one parish, or one diocese where for a time they may be informally tolerated, but they are not required by ecclesiastical statute. In that sense they are private activities, even though in many instances they may be performed in common. A further difference was noticeable, at least until the reforms introduced by the Second Vatican Council (1962-5): devotions were commonly in the vernacular, whereas the liturgy, the public worship of the Catholic Church, was in Latin. There is another distinction to be made. The central act of worship of the Christian Church, at least in the Catholic tradition, has always been and still remains the mass, the celebration of the Eucharist. Essential to this act of worship, again in the Catholic tradition though not necessarily in all other Christian traditions, has been an ordained ministry: one could not have the mass without the priest. That was not true of devotions in the sense defined above. Even when devotions were clerically inspired or clerically led, the acts which they entailed could usually be carried out without the aid of a member of the clergy. The **Stations of the Cross** performed in a church might usually be conducted by a clergyman, but did not have to be, and individuals could gain the same **indulgences** with which making the Stations had been endowed by walking around the Stations on their own. **Pilgrimages** to holy **shrines**, one of the most obvious and most demanding acts of devotion, have until modern times been basically solitary undertakings by lay people.

It has been common to see a division in the historical development of devotions marked by the sixteenth-century Council of Trent. Before the Council, it has been argued, devotions were local, tied not just to a particular parish but frequently to a spot in that parish where a statue may have been found or an **apparition** seen: the **saint** who was venerated was also a local holy man or woman. Through the shrine which grew up around statue, vision or saint, the people of the neighbourhood had direct access to the power which controlled their lives. **Confraternities**, which were also a form of devotion since they usually fostered the cult of a particular saintly **patron**, were means of organizing people's lives to meet the possibility of penury and the certainty of death. After Trent, the argument goes, devotions were much more generalized: saints had to be recognised in Rome, and so did visions. The indulgences which were associated with devout practices could not be gained unless the **rosary** or **medal** were blessed by a priest - and frequently not any priest but a member of a particular religious order, which meant that its influence increased. Indulgences flourished in the mid-nineteenth century as possibly never before: not, as they had been in earlier centuries, as a means of raising revenue for the papacy, but as a means of extending papal power. Indulgenced devotions, in other words, were a way in which the papal desire to centralize authority on Rome expressed itself.

There is much to be said for this argument, but it must be remembered that some of the most flourishing of nineteenth-century devotions such as those to the **Sacred Heart** and to the **Blessed Sacrament** had roots which lay in the Middle Ages.

In the years since the Second Vatican Council devotions have been in decline as attention has focused on the liturgical, rather than on the extra-liturgical, worship of the Church. In part this decline may also have been in response to the wish of the Roman Catholic Church to draw closer to other Christian Churches which, on the whole, did not find the forms of devotion in which Roman Catholics used to engage wholly sympathetic. There was, for instance, both during the Council and afterwards, a distinct down-playing of the role of the **Virgin Mary** in Catholic practice. Pope John Paul II has attempted to reverse this trend by his unabashed personal devotion to Mary, and his frequent visits to Marian shrines. At the same time, and particularly perhaps in Latin America, there has been an effort to revive popular devotions in an attempt to provide a more varied diet of worship and thereby counteract the influence of Protestant sects whose livelier, more popular forms of religious meetings have been attracting converts from Catholicism.

Dies irae, dies illa (= "A day of wrath that day will be"), a **hymn** commonly attributed to the Franciscan Thomas of Celano (1200-55), who was the biographer of St Francis, and though the ascription to him is by no means certain, it was probably written by a Franciscan: it certainly does not appear to predate the thirteenth century. It is based not only upon scriptural texts but also upon other medieval poems. The last six lines are an addition, the first four being taken from a hymn dating from the twelfth century or earlier. The whole is a meditation upon death and judgment, and, it is sometimes suggested, was probably first used as a **sequence** for masses in **Advent**, whose liturgy it fits rather better than that of the requiem where it is now found.

Dominic, Third Order of Saint, an association or **confraternity** which depends for its governance and spirit upon the Dominicans. It traces its origins to the Militia Christi ("Army of Christ") founded at Toulouse in 1206 by St Dominic himself and Bishop Foulque of that city to present an armed resistance to the Albigensians, and to protect the rights and revenues of the Church. Members of this Militia were drawn from confraternities of **penitents**, and it continued to be regarded as of that category after its formation. While members wore the black and white colours of St Dominic's Friars Preachers, the Militia differed widely from the Friars. Though the sanctification of its members was not ruled out, neither was it explicitly concerned with their spiritual progress until after the defeat of the Albigensians. Some sort of rule for Dominican tertiaries appears to have existed from the same year as that for the **Third Order** of Saint **Francis**, 1221, but it was extended and improved in 1228 and 1234, and a final version was produced in 1285 which was confirmed by Pope Innocent VII in 1405, and by Pope Eugenius IV in 1439. The Third Order flourished wherever the Dominicans themselves worked, including in missionary territories. Its basic rules and purpose are those of **Third Orders** in general, though it shares the specific task of the Dominicans of working for the salvation of the souls of others, and not only of its own members. Dominican tertiaries are required to say the Office daily, though this may be commuted to a form which consists only of the **Hail Mary** and the **Lord's Prayer** recited a number of times, or the **Little Office of Our Lady**, or the **Rosary** either in its entirety, or in part.

Dormition, or "Falling Asleep", **of the Virgin Mary**, one of the twelve great **feasts** of the Byzantine Church, which is celebrated on 15 August. It replaced the feast of the Maternity of Mary in the sixth century, and from it arose the Western-rite feast of the **Assumption**, although in the East it was also sometimes known as the *analepsis*, or Assumption. It reflects a story found in the apocryphal gospels that as Mary lay dying the apostles were brought to her bedside from all parts of the world, and accompanied her bier to the grave. Frequently shown in icons of the Dormition is the hand of a Jew who attempted to overturn the bier during the funeral procession; his hand stuck to it and was restored to him only when he confessed Christianity.

doxology, meaning "glory", from the Greek for that word, is used of the "Great doxology", the *Gloria in excelsis Deo* ("glory be to God on high ...") and of the "Little doxology", the *Gloria Patri et Filio* ... ("Glory be to the Father, and to the Son ..."). Forms of expressing glory to God occur in the Old Testament, at the end of each of the four books of psalms, for example, and frequently in the New Testament also. Such doxologies were, of course, in the Old Testament, directed to God alone. In the New they sometimes mention both God and Jesus Christ but not even in the earliest Christian liturgies is there reference to the Holy Spirit. In the middle of the second century St Polycarp is credited with a Trinitarian doxology in his Letter to the Smyrneans. The practice of ending **prayers** with a Trinitarian doxology, both within and outside the public liturgy, seems to be well established by the beginning of the third century, and at the end of psalms chanted antiphonally soon afterwards. That, however, accounts only for the first part of the prayer which is now in frequent use: "Glory be to the Father, and to the Son, and to the Holy Spirit, as it was in the beginning, is now, and ever shall be, world without end". In 529 the fifth canon of the Council of Vaison decreed that the second part of the doxology should always be recited, which was by that time in any case a common practice. The precise form of the little doxology as it is now said in English is a consequence of the Reformation: during the brief Marian restoration of Roman Catholicism in England, no attempt was made to alter the Protestant translations of this and other prayers which had become familiar to the people of England.

Dulcis Jesu memoria (= "Jesus, the sweet memory", though a well-known version starts "Jesus, the very thought of you with sweetness fills my breast"), a **hymn** used at **Vespers** on the **feast** of the **Holy Name**. It has frequently been ascribed to St Bernard of Clairvaux (1090-1153), but this is now thought to be unlikely. His authorship is not claimed in manuscripts before the fifteenth century, and the hymn itself does not appear before the early thirteenth. It seems likely, on the evidence of the manuscripts, that it was written around the year 1200 or a little earlier. The first manuscripts to contain the hymn are English, and it seems quite likely that it was written in England. Because the author would appear to have been well versed in the writings of Bernard, it is possible that he, too, was a Cistercian. In its original form it was of forty-two verses, and described the soul's search for Jesus - a name which occurs over and over again. In some versions **doxologies** have been added.

E

Earthquake, Our Lady of the, a **shrine** of the **Virgin Mary** in Quito, Ecuador. The title was given to the ancient stone statue of Our Lady of **Mercy** after the earthquake of 1755, in thanksgiving for the safety of the city, which was attributed to the intercession of Mary.

Easter, a celebration of the **feast** of Christ's death and resurrection. In its earliest manifestation it appears to have been a continuation of the Jewish feast of the Passover which commemorated the escape of the Jews from Egypt, and the liberation of the people. By the time of Christ (and indeed long before) this was the major feast of the Jewish calendar. As a Christian feast it does not unambiguously appear until the second half of the second century, at which time it appears to be a memorial of Christ's death, regarded as a triumph, rather than the resurrection and consists of a night-long vigil terminating in the celebration of the Eucharist. A major dispute in the second century, however, divided the practice in Rome from that in Asia Minor. In the latter an influential group, known as the "Quartodecimans" (= fourteenth), believing that Christ had died on 14 Nisan of the Jewish calendar, always celebrated Easter on that date, no matter what day of the week it happened to be. It is clear from the course of the controversy that in Rome and elsewhere in the West it had become the custom to celebrate Easter on a **Sunday**. It is also the case that a Sunday Easter had been established in Jerusalem and Alexandria quite independently of Rome, though whether this custom, apparently brought in by Greek bishops in the second century, was introduced before it began in Rome is not possible to establish. The Jewish Passover was accompanied by a **fast** for a quite short period of time leading up to the Passover meal. This would seem to be the origin of the Christian fast at Easter, though it lasted for a rather longer period, covering the vigil and ending with the Eucharist. When the Friday fast was associated with the Easter one, this resulted in a lengthy, two-day fast. During the third century the fast was extended to six days (the whole of **Holy Week** in other words), and during the fourth to a whole six weeks, though it is clear that in this prolonged period the final six days were of particular significance, and of those the final two days were more important than the first four. The celebrations continued on for eight days (Easter Week) after the main feast day. This practice may owe something to the Jewish custom of celebrating seven days of unleavened bread after Passover, but it probably also reflects the Christian concern to mark Christ's resurrection appearances. This period was the time when those who had been newly received into the Church were given their final catechesis, or instruction in the faith they had just embraced.

Echternacht, a town and Benedictine abbey, just over twenty miles from the city of Luxembourg, and still, though only just, in the Grand Duchy on the border with Germany. It houses the **shrine** of the founder of the abbey, St Willibrord, who died there in 739. His remains are buried in the basilica which is dedicated to him. The shrine is honoured annually, on the Tuesday following **Pentecost**, with a "dancing procession", the origins of which are uncertain, but go back at least to the mid sixteenth century. Those taking part line up in rows, linked each to his or her neighbour by holding a handkerchief between them. There are bands, and the procession moves forward with dancing steps, while repeating the special **litany** to Willibrord. The final step of each row of dancers is a leap past the tomb of the saint in the crypt of the basilica.

Einsiedeln, Our Lady of, a **shrine** of the Virgin Mary located in a monastery in Switzerland, founded, according to legend, by St Meinrad in the ninth century. Again according to legend, it was Meinrad who brought to the place the original miracle-working statue of the Virgin. This wooden effigy was, it is claimed, the one honoured by the monks of the monastery in the twelfth century, but it was destroyed by fire in 1465. The new figure proved to enjoy the same wonder-working power and Einsiedeln became one of the great **pilgrimage** centres of medieval Europe. The history of the monastery claims that the blessing of the abbey church on 14 September 948 was carried out by Christ himself, surrounded by a company of angels, and that when the bishop came to undertake the ceremony he was told by **angels** that it had already been done. The feast of the angels, established in 1466, became, and to some extent remains, one of the major occasions of pilgrimage to the monastery.

ember days, days on which Christians were expected to **fast** and to pray: they were observed on Wednesdays, Fridays and Saturdays. The word "ember" derives from their Latin name of *Quatuor tempora*, or "Four seasons", and represent a Christian blessing to the four seasons of the year as they begin. Their origins are unclear. When they first appeared in the **calendar** at **Rome**, probably at the end of the fourth century, there were only three periods of this sort, timed for the beginning of Summer, the beginning of Autumn, and the beginning of Winter to coincide with the harvests of grain, of grapes, and of olives. This may reflect a positive decision on the part of the Church to "Christianize" similar harvest festivals which had marked the pagan year, although an alternative suggestion links them to **feasts** of the Jewish calendar. Pope Gregory the Great at the end of the sixth century added a further period of **fast** to mark the beginning of Spring. These were "stational" liturgies, the congregation gather on Wednesday at the **station** of Santa **Maria Maggiore**, on Friday at the church of the Twelve Apostles, and on Saturday at St Peter's. Because of their solemnity and penitential character it became the custom to ordain men over this period, so that their names would be announced on Wednesday, they would be presented to the congregation on Friday, and the ordination would take place during the **vigil** on Saturday evening. From Rome this practice spread throughout the rest of the Church, being introduced into England in 747 by the Council of Clovesho. The greater the distance from Rome, however, the less the ember days coincided with the harvest. The same was also true of the "rogation days", held on the three days immediately before the **Ascension** to pray for a **blessing** on the earth. In the reforms of the liturgy which took place in 1969 the ancient ember days disappeared, as did rogation days, and the recommendation was made that the local churches should choose periods appropriate to their own cycle of harvests as a time for special prayer.

The masses appointed to be said on these occasions were such **votive** masses as might seem proper.

Epiphany, feast of, an occasion which now celebrates on 6 January the coming of the **magi,** but in the early Church was associated both with the **baptism of Christ** and with his nativity (and, in some instances, with the marriage feast at Cana). This feast began in the East and became part of the Roman liturgical calendar in the middle of the fourth century, only a few years before Rome's nativity festival (**Christmas**) began to be observed in the East. Even in some places in the West the Epiphany remained for a time a nativity festival, though generally it took over the theme of the coming of the magi - perhaps simply to divide between the two Winter feasts the story of Christ's birth.

Ergotism, Our Lady of ("Notre Dame des Ardents"), a **devotion** to the **Virgin Mary** at Arras in France, dating from the twelfth century. According to legend two knights who were deadly enemies were separately visited by a vision of a lady who told them to go to Arras where there were forty-four people dying of ergotism. At Arras they were to go at cockcrow to the church where a woman, dressed as in the vision, would give them a candle. The sick were to drink water into which some of the wax of the candle had been allowed to fall. They did so and were healed. A chapel in which the candle was preserved was built in 1215, and survived until the French Revolution. For the disease, see **fire, holy.**

Espousals of Mary, a **feast** which in origin appears to have been part of the **devotion** to St **Joseph** which in the fourteenth and fifteenth centuries was burgeoning in Germany and especially France under the influence of Jean Gerson (1363-1429), chancellor of Notre Dame in Paris. Gerson claimed it was already being celebrated on 19 March by Augustinians in Milan, and a friend of Gerson's introduced the liturgical observance of the feast of the Espousals of Mary and Joseph into Chartres. Under the influence of the Franciscans it became a festival of the **Virgin Mary** rather than of the marriage between Mary and Joseph. In 1537 the Franciscans were permitted to celebrate it on 7 March, and in the seventeenth century it spread more widely throughout the Church, the day of its observance being fixed on 23 January.

Eucharistic Heart of Jesus, Archsodality of, an association under the spiritual guidance of the Redemptorists dating from 1868, when Pope Pius IX gave this **devotion** tacit approval. A number of separate **confraternities** sprang up, which were united in an Archconfraternity in 1903, based upon the church of St Joachim in Rome. Members are expected to spend at least half an hour a week in meditation; to say on the hour "May the most holy sacrament be praised and adored for ever"; to receive communion on **Maundy Thursday**, and on the **feasts** of **Corpus Christi** and the **Sacred Heart**.

Eucharistic League, a pious union founded in the Carmelite Church of **Corpus Christi** in Milan in 1896. Members of this **confraternity** undertake to promote the Kingship of Christ in families and in the State, and to pray for the triumph of the Catholic Church, together with the conversion of schismatic and dissident churches so they may return to unity under the pope. There are varying degrees of membership. The basic obligation is to say certain prayers (including those proper to the League), to be present during **exposition** of the Blessed Sacrament at least once a month, and to spread the love and knowledge of the Sacrament especially within their own parishes. The higher rank of "zelators" have the task of spreading **devotion** to the Sacrament, spending an hour in adoration each day if at all possible, accompanying the priest when he takes the sacrament to the sick, providing decoration for the altar and so on. Above them again is the rank of "moderators" who have, in addition to an organizational role, the duty to make the League better known. See also **Priests' Eucharistic League**.

Exaltation of the Cross, a liturgical **feast** kept on 14 September according to the Western **calendar**, which began in **Jerusalem** on 13 September and appears to have marked the **dedication** of the basilica on the spot where Christ was crucified. The 13th was chosen because it was according to tradition the day on which the true **cross** was found by St Helena: on the following day (the 14th) the cross was **venerated** by the people. The Finding (or "Invention" from the Latin *invenire* = "to find") of the Cross was celebrated on 3 May in **Rome** from the beginning of the sixth century. By the middle of the seventh century 14 September was celebrated in Rome as the Exaltation as well as 3 May, and so it continued until 1960 when the feast of the Finding was suppressed. The celebration of the Exaltation in Rome came to be marked by a **procession** from the basilica of Santa **Maria Maggiore** to the **Lateran**, where the **relic** of the cross was kept at least from the time of Pope Sergius (687-701).

Expectation of the Childbirth of Mary, a **feast** of the **Virgin Mary** observed in some places on 18 December. Its early history coincides with that of the **Annunciation**, which was celebrated in Spain on 18 December until it came to follow the Roman **calendar** and was placed on 25 March. The December feast, a week before **Christmas**, then became known as the Expectation. By the end of the eighteenth century its observance was widespread, but it has never become a celebration of the universal Church.

exposition, a form of **devotion** to the Blessed Sacrament in which the host is displayed, usually in a monstrance while the laity venerate it. Its best-known form is that of the service of **Benediction**, but the practice derives its origins from the elevation of the host at the moment of consecration in the Mass which began towards the end of the twelfth century and became common by the start of the thir-teenth. It is commonly suggested that the elevation was introduced in response to denials, specifically by Peter the Chanter (d. 1197), that Christ was present in the host before the consecration of the chalice: hence the raising of the host for adoration as soon as the words "This is my body" had been said. In popular belief the simple sight of the host raised above the altar became a spiritual act, and miraculous cures were attributed to it. Theologians debated whether persons in serious sin could look upon the host (it was agreed they could not receive it), and decided that it was a meritorious act which might turn the sinner towards God. Exposition in churches and in **processions** had become so common by the fifteenth century that regulations had to be introduced to limit it: a synod in Cologne in 1452 forbids the practice except during the **octave** of **Corpus Christi**. In some German churches there were built "sacrament-houses", in effect highly ornate stone monstrances in which the host was permanently displayed. Also in Germany at the end of the fifteenth century, and in the Netherlands, there was the custom of exposing the host simply in order to give added solemnity to the celebration of mass. In more recent times a number of **confraternities** and religious congregations have undertaken the practice of "perpetual" **adoration** of the blessed sacrament. In some places the devotion known as the **Forty Hours** fulfils this function, since as the devotion finishes in one church it begins in another. The custom of exposition, and the devotions attached to it, has declined as a result of efforts by liturgical reformers to situate the sacrament more firmly within the context of the mass.

F

Families Consecrated to the Holy Family, Universal Pious Union of, an association which arose out of a number of individual societies, founded from the seventeenth century onwards, which brought together families which had determined to model themselves upon the Holy Family of Jesus, Mary and Joseph. It was, however, the **confraternity** founded in Lyons by the Jesuit François Philippe Francoz which became, by a decree of Pope Leo XIII in June 1892, the one to which all others had to be linked. The Pope also laid down a form of consecration. Members are expected to have some statue or other image of the Holy Family in their houses before which they pray, as a group, at least once a day, and to take the Holy Family as exemplars. The families are recommended to use frequently the invocation, "Jesus, Mary and Joseph, I give you my heart and my soul. Jesus, Mary and Joseph, assist me in my last agony. Jesus Mary and Joseph may I breathe forth my last in peace with you".

Family Rosary, Pious Union of the Daily, an association first established in the last century in the Basilica of St Mary Major, Rome, to preserve the faith and morals of the family through prayer to the **Virgin Mary**, and through her intercession as **Mediatrix of All Graces**, to pray for the conversion of sinners, the triumph of the Church, for the State, and for peace. Members of this **confraternity** are expected to say a third of the whole **Rosary** each day, except in the summer months, when those who are engaged in agricultural work may say the litany of **Loreto** instead. Each first Saturday of the month a member of the family is encouraged to go to Mass and receive communion. Families are also required to maintain high standards of morality in the home, for example, removing from the house any books which are opposed to the faith and morals of the Church.

fast, eucharistic, a practice of not eating or drinking before the reception of the eucharist. It goes back at least to the late fourth century and may be older, though in the earliest days of Christianity it seems that the eucharist was received in the course of a meal. The first legislation of which there is record dates from North Africa in 393, and this laid down that the eucharist was to be received before any other food or beverage that day. This was the practice until 1953, when a drink of water was allowed. In 1957 the limit of the fast was put at three hours - though water was still allowed at any time - and in 1964 that limit was further reduced to an hour before communion. The sick and those who look after them are not even bound by this provision, and priests are required to observe the fast only before the first mass they celebrate, if required to celebrate more than one.

fasting, the abstention from food for a period of time for devotional reasons. It was practised in Judaism with a fast leading up to the Passover meal, and, among the more devout, on Mondays and Thursdays as well. These days seem to have been chosen so that one was not fasting just before nor just after the sabbath. Early Christian practice was to follow the Jewish custom at Passover time by fasting at **Easter**, and on Wednesdays and Fridays according to the second-century text known as the *Didache*: days perhaps chosen so as to be different from the Jews or just possibly because it was believed that Christ had been arrested on a Wednesday and put to death on a Friday. A two-day period of fasting developed when the Friday fast was associated with the Easter one. During the third century the fast was extended to six days and a century later to a whole six weeks.

Fatima, a **shrine** in Portugal dedicated to the **Virgin Mary** after a series of apparitions on the 13th of each month from May to October 1917. The three visionaries were children, Lucia dos Santos, nine years old, and her two cousins, Francisco aged eight and Jacinta aged six. After the deaths of the last two, Lucia claimed they had also had a vision of an angel the previous year in the form of a thirteen-year old boy, who called himself an angel of peace and taught them to pray. This apparition appeared three times, the first and last time at Loca do Cabeco where the three were looking after sheep, and the second time in Lucia's garden. On the last occasion the angel was holding a chalice and a host, the latter he gave to Lucia, while Jacinta and Francisco drank from the chalice. The location of the 1917 visions was a mile and a half from Loca do Cabeco, at Cova da Iria, where the children were again pasturing their flock. They were saying the **Rosary** at midday when they had the vision of a young woman, some fifteen years old, hovering above a nearby tree. She was wearing a long white veil and was clasping a rosary. On the second occasion the children were accompanied by a number of people from the village. On this occasion the vision spoke of the need to say the rosary. The villagers did not see the apparition, but reported flickering lights crossing the sky.

By July the number of those accompanying the children had risen to six thousand. Again they saw nothing in particular though the woman in the vision, who had not yet named herself, promised to perform a miracle so that her presence would be recognized. She taught the children a prayer to say. Shortly before the vision due on 13 August, the anti-Catholic sub-prefect of the district put the children in gaol so they could not visit Cova on the appointed day. Despite that, however, eighteen thousand turned up. The vision appeared to the seers six days later, and promised that there would be a miracle on 13 October. The three had a further vision on 13 September in the presence of a crowd which had now risen to thirty thousand, but a month later, 13 October, the number of those present has been estimated as being between seventy and one hundred thousand, many of whom claimed to have seen the sun spinning in the sky through the rain clouds.

Both Jacinta and Francisco died soon after the apparitions: Lucia became a nun at the age of fifteen, entering the rather stricter Carmelite Order in 1946. She claimed that the apparition had given the children three secrets, the first in the June vision, the other two in July. The first concerned **devotion** to the **Immaculate Heart of Mary**, which was revealed in 1927 with the virgin's permission; the second was a vision of hell; the third has never been revealed, though it has been written down and sent to the Vatican. The Virgin also asked that prayers should be said for the conversion of Russia, and in 1946 the **Blue Army** was set up for that purpose. Devotion to Our Lady of Fatima was approved in 1930, though pilgrimages had continued to be made ever since 1917 despite official government hostilities at the time they occurred.

feast, within the Christian tradition, is a liturgical celebration of some **saint**, or of some historical event or even of some significant theological concept. The feasts of saints began with the annual celebration by a local congregation of the death of a martyr beside his or her grave: the earliest Roman **calendar** was a record of the annual celebrations at cemetery churches in the city. When the calendar was transplanted from Rome to other churches, when it migrated to France, for example, all contact with the origins of each feast was lost, and the individual martyrs and, by that time, confessors, were honoured only by a liturgical ceremony. The history of many of the feast days of the calendar is recorded elsewhere in this dictionary.

Feast of Fools, a series of festivities surrounding the **Christmas** season, of which the best known is perhaps the election of a **boy bishop**. The "Feast of Fools" (or sometimes "of asses" of even "of the rod" because the rod of the cathedral cantor, his symbol of office, was seized) proper seems to have occurred chiefly on 1 January, the **feast** of the **Circumcision**, a day which was ascribed in a special manner to the subdeacons: St Stephen's Day (26 December) was that of the deacons; the following day, the feast of St John, of the priests; and the Holy Innocents (28 December) of the acolytes. In some places the subdeacons' day was 6 January or even 13 January. It seems that the feast was observed not only by turning upside down the proper hierarchy, so the lower orders of clerics took charge, but by singing, dancing, riotous **processions** and bouts of drinking. Opposition to these celebrations began in the mid-twelfth century, and by the beginning of the thirteenth there was both papal and local ecclesiastical legislation outlawing them. Nonetheless they continued on certainly into the fifteenth century, much to the distress of church reformers, and in some places into the sixteenth. The Feast of Fools seems to have been celebrated widely, but was apparently particularly popular in England and France.

Fields, Archconfraternity of Our Lady of the, a society founded in 1887 in the diocese of Sées, in France, and constituted an Archconfraternity two years later under the title of "Notre-Dame des Champs". Members of this **confraternity** undertake to pray for God's blessing on those who work in agriculture, and foster Christianity in the countryside. Their only obligation is to say the **invocation** "Our Lady of the fields, pray for us" three times in the course of the day and to say a further specific prayer at least once a week.

Fifteen Saturdays, a **devotion** to the **Virgin Mary** cultivated by the Dominicans, which seems to have begun in the seventeenth century. Those performing this devotion are required to say the five decades of the **rosary** over the fifteen **Saturdays** immediately preceding the **feast** of Our Lady of the Rosary, and to go to confession and receive communion. **Indulgences** have been attached to this practice seemingly almost from the beginning.

fire, holy, the medieval name for **ergotism,** a disease occasioned by eating rye bread infected by a dark-violet fungus, which swept England and France in the twelfth and thirteenth centuries. It brought on gangrene with the sensation of being on fire - hence the name - often with convulsions. Epidemics of this disease gave rise to **pilgrimages** to **shrines** of the **Virgin Mary** at **Paris, Chartres** and elsewhere.

First Communion and Perseverance, Archsodality of a Good, an association under the spiritual guidance and direction of the Dominicans. It was founded in 1891 in the **shrine** of Our Lady of the **Rosary** at Prouille in the French diocese of Carcassone by Fr Antoine Doussot, O.P., becoming an Archsodality five years later. Its seat was moved to Rome in 1910 when it was put under the charge of the Master General of the Dominicans. The purpose of this **confraternity** is to ensure that children worthily receive their first communion, and continue so to receive the sacrament for the rest of their lives. Members, who are expected to receive communion at least weekly, are encouraged to visit churches regularly to pray before the tabernacle, and to encourage **devotion** to the sacrament in themselves and others. The **patron** of this confraternity is Blessed Imelda Lambertini, and a **medal** of her, suitably blessed, is given to members.

First Saturday Devotion, a practice of keeping the first **Saturdays** of each month as **reparation** to the **Virgin Mary** for the dishonours shown to her. Its popularity dates from the eighteenth century. In the nineteenth it was associated with the Saturday **Communion of Reparation**, which also became very popular and was granted numerous **indulgences**.

Five First Saturdays, a pious **devotion** arising from the apparition at **Fatima**, according to which the **Virgin Mary** undertook to obtain for those who say five decades of the **rosary** and make a fifteen-minute meditation on the mysteries of the rosary, the graces needed for salvation.

Five Wounds, the wounds in the side of Christ and in each of his feet and each of his hands. The first reference to these five as a group seems to be one made by St Peter Damian (1007-72). A century later Alfonso Henriquez proclaimed himself King of Portugal after defeating five Moslem Kings, and in 1139 put the Five Wounds upon his country's coat of arms in gratitude to Christ who, tradition claims, appeared to him in the middle of the battle. It was, however, the appearance of the **stigmata** in the hands, feet and side of St Francis of Assisi in September 1224 which focused attention upon the **devotion** to the Five Wounds. It was certainly known in Germany during the thirteenth century, and it was in German-speaking areas that the earliest liturgical celebrations of the **feast** appear in the fourteenth century. It became very popular. It was reported that the Mass had been written by St John the Evangelist, and revealed to Pope Boniface II (530-32) - perhaps significantly the first pope of German ancestry. If the Mass of the Five Wounds were to be said five times, it was thought, a soul was freed from **purgatory**, and the repetition of an act five times as a particularly holy gesture seems to be related to the Five Wounds devotion (Heinrich Suso, who died in 1366, is said to have drunk five times during meals). A great many prayers were composed in honour of the Five Wounds. It was recorded of St Clare, who died in 1253, that she knew the prayer to the Five Wounds composed by Sister Agnes of Oportulo, but such manuscripts as survive are later than the thirteenth century. By the fifteenth century specific prayers to the Five Wounds were common, frequently linked to a five-fold repetition of the **Lord's Prayer** and the **Hail Mary**. Both Franciscans and Dominicans attempted to link this devotion to that of the **Rosary** at the end of the fifteenth and beginning of the sixteenth centuries, while in more recent times the Passionists have introduced a rosary of the Five Wounds. Also by the end of the fifteenth century the iconography of the Five Wounds was well established. It displayed, in the centre of a shield, a heart pierced with a pair of hands above it and a pair of feet below. It was this emblem that those who took part in the Pilgrimage of Grace in England in 1536-7, a rising against the Reformation, put upon their banners, though the heart dripped blood into a chalice.

flagellation, a practice of beating the body with rods or a whip. It began as a disciplinary punishment for a serious failing in early monastic times: hence the use of the word "discipline" for the whip which came to be used from the eleventh century onwards, though in the first centuries a birch rod was more commonly employed. In civil law such beatings were a punishment reserved to slaves: in ecclesiastical law only senior churchmen were exempt, and not even these if the fault was serious. A monk who was judged guilty of some offence might be beaten until his back ran with blood, if the offence were grave enough. The same could be true also of nuns. The popularity of the discipline as a penitential practice is commonly attributed to the enthusiasm of St Peter Damian (1007-72) who in 1035 joined the extremely rigorous Camaldolese Benedictine monks of Fonte Avellana in Tuscany, a community reformed by St Romuald (c. 950-1027), and of which he became abbot c. 1043. Though there are occasional references in earlier saints' lives, the first systematic use of the whip as distinct from birch rods is recorded by Peter Damian in a life he wrote of his disciple Dominic Loricatus ("the mailed", so called because he wore a coat of mail next to his skin), who died in 1060. In 1057 Peter Damian became Bishop of Ostia and a Cardinal, and his subsequent travels, and his personal fame as an ascetic, gave him plenty of opportunity to spread the practice. He wrote a book in praise of flagellation for the monks of Monte Cassino, who were apparently unwilling to strip to their waists to be beaten by someone in the presence of their fellow monks. In the twelfth century the practice spread widely in religious communities, and in the thirteenth even among the laity. Birch rods continued to be used to the end of the Middle Ages, but the whip, often with knots in the leather thongs, gradually became more common. The use of the discipline as part of the rule of a religious community was generally restricted to certain days - commonly Fridays - and would continue for the period of time it took to recite some prayer, often the psalm *Miserere* (Psalm 51). It was often endured in a sitting position, though according to Jacques de Vitry, Mary of Oignies associated the discipline with that of **genuflection**, giving herself three hundred strokes for each genuflection. The practice of flagellation remained common in religious orders until the 1960s, but has since gone into decline, though without entirely disappearing.

Forty Hours, a period of prayer undertaken before an **altar** on which the **Blessed Sacrament** has been exposed. Though there has been a suggestion that the number of hours reflects the number of days of Christ's fast in the wilderness (the explanation offered by Pope Paul IV when he approved the **devotion** in November 1560), a more likely explanation is that the period was chosen to coincide with the widespread belief in the Middle Ages that forty was number of hours during which Christ's body lay in a tomb. And as that period extended over three days, the Forty Hours devotion is also extended over three days. The service was organized as follows: on the first day a Mass of the Blessed Sacrament was said, and the Sacrament remained in a monstrance, exposed on the altar. On the second day a Mass was said for peace, but at a side altar. On the third day came the "Mass of Deposition" and the Sacrament was returned to the tabernacle. At the same time, however, the Sacrament was being exposed in some other church, at least in big cities, so that the **exposition** would be continuous. Pope Clement VIII issued a decree to establish this "uninterrupted course of prayer" in Rome in November 1592. In doing so he made it clear that his purpose was to pray for peace in France, then at war with Spain, and for the defeat of the Turks. Likewise when, in 1527, Gian Antonio Beloti made the proposal while preaching in the church of the Holy Sepulchre in Milan that people pray before the Sacrament for forty hours, he did so in the hope that by their prayers they might obtain peace. In the churches of the Jesuits, however, an order which energetically promoted the Forty Hours, and indeed elsewhere, the service was associated with expiation for the sins committed during carnival. The decree of Clement VII does not suggest that the prayer was to be made before the exposed Sacrament, but as exposition had been a practice at least since 1550 among the Roman confraternities and earlier in Milan, it seems likely that even if he did not mention exposition, this was taken for granted. It has been suggested that more remote origins of a form of the Forty Hours was the practice in Zadar, a town on the north-east coast of the Adriatic where the "Verberati", a **confraternity** of Flagellants, kept a forty-hours' **vigil** during **Holy Week**. This may in turn reflect the widespread custom in England and elsewhere of the Easter Sepulchre where first a cross, and later the Blessed Sacrament, was laid on **Good Friday** while the faithful kept watch at the "grave". Later still, it seems that the Sacrament was kept in a veiled monstrance above the sepulchre. Though the Easter Sepulchre devotion was not of itself specifically limited to Forty Hours, the choice of such a period may have been influenced, as was noted above, by the common view that Christ had been in his tomb for that length of time, a conviction that goes back at least to St Augustine if not earlier.

Fourteen Holy Helpers, a group of **saints** - though the list varies somewhat from place to place - who were regarded as being particularly efficacious either against various diseases, or at the hour of death. **Devotion** to them as a group began in Germany and travelled to Hungary and elsewhere. Although there was a common **feast** day (8 August, until the reform of the **calendar** in 1969, when the feast was abolished), the fourteen were all well known - if in some cases mythical - and each had his or her own feast day as well. The list comprised most commonly Saints Acacius, Barbara, Blaise, Catherine of Alexandria, Christopher, Cyriacus, Denis, Erasmus or Elmo, Eustace, George, Giles, Margaret, Pantaleon or Panteleimon, and Vitus. All except Giles were, or were supposed to have been, martyrs.

Fourvière, Our Lady of, a **shrine** of the **Virgin Mary** at Lyon. According to legend, a **statue** of Mary had been brought to Lyon in the mid second century and placed in a cave opposite the temple of Augustus. Certainly a chapel in honour of Mary was in existence at Fourvière in the ninth century: the present basilica which surrounds the original chapel was begun in 1872.

Foy, Our Lady of, a **shrine** of the Virgin near Namur, where is venerated a stone statue of Mary found when an ancient oak tree was being cut down. Copies of the statue, made of the wood from the oak or of neighbouring trees, were rapidly circulated, and credited with miraculous powers.

Francis, Third Order of Saint, a **confraternity** of people, married or single, clerical or lay, who follow in a modified form the rule of St Francis of Assisi. The traditional account of the foundation of the **Third Order** attributes the initiative to a certain Luchesio, who in 1221 was converted by Francis's preaching and asked the Saint that a rule of life be drawn up for him: Luchesio and his wife Bona became the Third Order's first members. The year is not in doubt: in 1221 a *Manual for Penitent Brothers and Sisters Living in their own Homes* was composed for just such a confraternity. The *Manual* does not, however, imply any close liaison with the Franciscans, nor do any papal documents until the middle of the thirteenth century. There were already in existence in Italy in the early years of the century brotherhoods and sisterhoods dedicated to lives of chastity or penitence, and it seems to have been these which were united according to an adaptation of the Franciscan rule. This was probably undertaken first either at Florence or Bologna by Cardinal Ugolino of Ostia, the Cardinal Protector of the Franciscans. (It was Ugolino who, as Pope Gregory IX, **canonized** Francis in 1228, only two years after his death.) These groups of **penitents** could be unruly: to link them in this manner to an established religious order was a way of bringing them under some form of control.

The Third Order spread quickly - first throughout Italy, and then, after Francis's death, to France, Spain, Portugal, Germany and England. In 1289 Pope Nicholas IV brought it under the protection of the Holy See, which encouraged the confraternity's progress despite problems which arose when in the early years of the fourteenth century some of its members, over-zealous in pursuit of the ideal of poverty, were accused of heresy alongside other dissident groups. A number of privileges were granted to members, some of them in theory at least of considerable importance during the Middle Ages, such as exemption from extraordinary taxes, the right to be tried before ecclesiastical rather than civil courts, and immunity from the interdict. The Third Order of St Francis has continued to grow, enjoying particular success during the sixteenth and seventeenth centuries as Franciscan friars spread Christianity in newly-discovered lands of the Americas and the Philippines. There were distinguished martyrs among Franciscan tertiaries. More than other similar confraternities it has been endowed by the Holy See with a great many spiritual privileges in the form of **indulgences** - a number of popes, even in modern times, have been members of the Third Order of St Francis.

G

Gabriel the Archangel, recorded in the New Testament as the messenger bringing to the **Virgin Mary** the news of Christ's conception, seems to have been venerated from early Christian times, but was given a **feast** of his own only in 1921, which has since been removed from the Roman **calendar**.

Garabandal, a small village in the province of Santander, Spain, in which visions of the **Virgin Mary** - preceded by visions of an **angel** - are said to have taken place to four children at varying intervals from 18 June 1961 to 13 November 1965. During these visions the children went into trances, and heard messages, which they were to pass on to the world. The vision warned of forthcoming disaster.

George, Saint, patron of England, was martyred about the year 303 at Lydda in Palestine. Traditionally, and quite possibly, he has been thought to have been a soldier, and a vision of him together with St Demetrius was seen, it was claimed, by the crusaders during the siege of Antioch: King Richard I took George as his own, and his army's, patron, and although his cult had been known in Britain in Anglo-Saxon times, it was then that it began to spread, to be proclaimed, in 1415, one of the principal **feasts** of the Church's year in England. He was widely venerated elsewhere in Europe, and a number of other regions also took him as their patron. His fame was bolstered by the stories told of him in the *Golden Legend*, and in Germany he is counted as one of the **Fourteen Holy Helpers**. He is patron of soldiers and associated crafts such as armourers, and is invoked against the plague, leprosy and syphilis. The story of his slaying the dragon became popular in the twelfth century, and may have come from the story of Perseus slaying the sea-monster, which event is located near Lydda.

Golden Fleece, Order of, an order of chivalry founded at **Bruges** in 1439 by Philip the Good, Duke of Burgundy. It was instituted, said its charter, in honour of Christ and his Mother.

Gonfaloniere, Archconfraternity of, an association of nobles (*Gonfaloniere* = "standard bearers") in Rome dating back to 1264: its foundation is attributed to St Bonaventure. At that time it was called the *Raccomandati della Sanctissima Vergine*, but its name was changed to "Archconfraternitas Gonfalonis" after a rising of the people of Rome in 1354 when the members of the **confraternity** were believed to have defended the liberty of Rome, and justice for its citizens. Originally the members of this society paid the dowry for twelve poor young women about to marry, and formed the guard of honour for an image of the **Virgin Mary** when, once a year, it was brought out for veneration. It was raised to the rank of an Archconfraternity by Pope Gregory XIII (1572-85) who also gave it the role of redeeming captives from prison. Pope Sixtus V in 1586 commuted this task of redeeming prisoners held in the papal states for a sum of money to be paid annually to the pope. Over the years a number of other similar associations were founded in Rome, but they eventually came together into one society. Its members wear a white habit with, on the right, a white and red cross set against a blue background.

Good Counsel, Our Lady of, an **icon** of the **Virgin Mary** at Gennazzano, south-east of Rome. Its presence in the church was first reported in 1467, though according to tradition it had earlier been venerated at Skodra in Albania - of which country the Virgin under this title was declared **patron** in May 1915. The image is pain-ted on very thin plaster and rests upon a narrow ledge. Its survival in these conditions is itself regarded as miraculous by the icon's devotees. The church in Gennazzano is under the charge of the Augustinians who were first allowed publicly to celebrate the **feast** of Our Lady of Good Counsel in 1779. It became a feast of the whole Church in 1876. In Rome the feast is marked on 26 April, though elsewhere it is generally observed on 27 June.

111

Good Counsel, Pious Union of Our Lady of, a society approved by Pope Benedict XIV to honour the **icon** of the **Virgin Mary** under the title of **Good Counsel**. Members are expected to wear upon their persons, and to have in their houses, pictures or medals of this image of the Virgin. It is a **confraternity** of which a number of popes have themselves been members, and is under the spiritual guidance of the Augustinians, in whose church the image resides.

Good Friday, the Friday before **Easter Sunday**, and kept with particular solemnity as the day on which Christ died. At the end of the fourth century in **Jerusalem** there was a lengthy service beginning on Thursday evening, retracing Christ's steps as in the Gospel story, and ending on Golgotha on the Friday with the veneration of the **cross**. By the seventh century there was certainly a commemoration in **Rome**, though this would seem to have been of bible readings and prayers only as far as the papal liturgy was concerned. In other Roman churches, however, in addition to the prayers and readings, the cross was venerated by the people, and all received the eucharist, consecrated the day before and preserved for the purpose. Though this became the model throughout Europe, and in the papal liturgy as well, from the thirteenth century onwards only the priest received the eucharist, and the service took place not in mid afternoon but earlier in the day - from the sixteenth century in the morning. In 1955 the people were once again allowed to share in the eucharist, and the afternoon or evening became the appointed time for the service.

Gospa Sveta, a **shrine** of the **Virgin Mary** in Yugoslavia. According to legend, two knights were entrusted with a statue of the Virgin by the Bishop of Prague, Saint Vojtech, with instructions to take it to **Loreto** in Italy. When they arrived at Beljak in Carinthia they were ordered in a dream to take the statue back to Gospa Sveta and leave it there, When they awoke they both forgot the dream, but were unable to journey onwards until they had fulfilled these instructions. The statue of the Virgin venerated in the church dates back to the mid-fifteenth century.

"Gospel in Life", The Archconfraternity of the, a **confraternity** founded to honour, love and glorify the Gospel, and to bring all to live their lives according to its precepts. It was started in 1934 in the Basilica of the Sacré Coeur on Montmartre, and it was created an Archconfraternity the same year. It was placed under the patronage of the **Virgin Mary** as **Queen of the Apostles**, and apart from a particular invocation ("Queen of the Apostles, pray for us. Queen of the Evangelists, pray for us") members are required only to read at least once in the week, as a form of spiritual reading, either a page of the Gospels, or a commentary upon them.

Grace, Our Lady of, a title of the **Virgin Mary** which dates from the Middle Ages - sometimes as "Mother of Grace" - which apparently was first celebrated liturgically at Faenza in Italy. Though the date of the observance originally varied from place to place, it became fixed for 9 June. At Castellazzo, also in Italy, a **shrine** to Mary under this title became in the 1940s a gathering place for motorcyclists, and Pope Pius XII declared Our Lady of Grace of Castellazzo the **patron** of motorcyclists.

Graces, Society of Our Lady of, a society under the direction of priests of the Servite Order, and founded in September 1854 in their church of Saints Gervasius and Protasius in Udine, Italy. There had been a **devotion** to the **Virgin Mary** under that title (*Madonna delle Grazie*) in Udine since 1479, when a picture of the Virgin, said to be miraculous, came to the city. Members of the **confraternity** foster devotion to Mary, and pray for the dead, especially those of the society itself. They also undertake to make a financial contribution to religious services associated with the society.

Gregorian masses, also called "the Trental of St Gregory", was the custom of saying thirty masses in the course of a year for some recently deceased person. It was a practice particularly in vogue in the Middle Ages and was attributed to Pope Gregory the Great because of a legend in which he had been granted a vision of his mother. She was, she revealed, suffering great torments in purgatory because of her past sins (she admitted to having given birth to an illegitimate baby which she had murdered and secretly buried). The vision asked the Pope to say thirty masses. He did so, and was granted another vision in which his mother again appeared, this time in a splendour so great the Pope mistook her for the **Virgin Mary**.

Grieving Heart of Jesus, Pious Union of, an association founded in Guatemala City in August 1857 to foster **devotion** to the sorrowful heart of Christ, to promote a greater understanding of the value of the state of grace, and to spread the doctrine of the mystical body of Christ. To this end members of the **confraternity** undertake to preserve their state of grace; to receive communion on the 25th day of each month and to spend an hour in prayer; and at some moments of the day meditate upon the sorrows of the **Sacred Heart**, and pray for the conversion of sinners. Membership is divided by ages: from three to ten years of age they are called "consoling angels", from ten to fourteen "Gethsemane angels"; from fourteen to twenty-two "flames of the Sacred Heart", and the remainder "burning lamps".

Guadalupe, the Virgin of, a title of the **Virgin Mary** of which the best-known **shrine** is that in Mexico City, although the original, from which the latter takes its name, is in Estremadura, a Spanish province south-west of Madrid. There, in the fourteenth century, a cowherd went in search of one of his charges which had disappeared. He found the animal lying dead a short distance away from the rest of the herd, and began to cut it up for meat. As he did so, the animal suddenly sprang back to life and at the same time the Virgin appeared on the hillside, and told him to dig at the spot where she had appeared where a statue of herself lay hidden. He did not do so, but went back to his companions who were convinced of his story when they saw the marks of the man's knife on the cow he had begun to butcher. They did not immediately go in search of the statue but set off home, when the cowherd found that one of his children had died. He promised to consecrate him to the service of Our Lady of Guadalupe should the lad recover - which he promptly did. The cowherd then went to the priests to tell them his story, and they sent out a party to look for the statue, which they found in a cave. A shrine was immediately built around the spot, the cowherd and his family became its hereditary guardians and the Virgin of Guadalupe became the title under which Mary was most venerated in Spain after that of Our Lady of the **Pillar**.

114

Some two centuries later, in the early morning of 9 December 1531, a Christian Indian, a childless widower who lived near what was later to become Mexico City, was passing a hill known as Tepeyac while on his way to mass, when he heard singing coming from its summit, and a woman's voice calling out his name, Juan Diego. He climbed the hill and found an Indian girl of some fourteen years who declared herself to be the Virgin Mary. She said that she wanted a shrine to be built to her on the top of the hill, from which she would assist the Indian population of the country. This request Juan had to carry to the local bishop in Tenochtitlán. This he did, twice, but Bishop Zumárraga remained unconvinced. Juan Diego's uncle, Juan Bernardino, was suddenly taken seriously ill and on the Monday (the original **apparition** had occurred on a Saturday) Juan did not go to Tepeyac at all, and on the following day walked past at some distance to avoid encountering the Virgin. Nonetheless she came to meet him, declared herself his mother, promised to cure his uncle, and sent him to the top of the hill to collect some roses, although it was not the season for them. He did so. She tied them up in his *tilma*, or Aztec cloak, and sent him back to the bishop. In the bishop's presence he opened the cloak and the roses fell to the ground to reveal, on the cloak, an image of the Virgin. This convinced the bishop of the veracity of Juan Diego's story, and he undertook to build a shrine on Tepeyac. When Juan returned home he found that his uncle had been cured by the Virgin, who revealed to him that she wished to be venerated on the hill-top under the title of the Virgin of Guadalupe. Such is the traditional account to explain the Indian image of the Virgin still honoured in Mexico City. But this version is not corroborated by any contemporary evidence - Bishop Zumárraga does not mention it, for instance - and although a near contemporary account written in Náhuatl is attributed to an Indian, who studied with the Franciscans in the 1530s, named Antonio Valeriano, only fragments of this document date from the sixteenth century and the earliest complete written version of the story dates from more than a century after the events were reported to have taken place. On the other hand there is earlier evidence of a shrine to the Virgin of Guadalupe at Tepeyac. First accounts of it suggest that what was venerated there was not an image on a *tilma* but a statue of the Virgin known by the name of Our Lady of Guadalupe. That this title was used is perhaps not surprising because many of the *conquistadores* came from Estremadura, including Cortés himself, and would be likely to have a **devotion** to Mary under that name, which was in any case the most popular Marian title in Spain at the time. Under this title, the Virgin is **patron** of Mexico and of Central and South America. The **feast** day is 12 December.

Guápulo, a **shrine** of the **Virgin Mary** not far from Quito in Ecuador, which was created in 1581. **Devotion** to Our Lady of Guápulo was widespread in Latin America.

guardian angels, a class of angels who are charged with the safety of individuals. It is not a matter of Catholic doctrine, but has a long history and appears to have developed out of an Old Testament belief in such beings. It records them as looking after, for example, Moses, Lot and later Tobias. In the New Testament Christ is reported as saying of children that their angels are constantly in the presence of God (Matthew 18:10). It was a matter of discussion in the early Church whether everyone had a guardian angel, or only baptized Christians. Despite the constant tradition in the Church about such beings, a **feast** of Guardian Angels was a late addition to the calendar. In the sixteenth century a number of dioceses asked that such a feast be established, at least for themselves, and it entered the universal calendar in 1608 at the request of Ferdinand of Austria, though it was not an obligatory observance except in Imperial territories. It became so under Pope Clement X, and Pope Leo XIII raised it in rank. The day set for its celebration, 2 October, was chosen because it was at the time it entered the universal calendar the first free day after the much more ancient feast of St **Michael the Archangel,** observed on 29 September.

gunners, and all others associated with artillery, have as their **patron** St Barbara, whose life was believed to have been lived in the fourth century, though her story is now regarded as wholly mythical. She seems to have been chosen as patron of gunners, and also as protector against sudden disasters and calamities, particularly those in mines, because her father was struck down by a thunderbolt.

H

habit, the distinctive dress of those belonging to religious orders and congregations. Though there are variations, it is most often white, black, brown or grey and consists of a tunic with a girdle or belt, a **scapular** thrown over it, and frequently a cloak when out of doors. Men usually have a hood attached, women a variety of headdresses, depending upon the style of their congregation. In the Middle Ages, and to some extent even down to modern times, lay people close to death have asked, as an act of **devotion**, to wear the religious dress of some particular religious community. One of the earliest of whom this is recorded is Lothair I, who in 855 died in the monastery of Prüm. It became a very common practice in the Middle Ages, though the person wishing to take the habit on his or her deathbed was required to make a religious profession (seeking the permission of their wives, were they married, in order to do so) and become part of the community before the clothing with the habit. The religious community would thereby frequently benefit from the wealth of the person thus entering; the new member of the community would be guaranteed the prayers of the monks or nuns for the salvation of his or her soul. The person thus received would be buried in the habit. Burial in the habit has remained a privilege extended to those who are members of those **confraternities** or third orders attached to some of the older religious orders. Members of such confraternities are also usually expected to wear the scapular of the order to which they are attached, though admittedly in a highly modified form.

Hail Holy Queen, a **prayer** or, more correctly, a **hymn** to the **Virgin Mary** composed at the end of the eleventh century. The earliest versions are in almost the exact form in which the hymn is used today except that the word "mother" has been added to the first line (the original simply read "Hail Queen of Mercy"), and "Virgin" has been inserted in the final line. These additions to the text were, however, made very early - certainly by the thirteenth century. The music is thought to be contemporary with the text, and may be from the same hand. The earliest uncontrovertible evidence of the usage of the hymn comes from the Statutes of Peter the Venerable, Abbot of Cluny c. 1135, where it is stated that it should be sung during **processions** on the **feast** of the **Annunciation**, and also during processions on other **saints'** days. Despite this piece of evidence, spread of the custom of singing the *Salve Regina* is chiefly attributable to the Cistercians, among whom it became a required prayer from the beginning of the thirteenth century. The Benedictines were instructed to sing the hymn after Compline, which suggests that the notion of it being a processional hymn had been retained possibly because, as the Jesuit Herbert Thurston has remarked, its music was distinctly more tuneful, and presumably therefore more memorable, than other plainchant music of the time. It was, however, frequently said rather than sung, among the Cistercians, for example, at the end of mass in place of the opening of the Gospel of St John, possibly while the priest was on his way back to the sacristy from the **altar**. Thurston attributes the hymn's popularity among sailors to the same tunefulness, and cites references among accounts of Columbus' voyage to and from America in evidence of this popularity. It was possibly the fact that the hymn was sung at Compline, an office which the more devout laity may have attended, that led to its being widely used in the Middle Ages as the basis for an evening prayer-service, held in front of a statue or in the lady chapel. Guilds or **confraternities** were formed to encourage this practice, and it became part of the more formal service of **Benediction** of the Blessed Sacrament, especially those held on **Saturdays**, a day on which the Virgin Mary was particularly commemorated.

Hail Mary, a popular **prayer** to the **Virgin Mary**. As it is now recited, it clearly divides into two parts. The first part - "Hail Mary full of grace, the Lord is with thee, blessed art thou among women, and blessed is the fruit of thy womb, Jesus" - is constructed from the archangel Gabriel's greeting to Mary at the **Annunciation**, and Elizabeth's greeting to her at the **Visitation**. There is evidence that

Gabriel's words were used in private **devotions** at least from the eighth century and possibly a century or so earlier in the East, and in the West it appears in the Offertory of the mass for the fourth Sunday in **Advent**, in a **liturgy** traditionally ascribed to St Gregory the Great. As a popular form of prayer on its own, however, the Hail Mary does not seem to have come into use until the eleventh century when the **Little Office of Our Lady** came into vogue. That office made considerable use of the first part of the prayer, and in the course of the eleventh century it clearly became more widely known and used independently - as a hurried greeting when passing statues of Mary, for example, or before a Marian altar. As these were clearly very brief prayers, it may be that they ended with the words "among women", though certainly by the beginning of the twelfth century it continued to "fruit of thy womb". The second part of the prayer, "Holy Mary, Mother of God, pray for us sinners now, and at the hour of our death", developed gradually from the beginning of the fourteenth century onwards, and had become a fixed form by the end of the fifteenth century, in the words in which it is still recited. As a popular prayer, then, the entire formulary was not in use before the sixteenth century.

Hailes, a **shrine** of the **Precious Blood** in Gloucestershire. The shrine itself was located behind the high **altar** of the Cistercian abbey founded in 1251 by Richard, Earl of Cornwall, brother of King Henry III. The phial containing the **relic** was brought to Hailes in 1274 by Edmund, second son of Richard of Cornwall, who had received it from the Count of Flanders. The relic bore the authentication of the Patriarch of Jerusalem who had afterward become Pope Urban IV (1261-64). Because of the relic, Hailes abbey became a major centre of **pilgrimage** up until the dissolution of the monasteries. The Holy Blood was removed in 1538 and taken to London where, in a sermon preached by the Bishop of Rochester at St Paul's Cross, the relic was said to be honey coloured with saffron, and was poured out on to a fire.

hair shirt, some rough cloth - traditionally made out of goats' hair - worn either as a shirt or around the waist in the form of a belt. The Latin term for a hair shirt, *cilicium*, or the French *cilice*, has come to be used for a spiked bracelet worn either on the upper arm or round the thigh by members of some religious orders. In English the word frequently used is sackcloth. As a form of penitential practice it was much used in the early Church (perhaps in conscious imitation of the dress of St John the Baptist and his call to repentance), though it was not, perhaps surprisingly, commended to his monks by St Benedict, and Cassian was positively against them wearing it. In the Middle Ages, however, when increased discomfort was achieved by the use of wire mesh, it became common for members of religious orders to wear hair shirts, and many of the laity did likewise. Sackcloth was also worn by penitents, especially on **Ash Wednesday**, and in some instances even the **altar** was dressed with it. It has rarely been imposed by rule, and with the exception of members of a couple of the stricter religious orders, it has always been worn as a voluntary form of penance.

Hal, Our Lady of, a **shrine** of the **Virgin Mary** in Brabant (Belgium), where is honoured a black statue of the Madonna. A reputation for miracles made this shrine a major place of pilgrimage in the second half of the thirteenth century.

Hallowe'en, literally the **vigil** of All Hallows or, nowadays, **All Saints.** The latter feast is celebrated on 1 November, so Hallowe'en is marked on 31 October. The customs now associated with Hallowe'en, however, more properly belong to **All Souls Day,** 2 November, when masses and prayers are offered for the deceased still in **purgatory.** It was believed that those in purgatory would return to haunt people who had wronged them during their lives, and they could only be placated, and prevented from doing mischief, by gifts, particularly of food. Those returning to life on this day, it was believed, sometimes did so in the form of witches or toads. Other forms of marking All Souls Day included - and in some places still include - processions to cemeteries, to leave lights, flowers or food beside graves.

Happy Death, Archsodality of, an association that began in the church attached to the Jesuit headquarters in Rome in October 1648. It was the practice for people to come there on Friday evenings to pray for a holy death. From the Gesù the custom spread to other Jesuit churches, and from the nineteenth century onwards it became possible to establish other societies linked to the Roman Archsodality (which it had become in September 1729) of the Gesù in churches other than those belonging to the Society of Jesus. Members pray for a peaceful and holy death. They do so in particular by reflecting upon the suffering of Christ upon his cross, and upon the sufferings of the **Virgin Mary**. They are expected to undertake this exercise once a week, or at least twice a month, and to engage in the corporal works of mercy, especially those of visiting the sick and burying the dead.

happy death, patron of, is traditionally taken to be St **Joseph** because at his death he was attended by Christ and the **Virgin Mary**.

healing, patron saints of, those **saints** whose protection is, or was, commonly invoked against the threat of, or in the hope of a cure from, certain illness, included the following: Andrew Avellino (1521-1608) against death by apoplexy - from which he himself died, just as he was about to celebrate mass; Anthony of Egypt (251-356) was invoked by those who suffered from skin diseases or ergotism: his **relics** were supposedly translated to Constantinople and then to La Motte where an order of Hospitallers bearing his name was founded c. 1100, the place becoming a **pilgrimage** centre for sufferers from ergotism; Apollonia was martyred in 249 after having all her teeth knocked out: she was therefore invoked by those with toothache, but also by dentists; because Blaise (died c. 316, though evidence for him is no older than the eighth century) had saved a boy from choking to death when a fishbone was stuck in this throat, a blessing is given to throats in his name, and he is invoked by people with sore throats; the name of St Clarus, who died about 660, means "clear", hence he became the patron of those with short-sight; according to legend, after St Denis had been decapitated about the year 258, his corpse carried his head two miles from the place of martyrdom to the spot where the Abbey of St Denis now stands in Paris: he is therefore the patron of those who suffer from headaches; Fiacre (died. c. 670), because of a play on his name ("fic" is a small tumour in French), is patron of those suffering from haemorrhoids, though more importantly he is invoked against venereal disease, possibly because of his reputation as a misogynist; Giles (died c. 710) was wounded by an arrow, and crippled, so he was popular in the Middle Ages as patron of all those who were lame and, because those who were lame frequently had to beg for a living, of beggars too - and, by extension, - of lepers; Pope St Gregory the Great (c. 540-604) was elected Bishop of Rome in 590 during a plague, and because he was credited with overcoming it through organizing **processions** and **litanies**, he was thereafter hailed as protector against plague; as well as being patron of **hunting**, St Hubert (died 727) was invoked against rabies, though for no very obvious reason; in the legends surrounding John the Evangelist there is a story that the high-priest of the goddess Diana poisoned a cup from which he was to drink, but he survived unscathed: hence he protects against poison; as patron of the sick in general, and also of hospitals and nurses, the Church has chosen John of God (1495-1550), who founded the Brothers Hospitallers (before doing so, however, he had been a successful bookseller, and is also the patron of that, and associated, professions); the Evangelist St Luke is also regarded as a patron of the medical profession, because that was apparently his own role; likewise Pantaleon (or Panteleimon), martyred supposed c. 305, was a doctor and in the East in particular is regarded as the patron of the profession; Peregrine Laziosi (1260-1345) died of cancer, and is invoked by cancer sufferers; Pirminus (died 753) was believed to have been unharmed after a bite by a venomous snake, and was therefore called upon both against snake-bites, and against poisons in general; Roch (c. 1350-c. 1380) was particularly popular in the Middle Ages as a protector against plague both because he himself had cared for those infected by it, and because he was miraculously cured from it; Sebastian (martyred c. 288) was, like Roch, invoked against contagious diseases such as the plague, though it is unclear why this should have been so: possibly because of his constancy in facing the arrows which killed him, or perhaps because he was on one occasion successfully called upon for protection against plague; Thomas the Apostle was regarded as an especial patron of the blind because of his spiritual blindness in failing to accept the word of the other apostles that they had seen Christ; Ubald (c. 1100-1160) became Bishop of Gubbio, and was renowned in his lifetime for rescuing people from what was then regarded as demonic possession: it may be that it was by extension from this that he came to be prayed to as a protector against rabies; also a protector against rabies was St Vitus (martyred c. 300, though the story seems totally mythical), but for no apparent reason: he was chiefly invoked against St Vitus' Dance (Sydenham's Chorea), and it is probably from this that his wide-ranging patronage stems - it includes nervous diseases in general, epilepsy, even snake-bite.

Heart of Mary, a form of **devotion** to the **Virgin Mary** popularized, if not devised, by St John Eudes (1601-80) though historians of the cult see traces of it in the mystics St Mechtilde of Hachebron (1241-98) and particularly in St Gertrude the Great of Helfta (1252-1302). Other spiritual writers of the thirteenth and fourteenth centuries mention the Heart of Mary, but it suffered a decline in the fifteenth century to emerge again in the writings of the Carthusian Lanspergius (1489-1549), the Benedictine Louis de Blois (1505-66) and the Dominican Luis de Granada (1505-88). John Eudes, also a propagator of devotion to the **Sacred Heart** of Christ, put this devotion on to a new plane. In the years 1641-43 a conviction developed that he should organize the public cult of the Heart of Mary. He composed, and had printed, a mass and office of the Heart of Mary which he had performed for the first time in the cathedral of Autun on 8 February 1648, in the course of one of the popular missions for which he was famous, and for which he founded his Congregation of Jesus and Mary. His liturgy won the approval of several bishops who recommended it for private use. He went on to compose **litanies**, print and distribute pictures, dedicate churches of his congregation, and found **confraternities** for which he sought, and obtained, **indulgences** from the pope. He wrote books on the topic: *The Devotion to the Holy Heart and Holy Name of the Blessed Virgin*, published first in 1648, and his major treatise *The Admirable Heart of the Mother of God*, published only after his death in 1681. Despite his enthusiasm, however, the devotion failed to win acceptance by the Sacred Congregation of Rites in Rome. For this reason devotion to the Heart of Mary spread slowly. At the very end of the eighteenth century Pius VI gave permission to the Carmelites, to the Order of Fontrevrault and to the diocese of Palermo to celebrate the **feast**. Pius VII, in 1805, extended this permission to any diocese which asked. During the nineteenth century the devotion spread through Marian confraternities, and on 21 July 1855 the Congregation of Rites approved the form of office and Mass for the Heart of Mary. On 8 December 1942 Pius XII, influenced by the revelations at **Fatima**, solemnly consecrated the universe to the Heart of Mary in St Peter's basilica in Rome. On 4 May 1944 the Congregation of Rites made it a feast of the world-wide Church under the title "The Immaculate Heart of Mary", to be celebrated on 22 August. After the 1969 reform of the liturgy it became an optional memorial.

Help of Christians, Our Lady, a title of the **Virgin Mary** which has been an invocation in the **litany of Loreto** since the middle of the sixteenth century, but which only became a **feast** in the Church's **calendar** in 1815, when Pope Pius VII instituted it on 24 May in the papal states as a thanksgiving for their deliverance from Napoleon. Under this title Mary is the **patron** of both Australia and New Zealand.

hesychasm, a form of Eastern spirituality which emphasized prayer and contemplation as a means to interior peace ("hesychia" = "tranquillity"). Interior peace, however, was to be achieved in part at least by renouncing the world and all its distractions, so its ideal was that of the life of a solitary, rather than in a community of monks. A hesychast also renounced his own will through obedience to a spiritual teacher, and achieved union with God both through this tranquillity and by the constant repetition of a simple prayer - what became known as the **Jesus Prayer** - which enabled him to drive other thoughts away and turn the mind solely to God. The term is common in patristic and monastic literature from the fourth century onwards, though in its earliest appearance "hesychast" is synonymous with "hermit" or **anchorite**. The theory of hesychasm achieved its classical formulation in the writings of St Gregory Palamas (c. 1296-1359).

Holy Hour, the practice begun by St Margaret Mary Alacoque in response, she believed, to a command of Christ received in a vision in 1673. In this vision she was instructed to come down from her room every Thursday night and spend an hour in **meditation** upon the sufferings of Christ in the Garden of Gethsemane.

Holy Hour, Archconfraternity of, an association, founded by the Jesuit Father Debrosse at **Paray-le-Monial** in 1829. Its purpose was to continue the practice of the **Holy Hour** as begun by St Margaret Mary Alacocque. Members of this **confraternity**, which was later raised to the rank of an Archconfraternity covering France and Belgium, and in 1911 to cover the whole world, are required to keep this command of Christ, either individually or in groups, in any church or chapel, up to eleven o'clock at night. They pray to turn away God's anger from the world, asking forgiveness for sins, and offering consolation to Christ suffering. For membership all that is required is to have one's name (or for a religious community as a whole, the name of the community) in the register of members.

Holy Name of God, confraternity of, an association under the spiritual guidance of the Dominicans. Its origins are disputed, some dating it from the end of the twelfth century, others attributing it to the work of Andreas Diaz, O.P. during a plague in Lisbon in 1432, while some claim it did not begin until a century later, instituted among the students of a school in Burgos by Fr Didacus de Vitoria. The many **indulgences** which have been attached to this **confraternity**, as to others, include ones to be gained by undertaking the corporal works of mercy - and by admonishing those who blaspheme or rashly use oaths.

Holy Name of Jesus, a **devotion** which seems to have begun with the development of a more affective spirituality in the eleventh century, although the "name" had been invoked since early Christian times, sometimes in almost a magical fashion, as a means of exorcizing demons or as general protection. Though St Anselm (1033-1109) was not the first to use the name of Jesus in a devotional manner, his meditation, composed c. 1070, in which he dwells upon the name itself, was particularly important in the development of this form of devotion. His meditation, often incorrectly attributed, is frequently to be found in later prayer books and other manuals. It was picked up by St Bernard (1090- 1153), and piety towards the name spread rapidly, especially, it would seem, in England (there was an Office of the Holy Name at Salisbury c. 1260) and among the Cistercians, from which same background came the well-known hymn or "Jubilus" often wrongly attributed to St Bernard, the *Jesu dulcis memoria*. The custom of bowing the head at the name was already a custom in the middle of the thirteenth century, and it was commanded by a decree of the Second Council of Lyons in 1274. One participant in that Council was the Franciscan Guibert of Tournai (c. 1200-1284), and it was Guibert who wrote, as far as is known, the first complete *Treatise on the Holy Name of Jesus*. It is significant that Guibert was a Franciscan. Both they and the Dominicans were active in spreading the devotion, and in encouraging others to follow the prescript of Lyons II about bowing the head. Devotion to the name of Jesus formed a central motif in the mystical writings both of Richard Rolle of Hampole (c. 1295-1349) and of Henry Suso (c. 1295-1366). It reached new heights, however, in the sermons of the Franciscan St Bernardino of Siena (1380-1444). Bernardino's campaign of popular preaching in north Italy included holding up to the crowd who had gathered to hear him a plaque of the symbol for the name of Jesus, IHS. He was accused of heresy and his encouragement of devotion to the IHS symbol was declared by a Dominican to be superstitious. With the support of a brother Franciscan, St John of Capistrano, he combatted these charges, and was cleared of heresy by Pope Martin V in 1427. From then on the devotion went from strength to strength. The IHS symbol appeared everywhere - even in watermarks in paper - and Joan of Arc put "Jhesus Maria" on her battle standard. A number of different masses were composed during the fifteenth century, though there was no fixed date for the celebration of the feast - in Salisbury it was 7 August, elsewhere it was 15 January. An office was approved for use on 14 January by the Franciscans in 1530, and **Litanies of the Holy Name** likewise began to appear from the sixteenth century onwards. Several religious orders and dioceses had feasts of the Holy Name in their **calendars**, but it was not until 1721, at the request of the Emperor Charles VI, that Pope Innocent XIII extended the feast to the whole Church, fixing the feast day as the second **Sunday** after the **Epiphany**. In 1913 Pope Pius X changed the date to the Sunday which fell between 2 and 5 January, and if none occurred between those dates, then on 2 January. The feast was suppressed in 1969, though the missal still contains a **votive** mass. **Confraternities** of the Holy Name had been established from the thirteenth century onwards, but they greatly expanded in the sixteenth century under the direction of the Dominicans. The **Holy Name Society** has had particular success in the United States. The Society of Jesus, its title reflecting the personal devotion to the name of Jesus of its founder, St Ignatius Loyola, was also very active in encouraging this devotion, and the IHS symbol is widely to be found on the facades of Jesuit churches, while, of course, the name of the Society's best known church in Rome is the Gesù.

Holy Name of Mary, a **feast** of the **Virgin Mary** which began in Spain in the early years of the sixteenth century, but only entered the Roman **calendar** as an act of thanksgiving for the liberation of Vienna by John Sobieski on 12 September 1683. The feast was originally celebrated on the Sunday after the **Nativity of Mary**, but was fixed on 12 September early in the present century by Pope St Pius X.

Holy Name Society, or more officially the **Confraternity** of the Most Holy Name of Jesus, is an association under the spiritual guidance of the Dominicans. It traces its remote origins to an instruction to the Dominicans in 1274 by the pope to make **reparation** for blasphemies against the name of God, and the Dominicans appear to have established some form of confraternity for this purpose at Burgos in the middle of the fifteenth century, which was approved a hundred years later by Pope Pius IV, on 13 April 1564. Pope Clement VIII, however, limited the establishment of the confraternity, without dispensation, to parishes under the charge of the Dominicans, which tended to restrict its growth. In 1896 an American Dominican successfully petitioned Rome for this restriction to be removed, and there followed a great growth in the number of confraternities: each had to obtain its charter from the Master General of the Dominicans, but the authority of the local bishop was enough for the setting up of a confraternity. The purpose remains the same as that of 1274, namely to make reparation for blasphemy, but there is an additional end which is the sanctification of the members, through corporate attendance at communion on the second Sunday of each month, as well as involvement in various forms of Catholic action. A feature of the Holy Name Societies, at least in English-speaking territories, is the "Holy Name Pledge", a series of twelve pious promises, to which **indulgences** were attached in 1960.

Holy Rosary, Confraternity of, a society under the spiritual guidance of the Dominican friars which, it is sometimes alleged, can trace its origin to St Dominic, though no certain evidence can be found of the existence of such a society until the middle of the fifteenth century. Pope St Pius V in June 1569 restricted the right to establish these confraternities to the Master General of the Dominicans. They can, however, be erected in any church or chapel whatsoever, except private ones, and apparently those belonging to convents of nuns. Wherever the **confraternity** is set up, a chapel or at least an **altar** ought to be assigned to its members, on which is displayed either a statue or a picture of the **Virgin Mary** holding out the **Rosary** to St Dominic. The care of this altar is the task of the director, or rector, of the confraternity, whose duty it also is to encourage the public recitation of the Rosary, and public **processions** on the first **Sunday** of each month, and more particularly on the first Sunday of October. Members are expected to say all fifteen decades of the Rosary in the course of a week, praying for other members of the confraternity and for members of the Order of Preachers, the Dominicans.

Holy Saturday, the day before **Easter Sunday**, was originally kept as a quiet day, of **fasting** and meditation, though in some places by the late fourth century it seems that recent converts made public profession of their faith on that day, before being received into the Church at the Easter Vigil. From the sixteenth century until 1955, however, the vigil was anticipated in the morning of Saturday. From 1955 the vigil has been put back to a more appropriate time, and the Saturday is without any special celebration.

Holy Spirit, Archconfraternity of, an association founded by the Archbishop of Paris, Cardinal Guibert, in the church of Ste Geneviève, in 1884, and which two years later was raised to the rank of an Archconfraternity by Pope Leo XIII. Two years after that the seat of the **confraternity** moved to the main house of the Holy Ghost Fathers, whose Superior General, or those appointed by him, remains head of the association. Members undertake to pray for the grace of the Holy Spirit on the pope, and upon the Church's missionary activity. To this end they are expected to say some invocation in honour of the Holy Spirit each day and on the first Tuesday of each month to go to Mass and receive communion. Priest members are encouraged to say frequently the **votive** mass of the Holy Spirit, and lay members to attend it.

Holy Spirit, Confraternity of, an association first formally established in the church of Santa Anna, in Barcelona, to foster particular **devotion** to the Third Person of the Trinity, and to ask for the Spirit's heavenly gifts. The **confraternity** is divided into "choirs", each having seven members of the same sex and, as far as possible, of the same kind of status in civic life. Each one of the seven then recites one of the seven prayers on his or her appointed day, to ask for one of the seven gifts of the Holy Spirit. The association celebrates with particular solemnity the fourth **Sunday** of each month, attending mass and hearing a sermon, then, on bended knees, singing the **hymn** *Veni Creator Spiritus*.

Holy Spirit, Pious Union of, an association founded in Knechtsteden, Germany, by the Archbishop of Cologne in February 1914 to beg for the gifts of the Holy Spirit upon the Church, but more particularly upon its missionary enterprise; to ask for faith for those to whom the enterprise is directed; to ask for the conversion of sinners; and to ask for faith and charity, and the gift of fortitude, for all believers, but especially for members of the **confraternity** itself. Members are expected to attend **exposition** at least once a month; to pray for the Church's missionary work by saying the **hymn** *Veni Creator Spiritus*, and to keep each Tuesday as a day dedicated to the Holy Spirit. More zealous members also meet once a year for a Mass of reparation to the Holy Spirit for sins committed against it. There is a further association, "The work of charity of the Holy Spirit", whose members support missionary work by their almsgiving.

Holy Trinity, Archconfraternity of, an association founded in Rome under the inspiration of St Philip Neri in 1548. Its original purpose was chiefly the sanctification of its own members through the practice of the **Forty Hours** devotion, and to assist the poor among themselves. The year 1550, however, was declared a Holy Year, or **Jubilee**, which attracted many **pilgrims** to **Rome**. The **confraternity** undertook to look after the poor among these, providing them with food and accommodation. When the numbers visiting Rome diminished the following year, the members of the confraternity turned their attention to looking after the sick who had recovered sufficiently to be discharged from hospital, turning the hostels which had served the pilgrims into places of refuge for these. In recognition of its good works the popes bestowed many spiritual privileges upon the members, Pius IV conferring the title of Archconfraternity in 1562. Paul IV had granted the confraternity the church of St Benedict as its seat in 1558, but a new church of the Holy Trinity was built in 1570. The role of the Archconfraternity in caring for pilgrims and for convalescents declined over the years, and it eventually returned to its original purpose of the sanctification of its own members, chiefly through **devotion** to the Blessed Sacrament. The Cardinal Vicar of Rome is its moderator.

Holy Trinity, confraternity of, a **confraternity** associated with the Trinitarian Order for the Redemption of Captives, which has similarities with **Third Orders**. The early history of the Trinitarians is particularly obscure, and so is the origin of the confraternity whose members linked themselves to the work of the Trinitarians. This included, as well as the redemption of captives, missionary activity, the freeing of slaves, and the care of pilgrims and the sick in the Order's own hospitals. Members of the confraternity supported these undertakings through their prayers and almsgiving. They wear a **scapular** of wool, displaying a blue and red cross.

Holy Trinity, pious union of, an association or **confraternity**, founded in Madrid at the end of 1942 to bring together professional people and skilled workers who were divided into a number of distinct groups such as that of Saints Cosmas and Damian for doctors and pharmacists, those of St James or the Archangel Gabriel for telecommunications workers and so on. The members of this pious union undertake to exercise an apostolate among people of their own craft or profession, to encourage the study of moral theology and Christian philosophy, and to work among the poor, particularly through education and care for the sick in the parishes in the Madrid suburbs.

holy water, water which has been consecrated by a **blessing** and is used in ceremonies of various kinds. **Water** was frequently used, mingled with salt, in pagan Roman ceremonies as well as Jewish ones, and there is little doubt that Christians took over its use from such customs - with the difference that water for Christian use in this way had been prayed over. The earliest blessing of water, intended for use as baptismal water, comes from North Africa at the end of the second century. Prayers for the blessing of water, often coupled with oil, began to proliferate in the East in the third century and special mention was made in them of water being blessed so that it might cure illness. It is unlikely that the blessings were particularly solemn; they may have consisted of little more than a sign of the cross.

In both East and West the custom developed of washing hands before prayer, a form of ritual purity which may also have been taken over from the Romans or Jews. Basins for this purpose were placed at the entrance to churches from the fourth century at least, though at first probably filled with water that had not been blessed. In particular, the clergy washed their hands before beginning the ritual, and then in the course of it. It seems likely that the laity at one time also washed before receiving the sacrament. This cleansing became less important as the change took place to receiving the sacrament on the tongue, but the holy water remained as a form of ritual cleansing. It received for this purpose a special blessing.

Blessed water was used for a variety of purposes, and prayers of blessing appeared in the books of ceremonials at different periods. Pope Gregory the Great advised Augustine of Canterbury to sprinkle the pagan temples with it before turning them over to Christian use, and by the sixth century both in Rome and in Spain there were special prayers for blessing the water that was to be used to sprinkle houses: the Anglo-Saxons were accustomed to take water home with them to sprinkle their houses, possibly to drive away evil spirits. The use of holy water in this way did not become a general practice until about the tenth century. Later still the custom developed of an annual ceremony of the blessing of houses with water consecrated on **Holy Saturday**. (In the Eastern Churches a ceremony for the blessing of water has been performed on the **feast** of the **Epiphany** since the fourth century at least, though this is in remembrance of the **baptism of Christ** in the Jordan. Some of the faithful take this

"Epiphany Water" and drink it at meals or sprinkle it on their houses.)

Holy Week, the solemn celebration of the days leading up to **Easter**. The earliest accounts of Easter suggest that the one day, the **Sunday**, encapsulated the whole of the story of Christ's death and resurrection. If that is so then the articulation of the story over several days would appear to owe a great deal, if not everything, to the building programme begun by Constantine in Jerusalem in the early fourth century, and then the **pilgrimages** to the Holy Land later in the same century, accounts of which furnish vivid witness to the way in which the newly- constructed churches at such sites as that of the upper room where Christ celebrated the Passover with his disciples, the place of the crucifixion and that of burial, were used to dramatize the events as they unfolded over the course of the week. The days of Holy Week, **Palm Sunday, Maundy Thursday, Good Friday** and **Holy Saturday**, are all discussed separately.

holy year, or year of jubilee, appears to be distantly derived from the practice recorded in the Old Testament of celebrating the fiftieth year as a particular time of forgiveness and the remission of debt (see Leviticus 25:10), as indeed to some extent was every seventh year. There is evidence that in medieval times, even before the celebration of the first holy year in 1300, the fiftieth year was kept as a time of celebration, during which there was an especial opportunity for the remission of sins, and the penalties incurred by sin. When, on 22 February 1300, Pope Boniface VIII proclaimed a period in which great **indulgences** could be obtained by travelling to **Rome** and visiting the **basilicas** of St Peter's and St Paul's Outside the Walls once a day for fifteen days for visitors to the city, for thirty days for Rome's own citizens, he made vague mention of past customs, but these were unspecified. Boniface did not name his year a "jubilee", but it was certainly called that by some who commented upon the event - including Dante, who may have been there himself. The first holy year or jubilee was highly successful in attracting **pilgrims** to Rome, and although Boniface had clearly intended a Jubilee only once a century, Clement VI announced another one for 1350. For the jubilee of 1350 the basilica of St John **Lateran** was added to the list of those to be visited, and Santa **Maria Maggiore** became another in 1390 at the next holy year. The latter year was chosen on the ground that there should be a Jubilee within the average life-span, which was linked to the supposed age of Christ at his death. Hence the next one occurred in 1423. From 1450, however, they have been proclaimed every twenty-five years, only 1800, 1850 and 1875 being omitted because of political unrest in Europe in general, and Rome in particular. The last one was held in 1975. The best-known ceremony associated with the holy year is the opening in each of the four basilicas (on the **Christmas** Eve preceding the year, and by the pope himself in St Peter's) of a special door, which is sealed up again at the end of the period.

hopeless cases, patron of, is traditionally Saint Rita of Cascia (1381-1457) who led such a troubled life herself that she became a popular **saint** for those in very difficult situations. The much better known **devotion** to Saint Jude, one of Christ's apostles, appears to be of fairly recent origin. Although there is some evidence of a cult to Saint Jude existing in Europe, it was neither very active nor widespread. The modern appeal of Saint Jude appears to stem from a **shrine** to him in a Chicago parish, and the devotion was fostered from 1929 onwards as a means of raising funds for the activities in the United States of the religious order, the Claretians, who looked after the parish. Though it is difficult to say why the cult should have taken the special form of praying to Jude in times of great crisis (except, perhaps, that his name was so similar to that of the Judas who betrayed Christ that no one invoked him unless all else failed), the period at which this cult developed, the period of the Great Depression in the United States, may have helped to give it this particular slant.

hunting, patron saint of, or, more correctly, **saints,** for there are two patrons of hunting, both with similar stories: the two are Hubert, Bishop of Liège, who died in 727, and Eustace, of no known place or date, though his cult seems to have come from the East. According to the apocryphal stories of Eustace's conversion, he was a Roman general called Placidas, who encountered a stag with a **crucifix** between his antlers, which sight brought him and his family to Christianity. In the case of Hubert, the same story is told, apart from the detail that Hubert met the stag on **Good Friday**. The cult of both was highly popular in the Middle Ages, and Eustace was numbered among the **Fourteen Holy Helpers**. His **feast** day (20 September) has been suppressed. Hubert died on 30 May, which is kept as his feast, but more important is the translation of his **relics**, a celebration observed on 3 November.

hymns, religious words and music sung in churches and at other Christian gatherings. The first Christians used the psalms of the Old Testament, and this practice has continued down to the present day. But there were also specially composed hymns, some of which have left traces in the New Testament. There were certainly hymns written before St Ephrem (c. 306-73), but he is the first orthodox composer to be definitely identifiable. He was writing them to counter heretical songs, and this apologetic purpose influenced development thereafter. Hilary of Poitiers (c. 310-66), for instance, wrote hymns against the Arians. In the West St Ambrose (339-97) wrote hymns for his congregation in Milan in a simple metre which was easily remembered. Rome was slower to make use of this form of singing in its liturgy, though at the end of the sixth century the authorship of a number of hymns which still survive was attributed to Pope Gregory the Great. Hymns were written for the liturgy (**sequences** for example), for the Divine Office and for **processions**, but these were in Latin which, by the Middle Ages, was no longer the vernacular. Vernacular hymns seem to have developed out of the sequences at Mass, as a means of interpreting them to the congregation, but these had to develop alongside, rather than within, the liturgy. It was in fact the use of vernacular hymn-singing in Lutheran services which eventually led, for the first time, it would seem, in 1605, to permission being granted for vernacular hymns to be sung in Catholic services. It remains true, however, that the devotional singing of hymns has been a far greater part of the Protestant, than of the Catholic, tradition of worship.

I

icons, painted images ("icon" = "image"), most commonly on wood, whether portable or monumental. There was a dispute in early Christianity about the propriety of giving veneration to such images: the Old Testament had forbidden it (cf. Exodus 20:4), and refusal to worship the image of the emperor had been a reason for persecution. Nonetheless, the catacombs were painted with Christian scenes, and later on churches were decorated with them. The doubts about them did not go away, however, and led in the eighth and ninth centuries to iconoclasm - the rejection of the veneration of images, and indeed their destruction. The legitimacy of showing veneration to icons was asserted at the Second Council of Nicaea in 787. The oldest surviving icons date from the sixth and seventh centuries, and all come from St Catherine's Monastery on Mount Sinai.

Ignatius water, water which has been blessed with a particular prayer, and into which either a **medal** of St Ignatius Loyola, or some **relic** has been dipped. The custom is very old, and was much used as a protection against sickness, particularly in countries where Jesuits were active as missionaries. It was endowed with an **indulgence** in 1866.

Immaculate Conception, the belief that the **Virgin Mary** was conceived by her mother as free from any stain of original sin - a dogma of the Roman Catholic faith since Pope Pius IX's Constitution *Ineffabilis Deus* of 8 December 1854. 8 December was, and remains, the day on which the **feast** is kept. The doctrine had a troubled history. As a liturgical festival it began in the East with the feast of the Conception of the Virgin Mary, though celebrated as a feast of her mother, St Anne. According to the apocryphal Gospel, the

Protoevangelium Jacobi, and clearly in imitation of the conception of John the Baptist, Mary's mother was sterile, and was told only late in life by an **angel** that she would give birth. The feast therefore was sometimes called the Conception of St Anne, though what was being commemorated was Anne's conception of Mary. It was indeed sometimes known as the Annunciation of Mary, because of the visitation by the angel. The first evidence of this feast in the East occurs in the middle of the eighth century, but it was probably not universally observed in the Byzantine Empire until the end of the ninth century. At that time it was celebrated on 9 December. It seems to have come to the Western Church via England, where it was devoutly observed in certain dioceses before the Norman Conquest in the mid eleventh century, brought to England, possibly, by **pilgrims** returning from the Holy Land. The Normans put an end to liturgical celebration of Mary's Conception (it was not yet thought of as "immaculate", i.e., free of original sin). Eadmer (c. 1055-c. 1124), the disciple of St Anselm, Archbishop of Canterbury, is credited with the composition of the first detailed treatise on the Immaculate Conception. There may have been a particular reason for his writing it. It has been suggested that it was to defend the reintroduction of the feast into England by the Archbishop's nephew, also called Anselm, when he was appointed Abbot of the Monastery at St Edmund's Bury. Before Anselm came to England he had been Abbot in Rome, to which city the monks of the monastery of St Sabas, near Jerusalem, had fled from Saracen invaders. They had kept the feast of the conception for centuries in Jerusalem, and continued to do so in Rome, where Abbot Anselm had encountered them. Whatever the reason for Eadmer's treatise, Abbot Anselm's reintroduction of the feast brought about a considerable revival in England of belief in and **devotion** to the Immaculate Conception, a belief which then moved southwards on to the continent of Europe. There was opposition, particularly from St Bernard of Clairvaux (c. 1090-1153) and St Thomas Aquinas (c. 1225-74), but this scarcely delayed its progress as a devotion. As a theological problem it made somewhat slower progress, embraced enthusiastically by Franciscans (they adopted the feast in 1263) and Carmelites, opposed by Dominicans and Cistercians. But outside the last-named orders, the cult of the Immaculate Conception was universal by the mid fourteenth century. In 1477 Pope Sixtus IV approved for the diocese of Rome a Mass and office for the feast drawn up by a Franciscan, though he also had to issue an instruction to prevent those opposed to the doctrine from calling its protagonists heretics, and vice versa. The feast became obligatory for the Roman rite in 1708 - though officially it did not become the feast of the *Immaculate* Conception until after the dogmatic definition of 1854.

Immaculate Conception of Our Lady of Lourdes, Archconfraternity of, an association originally founded simply as the Society of the **Immaculate Conception** in 1872, and made an Archconfraternity the following year for France, and for the whole world in 1879. Its name was changed to add "of Our Lady of **Lourdes**" in 1910. The purpose of this **confraternity** is to honour the Immaculate Conception, and to commemorate the definition of this dogma in 1854. Members are also expected to support the **shrine** at Lourdes, including by almsgiving, and to pray for the conversion of sinners. They are expected to pray some part of the **rosary** each day, practise penance and humility, and work actively for the poor and the sick.

Immaculate Conception of the Blessed Virgin Mary, Confraternity of, an association established in the Theatine church in Rome in May 1894 to give honour to the **Virgin Mary** under the title of the **Immaculate Conception**. Members of this **confraternity** are expected to wear the Blue **Scapular**, and to keep the twelve first **Saturdays** of each month with special **devotion**.

Immaculate Conception of the Blessed Virgin Mary, Society of the, an association formally founded in June 1847 to commemorate the vision of St Catherine Labouré in which she was given the **miraculous medal**. The original constitution of this **confraternity** permitted its establishment in schools run for girls by the Congregation of the Sisters of Charity of St Vincent de Paul, to which Catherine Labouré belonged. Successive papal permissions widened the scope of the Society to include other schools, houses and parishes associated either with the nuns or with the priests of the Congregation of the Mission, the religious congregation to which the Sisters of Charity were linked. The purpose of the society is to honour the **Immaculate Conception** of the **Virgin Mary**, and particularly the virtues purity, humility, obedience and charity. Any woman may be a member from childhood onwards, though membership is divided into sections, one to include the young, another those who have married, and another any woman who is in any way sick or handicapped, particularly the blind, for whom members of this society are expected to show especial care. The insignia of the society is the miraculous medal, with which members are invested upon joining, and they are expected to celebrate the first Saturday of each month in honour of the **Immaculate Heart of Mary**. They are also required to keep **vigil** on the night of 18 July each year, to recall the anniversary of the founding of the society.

Immaculate Conception, Rosary of, a form of the **rosary** which consists of saying the **Hail Mary** twelve times, followed by the **doxology** said three times.

Immaculate Conception, Sodality of, an association founded in the church of Santa Maria in Ara Coeli, Rome, originally in April 1727, but refounded in 1842 to honour the **Immaculate Conception** and to spread **devotion** to the **Virgin Mary**. Members of this **confraternity** are expected to say at least once a week the **Rosary** of the **Immaculate Conception**, to pray a third part of the rosary for deceased members of the association, and to support it by almsgiving.

Immaculate Virgin of the Holy Medal, Sodality of, a society founded to commemorate the revelation of the **miraculous medal** to St Catherine Labouré. Membership of this **confraternity**, which dates from the mid-nineteenth century, is consequent upon the bestowal, in due form, of the **medal** itself. No obligations are iimposed by membership, though members are encouraged to use the **invocation** "Mary, conceived without sin, pray for us who call upon thee".

indulgences, a development of the notion of penance, allied with the doctrine of **purgatory**, according to which it lay in the power of the Church to remit from the sinner the punishment still due to him or her after death even for the sins which had been forgiven through the confessional. The term *indulgentia* become a technical expression for this type of remission of punishment only in the thirteenth century: before that time the word "remission" itself had sometimes been used, as likewise "relaxation" and "absolution". The earliest indulgences appear to come from Southern France in the first half of the eleventh century. In these instances they were granted for visiting churches or for giving alms, and they replaced part (a day, a week) of the penance which had been imposed by the Church for the sin confessed. At this stage the indulgence (remission of the ecclesiastical penance) was quite distinct in the minds of church authorities from forgiveness of sin, or remission from the consequences of sin in the next life. That was left to God, though the Church could and did pray that God would be merciful.

Early indulgences were generally quite modest in their claims, remitting a few days of penance, and papal ones were generally more restrained than those of bishops. Because they were intended to replace the ecclesiastically-imposed penance, some penitential practice was usually required. And possibly there was no more obvious form of commutation of penance than to go on pilgrimage - or on a crusade. When in 1095 Pope Urban II proclaimed the crusaders' indulgence, he pointed out that the journey was itself equivalent to any penance that might have been imposed. These were the first forms of "plenary" indulgences, and though crusading indulgences were not uncommon, they were granted very infrequently in any other circumstance - and they were also limited to the pope to grant. By the end of the twelfth century, however, Pope Innocent III was extending the crusading indulgence to all those who helped with the crusade, whether or not they went to fight.

A major development was the jubilee indulgence of 1300 when Pope Boniface VIII, at least in part for financial motives, granted a plenary indulgence to all who came to Rome in that year. It was intended by Boniface that such indulgences should be granted every century, but by 1470 Pope Paul II had reduced the intervals between jubilees to twenty-five years, thereby making it theoretically possible for most Christians to obtain full remission from the punishment still to come for their sins. But by that time it was not necessary to make the arduous journey to Rome. Already by the middle of the fourteenth century plenary indulgences, granting full remission at the hour of death, were available for individuals from the papal court in exchange for a fee.

Much of the devotional life of Catholics came to centre on the acquisition of indulgences, and a book was produced, the **Raccolta**, which encompassed them all. Prayer books regularly listed the benefits to be gained by saying certain formularies or performing certain actions. There were "toties quoties" (= so many times, that many times) indulgences, meaning that as often as one performed some action or recited some prayer, that number of times the indulgence might be gained. Others, however, might be gained only once a day, once a month, or once a year. There was a complex structure of plenary and partial indulgences, and the number of days remission came to be thought of as directly related to the number of days to be spent, or not as the case might be, in purgatory. Some of the language retained its links with the historical roots. It was possible to gain "quarantines", that is to say forty-day remissions, which clearly reflected the benefits gained by a penance performed during the forty days of **Lent**.

Long before their rejection by Luther, indulgences had been the subject of much controversy: Abelard, in a book written in the second quarter of the twelfth century, criticized bishops for their liberality in bestowing them in return for offerings. He was not alone in doing so, and other theologians of the same period, even while admitting they might be granted, saw them only as the commutation of one form of penance for another. Opinion in the thirteenth century, however, moved towards seeing an indulgence as a direct, rather than an indirect, remission of punishment due in purgatory. This might have been a difficult position to argue had it not been for the parallel development of the "Treasury of the Church", which argued that the punishment due to sin had been already borne by Christ and the **saints,** and their merits could be applied by the Church through indulgences to others. Thomas Aquinas taught that no link existed between what had to be done to gain the indulgence, and the indulgence itself: those in ecclesiastical authority could dispense them at will. This has not been the common opinion. All would agree that the recipient must be in a state of grace, and the gaining of indulgences frequently requires the reception of communion over and above the specific acts associated with a particular indulgence. The granting of an indulgence has therefore become disassociated from the sacrament of penance and linked instead to the fostering of devotional life among Catholics.

So far discussion has been about the history and theology of indulgences in themselves: the application of indulgences to the dead was a much later development, the first papal one of this kind not being granted, it seems, until 1457. Their validity was much debated and the view that indulgences simply release souls from purgatory has not won general acceptance. It is the more common view that indulgences are a way of asking God that a soul be freed, rather than operating directly.

As far as Catholic doctrine goes, the Council of Trent insisted, against the Reformers, that the Church had the power to grant indulgences, and that they were beneficial for the faithful. Current legislation concerning them is contained in canons 992-997 of the *Code of Canon Law*, and is very restrictive, limiting the power to grant indulgences to the pope, or to those delegated to do so by the pope.

Infant Jesus, Archsodality of, an association or **confraternity** established by the Brothers of the Christian Schools to pray and work for the christianization of the classroom, and for vocations, particularly to teaching. It began in Palestine at the beginning of this century, being canonically established by the Patriarch of Jerusalem in Bethlehem on 1 July 1907. It was raised to the rank of an Archsodality by Pope St Pius X in July 1909. It was intended to recruit not only boys in colleges run by the Brothers of the Christian Schools, but any other Christian children who might wish to join. At its most successful it was producing magazines aimed at its members throughout the world in a large number of different languages.

Infant of Prague, a **statue** of Christ as a child, holding in his left hand a globe with a **cross** upon it, and holding his right extended in **blessing**. Since 1628 this statue has been kept in the church of the Discalced Carmelites in Prague, Our Lady of **Victories**. The image, which is of wood and wax, and is about eighteen inches high, came to Prague from Spain in the sixteenth century, and nothing is known of its early history. It became an object of popular **devotion**, it seems, only after being placed in the Carmelite church. It was crowned in 1655, and many indulgences have been attached to it, thus adding to its popularity. A number of curious customs have grown up around the statue in some countries, such as standing it outside one's door overnight to ensure fine weather the following day.

Infant of Prague, Sodality of, an association or **confraternity** under the spiritual guidance of the Discalced Carmelites, whose purpose is to promote the spiritual life of its members, particularly through **devotion** to the **Infant of Prague**. It began in 1628 in the Monastery of Our Lady of Victories of the Discalced Carmelites in Prague itself, where it served to heighten devotion to the **statue** of the Divine Infant. From there it spread to other churches of the Order, but it was not until 1913 that it was formally established as a sodality.

Iona, an island off the West coast of Scotland where the Irish monk Columba founded a monastery in 563. The monastery was suppressed at the Reformation, but a community was refounded there by a Church of Scotland minister, George McLeod, in 1938. It has since become a retreat centre across denominational divisions, though still under the general jurisdiction of the Church of Scotland, attracting some quarter of a million visitors each year as pilgrims, and about 1,600 to stay for spiritual counselling.

Island, Our Lady of the, a **shrine** of the **Virgin Mary** near Solin in Yugoslavia, on a island on the River Jader. The shrine was begun by the Croatian Queen Helena, who died in 975. She built two churches, one of which, intended as a royal mausoleum, was dedicated to St Stephen, the other to Mary. Both disappeared in the wars against the Turks, but when their ruins were discovered at the end of the nineteenth century they became a centre of **pilgrimage**.

Itatí, a **shrine** of the **Virgin Mary** on the banks of the River Paraná in Argentina. The shrine appears to have been founded first in 1615 by Fray Luis de Bolaños, but was destroyed by Indians and the statue removed. This was found a few days later, however, by two Indian children, standing on a rock in the river, surrounded by light and music. The local people built a sanctuary for the wooden image, replaced by a much more splendid building now. The **feast** is celebrated on 9 July.

J

Jesus Prayer, a form of prayer which consists of the repetition of the name of Jesus, together with a short formula. A common usage is "Lord Jesus Christ, son of God, have mercy upon me" - another version, sometimes identified as the Russian form, ends "... upon me a sinner". The origins of the prayer are believed to lie in **hesychasm**, with its belief that perfection lies in constant union with God through prayer. The simplest way to achieve this end was by the unceasing repetition of a short formula. It is described by Diadochus, Bishop of Photike (c. 400 - c. 485) and by others in the fourth century, though without indicating a precise formula. Dorotheus of Gaza, however, just a hundred years after Diadochus, wrote of his disciple Dositheus that when Dositheus was seriously ill he repeated "Lord Jesus Christ have pity on me", or "Son of God, come to my aid". There is a slightly fuller description in St John Climacus (c. 579 - c. 650), and a much fuller one, though still without a prescribed formula, in Hesychius of Sinai, a monk whose dates are entirely uncertain except that he is later than John Climacus, and not later than the end of the tenth century. Though it is not entirely clear that he was doing more than using a metaphor, it seems possible that Hesychius's description of the prayer linked the repetition of the name of Jesus with rhythmical breathing. By the end of the twelfth century the formula appears to have been established, and certainly by the end of the thirteenth to be linked to rhythmical breathing. As such it was much in vogue on Mount Athos in the second half of the thirteenth, and throughout the fourteenth centuries, as witnessed by, among others, Gregory of Sinai (1255-1346), a monk originally of Sinai who spent a time on Mount Athos before moving on to Bulgaria, where he died. The system of the hesychasts was attacked by a Western theologian, later a bishop, Barlaam of Calabria, about the year 1337. Barlaam's criticisms were important because they occasioned a defence of hesychasm by St Gregory Palamas (c. 1296-1359), a monk of Athos who died as Bishop of Thessalonica. In this he defended both the prayer itself, and the method in which it had come to be recited. It was not so much directly from Mount Athos, however, that the Jesus Prayer came to be known in the West. From Athos it had spread, rather belatedly, into Russian Orthodoxy, where it was much in vogue during the nineteenth century. It is described in detail in the enormously popular *The Way of a Pilgrim*, first published in Russia c. 1870, but then regularly republished and translated into many other languages, including English. It is clear that there are convergences between this form of prayer and the chant of a *mantra*, but direct links between hesychasm and Indian spirituality are impossible to establish. It has, on the other hand, been pointed out that there are also similarities with Islamic spirituality for which it is much easier to account - by journeys of monks to Egypt, for example. But the association of a short formula of prayer with rhythmical breathing is perhaps so basic to spirituality that there is no difficulty in accepting that it could develop independently in several distinct religious cultures.

Jesus the Young Man, Archsodality of, an association or **confraternity** first established in the Salesian church in Nazareth in 1924, with the purpose of fostering piety among the young. It was recognized by Pope Pius XI in 1930.

Joseph, Archsodality of Saint, a society founded in Rome about the year 1860 and raised to the rank of an Archsodality in 1862. Its purpose is the promotion of **devotion** to, and imitation of, St **Joseph**, both in the individual members of the **confraternity** and in the Christian community at large. Its members are encouraged to show particular devotion during March, the month dedicated to Joseph, to say prayers in his honour for seven consecutive Sundays and to have some image of the saint in their homes. They are also expected to wear the "girdle" or belt of St Joseph.

Joseph, Model and Patron of Lovers of the Sacred Heart, Universal Archconfraternity of Saint, a society founded in Rome in March

1886 under the spiritual guidance of the **Sacred Heart** Fathers and raised to the rank of an Archconfraternity the same year. Its purpose is to foster **devotion** to St **Joseph**, particularly as a model of family life and to turn to him as **patron** in all that appertains to eternal salvation. Members of the **confraternity** are required to pray, morning and evening, the **invocation** "St Joseph, model and patron of lovers of the Sacred Heart of Jesus, pray for us".

Joseph of Beauvais, Archconfraternity of Saint, a society founded in Beauvais in January 1859 in the chapel belonging to the Brothers of the Christian Schools by a priest who was chaplain to the youths under instruction there. It became an Archconfraternity two years later and had great success in France and its then colonies. The **confraternity** exists to promote **devotion** to St **Joseph**, to seek his protection for all Christian families, Catholic countries, religious houses and communities, and against enemies of the Church. Devotion is also fostered to him to achieve a **happy death**.

Joseph of the Mountain, Pious Union of, a society founded in Barcelona, Spain, in October 1902, which seeks to promote in the Church by any appropriate means **devotion** to St **Joseph**. Members of the **confraternity** are divided into teams of men and women, and the "perpetual cult" of St Joseph which is the hallmark of the society is committed to the women. They are organized in groups of thirty, and once a month a statue of St Joseph is brought to each member's house for veneration for a day. This association had considerable success in Spain, and in Latin America.

Joseph, relics of Saint, the best known of which, his girdle or belt, was brought to France in 1254 by Sire de Joinville on his return from the crusades. He built a chapel for this yard-long stretch of grey hemp with an ivory buckle, and was buried there in 1319. It was an object of **devotion** until 1668 when it was accidentally destroyed. During the fourteenth and fifteenth centuries a number of other different places claimed to have the staff **Joseph** carried during the flight into Egypt. It was sometimes said that the swaddling clothes venerated at **Aachen** as having been used for Christ were in reality the foot-coverings of Joseph. As early as the year 1000 the town of

Chiusi claimed to possess the wedding ring Joseph had given to the **Virgin Mary**. On instructions from Pope Innocent VIII ownership of this object was transferred to Perugia in 1486.

Joseph, Saint, presented in the Gospels of Matthew and Luke as the husband of the **Virgin Mary**, though in neither, and particularly not in Luke, does he play a significant part, or appear outside the infancy narratives. Unlike that to Mary, **devotion** to Joseph was very late in developing. There was a **feast** in the Coptic Church on 20 July commemorating his death from the seventh century, but nothing in the West until much later, although his name occurs in a martyrology of the monastery of Reichenau, under the date of 19 March, during the second quarter of the ninth century. At roughly the same time the Irish monk Oengus composed his own martyrology, which included Joseph for the same day. The influence of Reichenau spread the inclusion of Joseph's name to the martyrologies of other abbeys until it became a commonplace, but this does not indicate there was any liturgical observance in honour of the saint. Indeed, there appears to be no evidence of this even when, in the early fifteenth century, a eulogy was added to the hitherto brief mention of Joseph in the martyrology. This addition has been ascribed to the efforts of Jean Gerson (1363-1429), Chancellor of the University of Paris. There had been a steady increase of writings by theologians, particularly Franciscan theologians, in which the role of Joseph was discussed, and, though not a Franciscan himself, Gerson was in the same tradition. He composed a Latin poem in honour of St Joseph and, in a sermon on the feast of the **Nativity of Mary** (8 September) 1416 before the fathers of the Council of Constance, urged them to establish a feast of Joseph as means towards repairing unity in the Church. He portrayed the Saint as a **patron** of all Christian families because of his preeminence in the family of Nazareth, and recommended him as a model for workmen. Gerson's close friend Pierre d'Ailly (1350-1420) wrote a treatise on Joseph's twelve prerogatives (the *Tractatus de duodecim honoribus*) which came to be used frequently whenever a liturgical office was to be compiled in honour of Joseph.

Parallel to this growth in theological writing, Joseph was given increasing prominence in devotional literature, though largely through pious lives of Christ or to some extent through lives of Mary which drew heavily upon apocryphal gospels. The same sources were used for the wide variety of mystery plays which entertained the townspeople of medieval Europe. The role of Joseph was not particularly stressed, but he was certainly present, usually represented as an old, possibly even senile, character. In some of the later German plays, on the other hand, his comes to be something of a comic part, even that of a drunkard. From the fifteenth century prayer books included prayers to Joseph drawn from the writings of St Bernard (1090-1153) and d'Ailly, and in the early sixteenth century a devotion to the seven sorrows (the "sorrows" were unspecified) of Joseph was proposed by an Italian Franciscan. There were also a handful of medieval guilds or **confraternities** dedicated to him, not surprisingly including those of carpenters.

It seems likely that the first church with a **dedication** to Joseph was built at Bologna about 1130, and a decade later he was listed as the secondary patron of a Benedictine church at Alcester in Warwickshire.

In about 1300 the church in Bologna came into the charge of the Servites, and it seems likely that they were the first to celebrate a feast of St Joseph (on 19 March), and were doing so by the year 1324. In 1350 they added the name of Joseph to the **Litany of the Saints**. There was a feast in Avignon about 1375, and the Franciscans had adopted it by the end of the fourteenth century. A letter of Jean Gerson's in 1416 claims that the Augustinians were celebrating the feast in Milan by that time, and so were the English - though on 9 February, the **octave** of the Purification (**Presentation in the Temple**). Much earlier (late thirteenth century) there was a **votive** mass written for the monastery of St Florian in Austria which could be used according to the personal devotion of the clergy, but this was not attached to any particular date, and was in no way obligatory. In 1479 Sixtus IV included the feast of St Joseph in the calendar of the church in Rome, though with the lowest rank, and from Rome it spread first to other Italian dioceses and then across Europe.

The liturgical reforms of the Council of Trent (1545-63) imposed the Roman calendar on the Western Church, thus completing the extension of the feast of St Joseph throughout the Catholic world. Thenceforward devotion to the saint grew rapidly. The Carmelite reformer Saint Teresa of Avila (1515-82), was especially committed to him, putting a dozen of the seventeen monasteries she founded under his patronage. The Carmelite fathers put the whole order under his patronage in 1621, and obtained permission to celebrate the feast of this patronage on the third Sunday after **Easter**. Other orders followed suit, many new foundations both for men and women taking their titles from him, such as the Congregation of the Sisters of St Joseph founded in 1650. The feast which had been included in the Roman calendar in 1479 with the rank of "Simple" had been raised to the rank of "Double" by Sixtus IV's successor, and to "Double of the second class" by Pope Clement X in 1670. Joseph was included in the Litany of Saints in 1726, and on 8 December 1870 Pope Pius IX declared Joseph to be the Patron of the Universal Church. A special Litany of St Joseph was approved in March 1909, and in 1962 the saint's name was added to the "Roman Canon" (Eucharistic Prayer 1). In the meantime, however, the liturgical observance of the feasts of St Joseph had undergone a number of changes. There had developed two quite separate feasts, that on 19 March and the "Patronage" (which became the Solemnity) of Joseph. In 1847 Pius IX had extended the latter to the whole Church. In 1913 it was transferred from the third Sunday to the third Wednesday after Easter, but was abolished entirely in 1956 to be replaced with the feast of St Joseph the Worker on 1 May. This was a conscious attempt by Pope Pius XII to give a Christian meaning to the day observed as a workers' festival. In the reforms of 1969 it has been reduced in rank to a memorial, the older feast of 19 March remaining as the main celebration in honour of Joseph.

K

Kevelaer, a **shrine** of the Virgin Mary located in a small town north of Cologne, and perhaps the most popular place of **pilgrimage** in Germany. It dates from the mid-seventeenth century when two soldiers brought to the town a picture of a statue of Our Lady **Comforter of the Afflicted** which had been erected in the city of Luxembourg by a nun who had been cured of the plague. The picture was acquired by a woman of the town - or, according to other versions, set up in a chapel beside the road by the soldiers themselves. People almost immediately came to pray before the picture for protection during the Thirty Years War.

Kibeho, a town in Rwanda, where it is claimed the **Virgin Mary** appeared to a number of schoolchildren (about a score claimed some kind of experience, though the principal visionaries numbered seven). The apparitions began with the appearance of the Virgin to Alphonsine Mumureke on 28 November 1981, and they then spread to others. There have also been claims that Jesus has appeared several times and that, as at **Fatima**, the sun was seen to dance in the sky. The **apparitions** lasted over a number of years, but by the end of 1983 they were over - although some visionaries claimed to have received special messages from time to time and one of them, Emmanuel Segatashya, has made it his special mission to preach the Virgin's message of prayer and penance not only in Rwanda but also in the neighbouring countries of Zaïre and Burundi.

Kingship of Our Lord Jesus Christ, Pious Union of, an association, limited to forty members, founded by a group of men at the University of the **Sacred Heart** in Milan, in 1928. The purpose of this group was to foster among individuals and in families knowledge of the kingdom of Christ and the Catholic Church (which they, it seems, believed to be identical). This they did by a variety of means, including promoting the celebration of the **Feast** of **Christ the King**, and by fostering loyalty to the pope. They also undertook to promote the social doctrine of the Catholic Church. In addition to the forty full members, there is also a group of "Friends", divided into various categories, made up of men who accept the general principles of the association.

Knock in County Mayo, in the north-west of Ireland, is usually regarded as a shrine to the **Virgin Mary**, though it began as an **apparition** of three figures of whom one was Mary, the others being identified as St **Joseph** and St John the Baptist. The vision occurred on 21 August 1879, and was seen in the early evening by Mary McLoughlin, the priest's housekeeper, and a friend called Mary Byrne. It showed the three figures hovering a foot or two above ground level against the gable-end of the church, with, to the left of St John, an altar with a lamb and a cross upon it. A small crowd gathered, all of whom witnessed the apparition, though none heard any words spoken. It seems to have lasted about three-quarters of an hour. The figure identified as the Virgin Mary was slightly taller than the others, and was crowned; the St John figure held a mass-book, and was wearing a mitre. A commission of enquiry was promptly established, and it was tacitly accepted by the Archbishop of Tuam that a vision of the Virgin had occurred. This decision was endorsed by a subsequent commission of inquiry in 1936, when some of the visionaries were still living. From the start, Knock was treated as a second **Lourdes**. Great numbers of pilgrims began to make their way there, and cures were almost immediately claimed - the first, of a deaf girl, only ten days after the apparition. These cures were meticulously recorded by the parish priest. It became the practice to prise away little bits of cement from the gable wall, and it was frequently these mementoes which were attributed with the healing powers. The gable-end of the old parish church is now covered by glass, with replicas of the figures as seen by the visionaries behind the glass. A **Basilica** of Our Lady of Knock which will hold 15,000 pilgrims has been opened nearby, recalling in its structure the four provinces of Ireland, and its thirty-two counties.

Knock, Pious Union of Our Lady of, a society founded in August 1935 by the then Archbishop of Tuam, primarily to look after the **pilgrims** and the **shrine** of **Knock**. It is divided into two parts: "the Stewards" care for the sick, and organise the ceremonies; "the Handmaids" also care for the sick, but are also directly concerned with looking after the sanctuary, and working in the kitchen. Members of the confraternity are expected to attend the shrine one day a month; they are also required to say the entire **rosary** daily.

L

La Chapelle, Our Lady of, a **shrine** of the Virgin in the parish church of La Chapelle at Brussels. The statue venerated there is the one before which a penitent was bidden to pray by his confessor, after admitting that he had sold his soul to the Devil. As the priest said Mass, an enormous spider descended to the altar and dropped on to it the contract which the penitent had signed with the Devil.

La Naval, Our Lady of the Rosary of, a **devotion**, particularly among sailors in the Philippines, to the **Virgin Mary**, which dates from the Spanish-Dutch war of the mid seventeenth century. In 1646 a Dutch fleet attacked Manila, which was defended by only two ships. The Filipino crew prayed to the Virgin, and took a vow that, should their defence of the city be successful, they would go barefoot in procession to a **statue** of Our Lady of the **Rosary**. Their defence was successful, and the sailors carried out their vow, walking to the chapel of Mary in the church of St Dominic. The procession is repeated every second Sunday in October. The image which is venerated under the title of "La Naval" dates from 1588. It is of wood, though the hands and head are of ivory. According to legend, it was carved by a Chinese who heard, as he cut into the wood, a voice saying, "Do not strike so hard, you are hurting me" - to which event he attributed his conversion to Christianity.

La Salette, Our Lady of, a **shrine** of the **Virgin Mary** in the French Alps south of Grenoble, where a vision appeared to fourteen-year-old Mélanie Calvat and her eleven year-old companion Pierre-Maximin Giraud on 19 September 1846. The two children were on the mountainside in charge of flocks of sheep and cattle respectively when, at about 3.00 pm Mélanie awoke from sleep to see a round light with the figure of a lady at the centre. The white-clad figure warned the children that if people did not repent - in particular of working on Sundays and of blasphemy - they would be punished. There would in any case, she told the children, be a potato famine that winter. The children were told to pray, and to pass on the message. When they related the story to the parish priest he immediately told them they had seen the Virgin Mary, and the apparition was officially approved by the Bishop of Grenoble five years later.

lance, holy, a **relic** of the passion of Christ. According to the Gospel of St John a soldier, surprised to see that Christ appeared to be already dead when he was sent to break the legs of those crucified, pierced his side with a spear or lance, and blood and water flowed out. Tradition has it that the soldier was later converted to Christianity. The existence of this **relic** is not recorded before the visit to Jerusalem of St Anthony of Piacenza about the year 570. When the Persian King Chosroës II captured Jerusalem in 615 the lance was taken away along with other relics, including that of the **cross**. It was returned in 629 after the defeat of the Persian armies by Heraclius, and placed in the church of the Holy Sepulchre. Before this time, however, the tip of the lance had been broken off and taken to Constantinople by Nicetas, who placed it in the church of Sancta Sophia. This point went to Paris in 1241 in payment of a debt to the French King Louis IX, and was eventually enshrined in the Sainte-Chapelle. It disappeared without trace at the French Revolution. The main body of the lance seems also to have been transferred to Constantinople at an unknown date: it ceases to be recorded at Jerusalem. When Constantinople fell to the Turks in 1453 it was removed from the city, but in 1492 was sent as a gift to Pope Innocent VIII and has since remained in the Vatican. There are other claimants to be the spear which pierced Christ on Calvary. The Nüremberg Lance, taken to that city in 1424 though now housed in Vienna, may possibly be a spear used at the Imperial Coronation of 1273, in which case it contained a fragment of one of the **nails** with which Christ was fixed to his **cross**, and therefore may have been revered for that reason. Another lance was discovered at Antioch in 1098, during the first crusade, by Peter the Hermit. This may be the relic preserved by Armenian Christians.

Lateran basilica, so called because it stands on the site of a palace which belonged to the Laterani family, is the cathedral church of **Rome**. The original **dedication** was to the Holy Redeemer, but after it was rebuilt at the beginning of the tenth century it was dedicated to St John the Baptist. It was almost entirely destroyed by fire in 1308 and again in 1360, and the present structure dates from the restoration begun in 1586 of both the palace, the usual residence of the popes from the fourth century until the departure to Avignon in 1309, and of the **basilica**. It contains some **relics** of **Christ**, and the **Scala Sancta** which is the only surviving part of the original building. As the cathedral church of Rome the **feast** of its dedication is observed throughout the Western Church on 9 November: it is said to be the oldest church in the West, and the first in dignity. However, the feast of the dedication of the Lateran was not commemorated in Rome, as far as is known, before the eleventh century.

Lauda, Sion salvatorem (= "Sion, praise your Saviour"), a **sequence** written by St Thomas Aquinas in 1264 at the request of Pope Urban IV for the mass of **Corpus Christi**, a **feast** then newly instituted. Its theme is calling the Church ("Sion") to the worship of the eucharist, and closely follows the theology of the eucharist as it is contained in Thomas's *Summa Theologiae*. Thomas has modelled the structure and metre of the **hymn** on the *Laudes crucis attollamus* written for the feast of the **Finding of the Cross** by Adam of St Victor, who died in the last quarter of the twelfth century and was renowned as the writer of sequences. The *Lauda, Sion* is still used in the Corpus Christi Mass, and has frequently been translated into English, most successfully perhaps in the hymn which begins "Laud, O Sion, thy Salvation".

laudes regiae, a type of **litany** used in the Church of Gaul (France), which differs from other litanies in that it is a chant of triumph rather than one of a penitential spirit. In its classical (Western) form it begins and ends with the three phrases *Christus vincit, Christus regnat, Christus imperat* ("Christ conquers, Christ rules, Christ commands"). Much of the *laudes* reflects Roman imperial liturgy, with "Hear, O Christ" replacing "Hear, O Caesar", but the *Christus vincit/ regnat/imperat* has a more complex history. The first two parts of the chant may have originated in the Eastern Church, and possibly even the final phrase may have been an attempt to render more accurately into Latin the full meaning of the Greek, but such suppositions can only be tentative. In the West the formula appears in the second half of the eighth century in Gaul, and in Rome, which was then very much under Frankish influence. A Frankish origin is supported by the form of the acclamation, which is distinctly military in tone, and in no church more than the Frankish does the liturgical blessing of weapons and battle standards play so a large a part. The combination of the *Christus vincit* with the Litany of the Saints seems to have occurred in France in the third quarter of the eighth century, as part of the campaign to sanctify kingship, but their use became widespread at coronations of Frankish, Norman, and other rulers, and was also used for popes and bishops.

lawyers, and all engaged in the legal profession, have as their **patron** St Ivo of Kermartin (1253-1303), who was himself a distinguished lawyer. His **feast** is celebrated on 19 May.

League of Daily Mass, an association which began in the Dublin church of the Society of Jesus in the early years of the twentieth century, and was formally recognized by Pope Benedict XV in 1915. Members of the **confraternity** undertake to attend Mass daily, though this commitment is not binding. Their purpose is to make reparation for offences against Christ in the Sacrament, to give glory to God and to thank him for graces received, and to pray for the dead.

League of Prayer for Union under the Protection of Our Lady of the Atonement, a society formally approved by Cardinal Francis Spellman, Archbishop of New York, to work and pray for the unity of Christians, and for the return to the Catholic Church of those who had fallen away. The society is under the guidance of the Superior General of the Friars of the Atonement.

Legion of Mary, a society founded in Dublin by a layman, Frank Duff, on 7 September (the eve of the **feast** of the **Nativity of the Blessed Virgin**) 1921 for the sanctification of its members and the service of the Church. Its original name was the Association of Our

Lady of **Mercy**: the name by which it is now known was chosen in November 1925 to reflect the somewhat militaristic language of the **confraternity** whose purpose is "to destroy the empire of sin, uproot its foundations and plant on its ruins the standard of **Christ the King**", as the Legion's handbook describes it. In keeping with this Latin title, the structures of the organization have been given similarly Roman names. Thus the basic unit, normally at parish level, is a *praesidium*, over two *praesidia* or more there is a *curia*, over several of those a *concilium*, and the Dublin headquarters is known as the *Senatus*. In addition to the active members, there are also "auxiliaries" who assist the work of the Legion through their prayers and financial support. Meetings take place around a simple **altar**, a **statue** of the **Virgin Mary** as the **Immaculate Conception**, placed between two candles and flowers. A meeting consists both of prayers and of an account by the individual members of the work they have undertaken in the course of the past week. This work includes visiting the sick, assisting the poor and other such activities, but members are also encouraged to help the parochial clergy in any way that they can. Much of the inspiration for the structure of the work and of the meetings was taken over from the St **Vincent de Paul Society**, but the specific Marian emphasis reflects Frank Duff's interest in the True Devotion to Mary taught by St Louis Grignion de Montfort. There is a particular **devotion** to the Virgin under the title of **Mediatrix of All Graces**.

Legion of the Immaculate Heart of Mary, Pious Union of, a society founded in Brion-près-Thouet in the diocese of Poitiers, France, to encourage both **devotion** to the **Immaculate Heart of Mary** and the spreading of the Kingdom of God. They aim to achieve the first by an act of **consecration** to the Immaculate Heart, and the latter by glorifying the **Sacred Heart** and working for the increase of vocations to the priesthood. There are two grades of membership of this **confraternity**. The first undertake to say the act of consecration when they become members, the second to repeat it frequently, and to say prayers for the society's intentions, particularly on the first Saturday of each month, and in the month of August, which is dedicated to the Immaculate Heart. Members are expected to wear the **medal** of the society. Those who join while still boys are called

"Angels of the Immaculate Heart", priests are "Priest Apostles", and the remainder are known as "Legionaries".

Lent, the six-week period just before **Easter.** The word comes from the Middle English "Lenten" meaning "Spring", but the Latin equivalent is *Quadragesima*, meaning "forty", and clearly refers to the length of the **fast** (forty days) by which Christians prepared themselves for the **feast** of Easter. The origins of Lent are particularly obscure. It seems likely, however, that there was from very early times in some parts of the Church a fast of forty days in commemoration of Christ's forty days in the wilderness and which followed immediately upon celebration of the **Baptism of Christ** on 6 January, now the **Epiphany.** The forty days attached to Easter began to appear in Rome and elsewhere shortly after the Council of Nicea of 325, and although no reference is made in what passes for the Acts of this Council to the establishment of such a fast, it is possible that it was ordered by the bishops gathered at Nicea. For a long time there was no agreement as to when the fast should begin and end. In Rome, for example, there was no fasting on Saturdays or Sundays, so in order to accommodate the forty days the fast was extended backwards from the first Sunday in Quadragesima to what is now known as **Ash Wednesday.** In other places the fast ended before the beginning of **Holy Week,** and the Saturday and Sunday before Easter were observed as the festival of the raising of Lazarus, and as **Palm Sunday.** The practice of baptizing new members of the Church at Easter was in force in Rome and North Africa in the third century, and throughout the Church by the fourth century, and the Lenten season therefore became the appropriate opportunity for final instruction and preparation. The candidates were expected to fast before their baptism, and the early document known as the *Didache* recommends that all Christians keep the fast with them, which no doubt gave added impetus to the penitential aspect of Lent.

Liesse, Our Lady of, a **shrine** of the **Virgin Mary** in the Ardennes. According to legend, in the year 1134 three knights from Picardy, the lords of Marchais, Eppes and Coucy, were captured in the Holy Land, and sent to Cairo where they were alternately threatened and bribed to deny Christ. This they steadfastly refused to do. When

Ismérie, the daughter of the Sultan, was sent to tempt them, they converted her to Christianity by relating stories of Mary and she helped them escape. She travelled with them, but when she lay down to rest angels came carrying a statue of the Virgin. The angels transported all of them back to France, and at Liesse the knights built a church, placing the statue inside it. Ismérie was baptized with the name Mary, and died shortly afterwards. The shrine became a major place of **pilgrimage** in France, though the first records of it being so date only from 1338, by which time, it seems, the pilgrimage was already well established. It remained the main sanctuary of the Virgin - portrayed as black - until the nineteenth century, and was patronized by the French royal family as well as by the populace in general.

Limpias, a town near the northern coast of Spain, lying between Bilbao and Santander, where it was claimed the figure of the crucified Christ was observed to open and shut its eyes, and look around the congregation. The occurrence was first reported by two young girls on 30 March 1919, at the end of a mission preached by two Capuchin priests. Subesquently large numbers of people who came to the parish church claimed to have witnessed the figure's eyes move. **Pilgimages** were organized, especially from the surrounding countryside, but without formal approval by the Church these tailed off by the mid-1920s. **Devotion** to the Christ of Limpias has not, however, entirely died out, and survives in particular in Latin America, while the shrine still attracts a small number of visitors.

Lindisfarne, sometimes known as Holy Island, is an island just North of Bamburgh Head, off the north-east coast of England. A monastery was established on the island, which is joined to the mainland by a causeway except at high tide, by St Aidan, a bishop from **Iona**, in 635. As a monastic community it was remarkable both for its scholars and its saints, the best known of the latter being undoubtedly St Cuthbert, who died in 687. In 875 the monks were forced to flee after repeated attacks by Vikings. They went first to Chester-le-Street and then to Durham, carrying with them the coffin of St Cuthbert. The great cathedral of Durham was built over the grave of Cuthbert.

Lisieux, a **pilgrimage** centre 110 miles west of Paris, and a **shrine** in honour of St Thérèse, a Carmelite nun who died on 30 September 1897. She had been born into a pious family at Alençon, some distance south of Lisieux, on 2 January 1873, but moved to the town after the death of her mother. Her sister Pauline joined the Carmelites there, and Thérèse determined to follow her. When she told her father this he plucked a flower and said that God would protect her as he had this little flower - the Saint later became known to her devotees as "the Little Flower". The prioress of the convent refused to admit anyone so young, and was supported by the bishop. When on a pilgrimage to Rome, Thérèse petitioned Pope Leo XIII for permission to enter: she became a Carmelite on her fifteenth birthday. Although of remarkable piety, it was her diary, *The Story of a Soul*, which attracted attention to her. She was canonized on 17 May 1925. Her shrine is in the convent, but a massive church has been built nearby to cope with the crowds - Lisieux is the most popular centre of pilgrimage in France after **Lourdes**.

litanies, a form of prayer widely used in the early Church and down to the present day. The word in its original Greek means a "supplication" or "petition", and petitionary prayers are to be found in the fourth-century liturgy used at Antioch. The deacon called for prayers for various categories of persons and the people answered "Lord have mercy" (*kyrie eleison*). This happened after the reading of the gospel, where the prayers of petition or "bidding prayers" now occur in the modern Roman Catholic liturgy. The practice spread from Antioch to other Eastern Churches, and thence to Rome. By about the year 400 in Rome there was a series of petitions included in the liturgy to which the response, addressed to God, appears to have been "Lord, hear and have mercy", a translation into Latin of the *Kyrie* of the Greeks. This was expanded over the years and a lengthy version known as the *Deprecatio Gelasii* is attributed to Pope Gelasius, Bishop of Rome at the end of the fifth century. The *Kyrie* in Greek did not itself disappear, however, and a letter of Pope Gregory at the end of the sixth century makes it clear that this was said, together with *Christe eleison*, as a form of litany in the mass, the *Deprecatio Gelasii* form eventually being dropped.

This supplicatory prayer, though it may have developed as part of the mass, was not confined to it, and by the end of the fourth century was in use as part of the **office**, at least in some places, and from the sixth century the *Kyrie eleison* was an obligation imposed upon monks by the rule of St Benedict and other monastic ordinances. The litanies were also used as part of **processions**, particularly penitential processions. This again appears to have originated in the East, at least by the end of the fourth century, and there processions were known as litanies, so close was the identification of processing and supplicatory prayer. In the West the practice began a little later, apparently at Vienne under Bishop Mamertus where they were called **rogations**, a latinized form of the Greek "litany". It is not clear what prayers were said in Vienne, or later in Rome, during these processions, but by the time of Pope Gregory they undoubtedly included the *Kyrie*. This form of prayer was brought to England by St Augustine in 597.

The litanies so far discussed consist of a series of petitions to which the response was "Lord have mercy", or some variant: they are not the litany of **saints** as such. Petitions to the saints - the **Virgin Mary**, John the Baptist, apostles, prophets and martyrs - were included in the Antioch liturgy in the fourth century. The fullest surviving one of early date, however, comes from the seventh century and is in Syriac, though reflecting a Greek original from the patriarchate of Antioch. In this instance the petitions are addressed to Mary, the archangels, John the Baptist and then through various categories, ending with an appeal to all saints. It has been argued - and convincingly - that a version of this Greek litany came to England in 668 in the luggage of St Theodore (c. 602-90) when he was appointed Archbishop of Canterbury. Certainly by the early eighth century the litany of the saints was well known in England, though various forms of it are known to have existed. The lists of saints varied, and so did the position of Mary in the sequence of petitions. By the first years of the ninth century the petitions *Kyrie eleison* and *Christe eleison* had been added at the beginning. It would seem likely that it was from England, and probably by way of Ireland, that the - originally Greek - litany of the saints was spread in Europe at large. This was happening by the end of the eighth century, and a hundred years later the lengthy appeal to the persons of the Trinity individually, as well as the *Kyrie eleison* and *Christe eleison*, had appeared.

These prayers were used for a wide range of liturgical occasions, as well as for penitential processions, for visiting the sick and the dying, or for private devotion. They were combined in the *laudes regiae*, and produced in metrical versions that were sung in processions. A number of types of litanies other than that of the saints have been compiled, most particularly the **litany of Loreto**.

Litany of the Holy Name, a series of invocations of the **Holy Name of Jesus**. A form of these **litanies** was to be found in Books of Hours from the sixteenth century onwards. By that time litanies for each day of the week were regularly prescribed for recitation by the laity: those of the Name of Jesus were to be said on Wednesdays. Such was the proliferation of this form of **devotion** that in 1601 Pope Clement VIII forbade public recitation of any except the **litany of Loreto** and the litany of the **saints**, unless prior permission had been obtained from the Holy See. Such permission was asked from time to time, but was refused until in 1862 Pope Pius IX granted permission, but only to those dioceses which explicitly sought it. In 1886 Pope Leo XIII extended the permission to the whole Church. Both Popes granted **indulgences** to the saying of the litany.

Little Office of Our Lady, a form of **prayer** to the **Virgin Mary** modelled on the divine office, containing the usual division into "Hours", but considerably shorter. It makes use of psalms, for the most part the same ones each day of the week, thus making for simpler recitation, and also of the **Hail Mary** and of **hymns** to Mary. Its use is first recorded in the tenth century, in the life of Bishop Ulrich of Augsburg, who died in 973 and has the distinction of being the first **saint** to be **canonized** by a pope. When Peter Damian (1007-72) wrote a treatise on the office, he strongly recommended the Little Office, and in 1095 Pope Urban II ordered it to be said for success in the first crusade. It was taken up by monks as part of their round of prayer, and spread to the laity, particularly to members of **Third Orders**, its propagation bolstered by collections of Marian legends in which miracles attested the efficacy of saying the Office. It was retained in the Breviary, when that was reformed in 1568 in the wake of the Council of Trent, though any obligation under penalty of sin on either the clergy or the laity was removed at that time. On the other hand Pope Pius V attempted to encourage its recitation by the granting of an **indulgence**.

"little way", the spiritual doctrine of St Thérèse of Lisieux (1873-97), worked out during the last four years of her life while she acted as novice mistress in the Carmelite convent of **Lisieux**.

Living Lamps, a pious union which was established at the beginning of this century to provide constant adoration of the Blessed Sacrament in churches outside the times of public liturgies. When members join the **confraternity** their names are inscribed in a book, together with the period of the week during which they intend to keep watch before the tabernacle. They are given a **medal** proper to the "Lampades Viventes" which they are expected to wear about their necks while fulfilling their obligations before the altar.

Living Rosary, Association of, a society founded in Lyons in 1826 by Pauline Jaricot and eventually placed by Pope Pius IX under the spiritual guidance of the Dominicans. At the beginning of each month one of the fifteen decades of the **rosary** is assigned to a member of the **confraternity** who undertakes to say it daily. Responsibility for organizing this distribution falls on the "zelator", under the guidance of the priest who has been appointed director. The teams are therefore made up of fourteen people and the zelator: the **indulgences** granted to this association depend upon the team being complete. If a member drops out, the zelator has only the space of one month to find a new recruit. An offshoot of this confraternity has been the Society of the Living Rosary for Children, which was started by Fr Ignace Body, O.P. in 1900 in France, and has since spread to other countries.

Lord's Prayer. Although English versions of this are known before the Reformation, there is no evidence that there was any such thing as an official form, nor a single one hallowed by use, though equally there is no doubt that many translations existed. It seems likely that the *Pater Noster*, as with other familiar prayers, was taught to children in Latin, even though neither they nor their elders could understand the words they were expected to repeat by rote. So much was this that case that in medieval times common **prayers** were known by their Latin names - a **rosary**, for example, was known as a "paternoster". Though they may not have understood the words, efforts were made to ensure that those who used them understood the sense: the clergy were regularly required to instruct their flocks in the vernacular in the meaning of the prayers they were saying. The first authoritative English text appears in the 1539 *The Manuall of Prayers or the Prymer in Englyshe*, and this version was that taught to the people in churches throughout England, with a minor variation in the first Prayer Book of Edward VI of 1549. The **doxology** was added in the reign of Charles II. During the (brief) attempt to restore Roman Catholicism under Queen Mary, the form of the Lord's Prayer to which English people had become accustomed was retained.

Loreto, a **shrine** of the **Virgin Mary** in Italy and the resting place of the Holy House of Nazareth. According to legend, the dwelling place of the Virgin where the Annunciation took place was transported from Nazareth by angels in 1291 first to a spot on the Dalmatian coast between Fiume and Tersato and then, on 10 December 1294, to Loreto, some fifteen miles from the port of Ancona on the Adriatic. The earliest account of these events dates only from 1465 or thereabouts, though the earliest recorded **pilgrimage** occurred in 1313. From then onwards Loreto became one of the major pilgrimage sites of Europe: a bull of Gregory XI dated 2 November 1375 granted **indulgences** to the "great multitude of the faithful" who went there. In addition to the Holy House, a statue of the Virgin Mary is much venerated, and Our Lady of Loreto was declared the **patron** of all those involved in flying by Pope Benedict XV and confirmed by a decree of the Sacred Congregation of Rites in 1920. The House itself is a small, rectangular building encased in marble, but originally constructed from materials not to be found in the vicinity of the domed basilica which now surrounds it. A local feast of Our Lady of Loreto was permitted in 1632, and its celebration gradually spread from Loreto itself to the rest of Italy, and then elsewhere: the feast of the "Translation of the Holy House of Mary the Mother of God in which the Word was made flesh" entered the Roman Martyrology for 10 December as a result of a decree of 31 August 1669. The original statue of the Virgin was destroyed by fire in 1921, and has been replaced.

Loreto, litany of, a **litany** of invocations in honour of the **Virgin Mary**, and by far the most popular of the litanies. In its present form it appears first to have been published in a book of prayers printed at Dilingen, possibly under the influence of St Peter Canisius, in 1551. An earlier, and much longer, version of it has been found at the end of a missal printed at Avignon for Armenian monks in the mid-fourteenth century: this group had a house at Ancona, close to Loreto. Remoter origins are, of course, the litany of the **saints**, which always contained a number of invocations of Mary.

lost articles, patron saint of, is St Anthony of Padua (1195- 1231) to whom on that ground, there has remained a considerable **devotion**. The reason for this "patronage" is difficult to say, though there is one suggestion that it arose because a novice, who had borrowed the **saint's** psalter without permission, hurriedly returned it when visited by a fearful apparition.

Lough Derg, a **pilgrimage** centre near Donegal in the north-west of Ireland, close to the border with Northern Ireland. The lake itself is some four miles wide and six long, and St Patrick's **Purgatory** is the largest of the many islands which dot the lake. According to tradition, after **Patrick** had driven evil spirits out of many places in Ireland they fled to the island in Lough Derg, and he went there to do battle with them despite attempts to prevent him doing so by people who feared they would never see him again. After twenty-four hours he returned successful. Patrick was also credited with having created the "cave" for which the island was famous in medieval times by drawing on the ground, whereupon the ground gave way to reveal a view of purgatory and so frighten his followers into penance for their sins. The height of Lough Derg's "popularity" was between the twelfth and fifteenth centuries, a popularity which arose at least in part from the experiences of Knight Owen in 1147 who claimed to have seen heaven after doing battle with the Devil in the cave. This story was put into a ballad in England, and the poem was circulated all over Europe - Dante is thought to have used it while writing his *Inferno*. Pilgrims flocked to the island from all over Europe, and in great numbers, to spend fifteen days there living on bread and water, twenty-four hours of which, as part of a seventy-two-hour total fast, were spent in the cave. This was a small structure in which it was impossible to stand upright, rather like a sepulchre, and indeed one medieval account suggests that a person entered it after the celebration of mass for the dead. At the end of the fifteenth century the cave was closed by order of Pope Alexander VI, but was reopened shortly afterwards. In the sixteenth century the length of the pilgrimage was reduced to nine days. As part of the government's attempts to eradicate Catholicism in Ireland, the buildings of the pilgrimage site, including the "cave" were destroyed in 1632, though this did not stop pilgrims coming. There was a revival in the early twentieth century which still continues. Now, however, the duration of a stay on the island has become three days, only on the second night of which is the pilgrim allowed to sleep. He or she travels to the island fasting from the previous midnight, and once on it is allowed only one meal a day of some dry bread and black tea. Much of the time is spent walking barefoot round six rings, the remains of cells for hermits, dating from about the time of St Patrick, near the edge of the lake. The night-long vigil is spent praying inside the basilica of St Patrick, which was consecrated in 1931 and holds twelve hundred people.

Lourdes, Our Lady of, a **shrine** of the **Virgin Mary** in the French Pyrenees. A fourteen-year-old shepherdess, Bernadette (properly Bernarde-Marie) Soubirous had a vision of a "Lady" in a cave at Massabielle, beside the River Gave which runs through Lourdes. These visions, of a woman dressed in blue and white, continued from 11 February 1858 until 16 July the same year. In the course of these visions, the Lady called for repentance, and for a chapel to be built on the spot at which they took place. On 25 March, the Feast of the **Annunciation**, she named herself, speaking, as she commonly did, in the local dialect: "I am the **Immaculate Conception**", a doctrine declared binding on the belief of all Catholics four years before. The authenticity of the appearances was rapidly accepted, and a statue of the Virgin, made to Bernadette's description, was unveiled in the cave in April 1864. Two years later Bernadette became a nun in the Congregation whose school she had attended, and was sent from Lourdes to Nevers, where she died in 1879. She was canonized in 1933. Lourdes has become the most important **pilgrimage** centre for Christians after Rome. It is particularly renowned for the number of apparently miraculous cures which have occurred there. The sick started to come to Lourdes in considerable numbers only in 1874 - though the first miracle was reported a year earlier - and a hospital was built in 1875. The sick are now bathed in, and the pilgrims drink, water which comes from a spring which seemingly came into being at the site of the visions, only in the course of them - on 25 February.

Love and Charity, Pious Union of, a society founded at Vélez Sarsfield in the Archdiocese of Buenos Aires by Fr Fortunato Tedesco in October 1942. The idea of this association came to Fr Tedesco when he was confined to bed through sickness, and was reflecting on the problems faced by other clergy in similar circumstances. His association, which began with seventy-six priests, has a two-fold aim: its members undertake to visit each other when they are ill to give them spiritual help; and secondly they provide material assistance to speed their recovery. Members must be in sufficient health to be able to practise their priestly ministry at the time of joining. Any member who is sick for more than eight days may seek financial assistance from the association: those suffering from longer illness may be sent to a place where recuperation would be swifter. No money is asked of the clergy themselves: all is sought by donations and legacies.

lovers, their **patron saint** has been since the end of the fourteenth century St Valentine, whose **feast** falls on 14 February. There is no reason for this in what little is known of the lives of either of the Valentines commemorated on that day, and the origin of the link may very well be a poem by Chaucer.

Luján, Our Lady of, a **shrine** of the **Virgin Mary** in the small town of Luján, some thirty-five miles west of Buenos Aires. According to tradition, in 1630 a Portuguese landowner in Córdoba, Argentina, wished to build a church in honour of the **Immaculate Conception**, and asked a friend in Buenos Aires to send him an appropriate statue. It seems that two terracotta images were sent, one of which arrived at Córdoba. The other was left behind after two days travelling when, on the third morning of the journey, the oxen refused to move until the case containing the statue had been removed. Don Rosendo Oramas, a local landowner, constructed a shrine for the statue in his own house, which was looked after by one of the black slaves who had been in the party transporting it to Córdoba. The first church was completed by 1685. A second was built as a thank-offering after a miraculous cure in 1754, and a basilica, begun in 1887, was completed in 1930. **Devotion** to the Virgin of Luján is strong throughout South America, and she is the **patron** of Argentina, Uruguay and of Paraguay, formerly all part of the same administrative province. Her **feast** is celebrated on the Saturday before the fourth Sunday after Easter.

M

magi, the three, sometimes called the three kings, or three wise men, are mentioned only in the second chapter of St Matthew's Gospel. No number is mentioned by the evangelist, but they presented three gifts, according to the text, of gold, frankincense and myrrh. One of the magi was associated with each gift, and after their names had been fixed by the ninth century, to Caspar (or Gaspar) was attributed the gift of gold, to Balthasar that of frankincense, and to Melchior myrrh. From the fourth century they were taken to be kings to fulfil the apparent prophecy of Psalm 72:10, "May the kings of Tarshish and the isles render him tribute, may the kings of Seba and Sheba bring gifts!" However, the Gospel does not call them kings but "magi", meaning wise men, perhaps astrologers. The depiction of one of them as black dates from fairly recent times. Their giving of the gifts is celebrated by the **feast** of the **Epiphany**. Their **relics** are venerated in Cologne, having been first discovered, according to legend, by St Helena, the Emperor Constantine's mother, and brought to Constantinople. From Constantinople they were taken, so the story goes, to Milan at the end of the fourth century, though other versions claim they were moved directly to Milan from the Holy Land during the crusades. When Milan was entered by Frederick Barbarossa in 1164 the relics were sent to Cologne where they were placed in a golden reliquary of considerable size arranged in the form of a basilica, with a central and two side aisles. It is located behind the high altar of the cathedral, and is known to have been the work of Nicholas of Verdun. These relics were the object of great **devotion** in the Middle Ages, and Cologne became one of the major **pilgrimage** centres.

mandatum, the command (hence *mandatum*) to wash one another's feet given by Christ to his apostles at the Last Supper. It was carried out liturgically, though with varying degrees of solemnity, at least since the third century, for the Synod of Elvira at the beginning of the fourth lays down the rule that the feet of those who are about to be baptized should be washed by people of lower rank than priests. The Rule of St Benedict requires that the feet of the community be washed once a week, and the community itself is to wash the feet of guests. As a full, liturgical, action it was established fairly late. By the end of the twelfth century the pope was washing the feet of twelve subdeacons after Mass and of thirteen poor men after his dinner: the whole affair became one of high ceremony with ambassadors and other dignitaries of Church and State nominating the individuals whose feet were to be washed by the pope.

Maria Maggiore, Santa, the Roman **basilica** which claims to have, in addition to other **relics** of the Nativity of Christ, the manger (**crib**) in which he was laid. It was founded on the Esquiline hill by Pope Liberius (352-66), and was therefore first known as the "Liberian basilica", but it was splendidly reconstructed by Pope Sixtus III (432-40) to commemorate the Council of Ephesus of 431, when Mary's title as Theotokos or "God-bearer" was vindicated. There is a legend that its outline was traced on the hill by a fall of **snow**.

Maria Stein, a **shrine** of the **Virgin Mary** some thirty miles south of Basel, in Switzerland in the side of a cliff down which a child fell in the fourteenth century. The child was unharmed, and local inhabitants placed a statue of Mary in the cave beside which he landed. The escape was regarded as miraculous, and people began to come to the spot on **pilgrimage**. When, in 1540, the same thing happened in exactly the same place, the crowds increased, and a monastery was established to look after them.

Maria Taferl, a **shrine** in Austria dating from the seventeenth century when a farmer attempted to cut down an oak tree next to a large stone on a hill-top, possibly a pagan holy place which had been "christianized" by a painting of the **crucifix** attached to the oak. The farmer failed to cut down the tree, injuring himself in the process, and ceased his efforts when he noticed the picture of the crucifix. He fell on to his knees and begged forgiveness - at which his bleeding stopped.   Pilgrims began to visit the spot, and the crucifix was replaced by a picture of Our Lady of **Sorrows**. A church was built, and apparitions of figures dressed in white were reported. The chief **feast** celebrated at the shrine is that of Our Lady of Sorrows, 15 September.

Marian years, two (so far) twelve-month periods dedicated to encouraging **devotion** to the **Virgin Mary**. The first was called by Pope Pius XII in 1954 to mark the centenary of the definition of the dogma of the **Immaculate Conception**; the second, called by Pope John Paul II, ran from **Pentecost** 1987 to the **feast** of the **Assumption** 1988. They have something of the nature of a **holy year.**

Mariazell, a **shrine** of the Virgin in Styria, Austria, founded when a statue of Mary was erected by a monk who had been sent to minister to miners in the district. It has served as a centre of devotion for Yugoslavs and Hungarians, and particularly for Austrians. The House of Habsburg has had an especial devotion to the shrine, and Our Lady of Mariazell was titled "the Great Mother" (*Magna Mater*) by the Emperor Ferdinand II.

Martha of the Hotels and Taverns, Confraternity of Saint, a society which seems to date back to the thirteenth century, though the first documentary evidence dates from 1455. In its present form, however, it began only in 1945. It exists to promote good relations among those who work in the hotel trade in any capacity, and to foster **devotion** to Saint Martha, the **patron** of the **confraternity**.

Mary Magdalen, Saint, identified with the "sinner" of the New Testament who, according to legend, after Christ's death went to France to expiate her sins. She died there and was buried at St-Maximin la Sainte-Baume, though her body was later removed to Vézelay. The great church at Vézelay became a profitable centre of **pilgrimage**, partly as a result of the claim to be the **shrine** of Magdalen. In December 1279, however, the monks of St Maximin claimed that they had found the true body of the saint in their own crypt, and that the relics taken to Vézelay in the eighth century were of someone else. From then on St Maximin became the focus of **devotion** to Mary Magdalen.

Mass of Reparation, Archsodality of, an association first founded in Paris in 1862, and raised to the rank of an Archconfraternity in 1886. Members of this **confraternity** - and a number of similar ones with identical titles were subsequently founded elsewhere in Europe - undertake to attend not only the mass on Sundays or other festivals to which they are obliged, but a second mass, to make up for all those who fail to attend at all. If, however, there is only one mass which they can attend in the local church, members are permitted instead of attempting to find a second mass, to spend a little longer in prayer in church either before or after the celebration of mass.

Matariah, a **shrine** of the **Virgin Mary** close to Cairo, where, according to a tradition preserved in the apocryphal gospels, the Holy Family rested on their flight into Egypt. A tree leaned downwards to provide fruit for them to eat, and water sprang up from the ground to give them drink. In the past the church there was a major centre of **pilgrimage** for Egyptian Christians.

Maundy Thursday, a name derived from *mandatum*, meaning "command", and used for the Thursday before Easter, on which day it is the practice to carry out Christ's "new command" to demonstrate love for one another through the washing of feet. The earliest record of the Thursday observances in **Holy Week** comes from Jerusalem at the end of the fourth century. There were at the time two Masses, one to mark the end of **Lent** and its **fast**, the other, on Calvary, to celebrate the institution of the eucharist. Gaul (France) was following a similar pattern from the fifth century. In Rome, on the other hand, even as late as the sixth century, there would seem to have been no mass to commemorate the eucharist. This came in during the following century, and it was during this mass that the pope, as bishop of the city, consecrated chrism, and blessed the oils of the sick and of exorcism. This was at midday. He also washed the feet of his household and reconciled penitents. Eventually, from the end of the seventh century it would seem, the practice of having only one mass prevailed, though this combined all the elements (the end of Lent, the reconciliation of penitents, the washing of the feet, the celebration of the eucharist and, in cathedral churches, the consecration of chrism). After the reforms following the Council of Trent, the service had to take place in the morning, which had the effect that the eucharist had to be reserved for a long period. The "altar of repose" therefore became the centre of attention. In 1955 the practice of having two masses was restored: there was in cathedral churches a "chrism" mass, and there and elsewhere "the mass of the Lord's Supper" was to take place in the evening. The altar of repose was to be a much more discreet part of the ceremony, though "watching" at the altar of repose, which had played a large part in pre-1955 piety, was allowed until midnight.

Maximus, Pious Union of Saint, a society founded in Turin, Italy, in 1869 to promote the work of parish missions, the making of retreats and so on in the Turin Archdiocese, and throughout its ecclesiastical province. Members of this **confraternity** are divided into the priest missioners, and those - either clerical or lay - who support the work of the society through prayers and almsgiving.

May, the month in the **calendar** in which particular **devotion** is shown to the **Virgin Mary**. While the origins of this practice are unclear, it may reflect an attempt to "christianize" Spring festivals celebrated throughout Europe. The earliest association of May with Mary seems to be in Spain during the latter part of the thirteenth century. Shortly afterwards the Dominican mystic Henry Suso (c. 1295-1366) is recorded as weaving a crown of flowers for the statue of Mary, a custom which eventually became widely practised. "May devotions" began to appear, possibly first in Italy, in the sixteenth century, and early in the eighteenth century a Jesuit published a small book, *The Month of Mary, or the Month of May*, which surveyed all the different devout observances, such as decorating statues, saying the **rosary** or praying the **litany of Loreto**, which were now common. Though they were common, they were still private rather than public devotions. This began to change from the mid-eighteenth century onwards until, a hundred years later, it had become a custom throughout the world.

medals, the practice of wearing which was at one time a very common form of **devotion**. There seems to be some evidence of religious medals in the early Church, but possibly only because the pagan practice of wearing amulets or charms was difficult to forbid. Certainly medals of a sort were purchased by **pilgrims** at their destinations, as a form of proof that they had indeed reached the **shrine** they had made the journey to visit, but these were not devotional objects. Religious medals as such began to appear in the fifteenth century, and so did celebratory medals, to mark, for instance, the 1475 **holy year**. Medals were therefore not uncommon in themselves, but it does not seem likely that they were blessed, or that **indulgences** were attached to them, until the late sixteenth century. They became much more common through the popularity of the **miraculous medal**, and in the present century through the permission granted to wear a medal in place of a **scapular**.

Mediatrix of All Graces, a title sometimes given to the **Virgin Mary**, and, as the entry on the Virgin Mary makes clear, one with a long pedigree. The *Glories of Mary* produced by St Alphonsus Liguori in 1786 insists that all graces come to men and women through Mary, and the influential German theologian Matthias Scheeben (1835-88) argued that no prayer would be answered without Mary's intercession on the petitioner's behalf. There was even papal approval for such a notion. In an encyclical of September 1891, Pope Leo XIII confirmed that no grace came except through Mary. Since the Second Vatican Council (1962-65), however, this doctrine - which has certainly never been given formal approval by the Church - has been played down.

Medjugorje, the site in Bosnia-Hercegovina on the borders of Croatia, of alleged apparitions of the **Virgin Mary**. They began on 24 June 1981 to two children, Ivanka Ivankovic, who was fifteen years old at the time, and Mirjana Dragicevic, who was sixteen. Eventually, however, eight children in all were involved. The vision also appeared to the Franciscan parish priest of the time, Fr Jozo Zovko, but did not speak. To the children she revealed herself as Mary, and called herself the "Queen of Peace". The Communist authorities of the time forbade the crowds to gather on the hillside where the apparition had first been seen, and the visions then transferred to the village church. When in 1985 the local bishop forbade the church to be used for this purpose, they continued in the parish house. Ten secrets have been entrusted to the children, not all of whom continue to see the vision, and enormous numbers of **pilgrims** have been attracted to the spot (which made the Communist authorities rather more sympathetic as foreign currency rolled in). The visions at Medjugorje have been complicated not so much by the somewhat apocalyptic messages but by the conflict between the Franciscans who run the parish and the local bishop.

Melleray, a "grotto" in the style of the cave at **Lourdes** near the Cistercian monastery of Mount Melleray in Ireland, where two young boys, Tom Cliffe and Barry Buckley reported having seen an **apparition** of the **Virgin Mary** for five consecutive days in August 1985. The reported visions, which occurred some six months after newspaper reports of "moving statues" of Mary at Ballinspittle and elsewhere in the Republic, attracted large crowds.

memorare ("Remember, O most loving Virgin Mary"), a commonly-used **prayer** to the **Virgin Mary**, the composition of which is frequently attributed to St Bernard of Clairvaux, though without any justification. Fr Herbert Thurston, S.J. has suggested that the attribution may have arisen from a confusion with a holy preacher, Claude Bernard (1588-1641), who had an intense **devotion** to this form of prayer, and believed himself to have been cured of an illness through its use. He had great numbers of copies of the prayer printed and distributed. Claude Bernard was not himself the author of the prayer - he claims to have learned it from his father - but no author is identifiable. It has been shown, however, that the prayer as it is now said in its Latin version formed part of a much longer prayer to Our Lady, beginning *Ad sanctitatis tuæ pedes, dulcissima Virgo Maria*, which is to be found in books of devotions from the last quarter of the fifteenth century. It was not known in English-speaking countries until the middle of the nineteenth century, when it was given an

indulgence by Pope Pius IX, at first for France alone but later the same year (1846) for the whole Church. The most frequently used version in Britain was translated for the 1886 *Manual of Prayers for Congregational Use*, approved by the cardinal and bishops. A version by Fr Ambrose St John had been published in his translation of the **Raccolta** of 1857, and it is Ambrose St John's form which became common in the United States.

mental handicap, patron of, is Dympna, a saint of doubtful authenticity. Her mother died when she was young, her father was physically attracted to her, and to escape his attentions she fled, possibly from Britain, to Antwerp with her confessor, St Gereburnus. Her father caught up with them where they were living as hermits at Gheel, twenty-five miles from Antwerp, and killed his daughter and his companions killed the priest. The supposed bodies of the two martyrs were removed to a **shrine** in the thirteenth century, an event which was accompanied by many miracles, in particular of those apparently suffering from mental illness. As a consequence, Dympna became the **patron** of all such sufferers. The place where the martyrdoms took place, Gheel, has become a centre for the care of those suffering from a wide range of mental illnesses, who are cared for in the homes of those living in the town.

Mercy, Confraternity of Our Lady of, an association under the spiritual guidance of the Mercedarians which claims to date from before the middle of the thirteenth century, and which was formally recognized by Pope Innocent IV. Like the Order of Our Lady for the Redemption of Captives itself, the **confraternity**, which had first supported the Order it its efforts to ransom Christians who had fallen into the hands of non-Christians, turned its activities to supporting the Order in its missionary activity. Members are invested with a white **scapular**, on which is imposed a picture of Our Lady of **Ransom**.

Mercy, Our Lady of, a **devotion** which is associated with the Mercedarians, founded in the thirteenth century for the ransoming of Christians held captive or as slaves by the Saracens. Members of the Order celebrated their **feast** on 8 September, the **Nativity of**

Mary, but as this title of the **Virgin Mary** came to be more widely commemorated - Innocent XI extended its observance to the whole of Spain in 1680 - the date had to be changed to 24 September. It was made a feast of the universal Church by Pope Innocent XII in 1696. It was removed from the **calendar** in 1969. There is an alternative account of the origin of the title. A vision of Mary in 1536 promised "mercy not justice" to the people of Savona, Italy, should they repent of their sins. Under this title Mary is **patron** of the Dominican Republic.

Michael the Archangel seems to have been revered from very early Christian times, quite probably drawing upon the role played by the archangel in Jewish apocryphal literature. One legend records an appearance by St Michael on Monte Gargano in Apulia, showing himself to people looking for a bull which had strayed from a herd, and asking that the place should be consecrated to him: this event used to be celebrated on 8 May in the Roman **calendar** with the **feast** of the Appearing. A feast which seems to have been almost as old, if not older, is that of 29 September (Michaelmas Day), with the **dedication** of the **basilica** of St Michael on the Salarian Way, six miles north of Rome. This event has been commemorated ever since the sixth century, though it has sometimes been confused with the dedication of the church on Monte Gargano.

Minims, Third Order of, an association or **confraternity** linked to the Minims, the Order of Friars founded in 1435 by St Francis of Paola. The origins of the **Third Order** seem to date from shortly after the Minims themselves, but it formally dates its beginning to the Bull of Pope Alexander VI of 1501 which approved the rule they had received from Francis de Paola. It attracted a large number of members, some of them - such as Henrietta Maria, the wife of Charles I of England, very distinguished by birth and others such as Saints John of God and Francis de Sales, for the holiness of their lives. The lives of tertiaries are expected to be distinguished by humility and by a spirit of penitence.

miraculous medal, a medal of which the design was revealed by the **Virgin Mary** to St Catherine Labouré on 27 November 1830 in the chapel of the convent of the Daughters of Charity of St Vincent de Paul on the rue du Bac, Paris. Catherine had been the recipient of a series of visions from the start of her noviceship seven months earlier, and they were to continue for almost another year. She reported them to no one except her confessor M. Aladel but he, acting upon the instructions given to the **Saint** by Mary had a **medal** struck and distributed at the end of June 1832. In 1836 a tribunal in Paris approved the medal as of supernatural origin. The vision which Catherine reported, and which was, and is, reproduced on the medal, shows on one side Mary standing upon a globe, her feet crushing a serpent's head. Rays come from her hands and around the image are the words "O Mary, conceived without sin, pray for us who have recourse to thee". On the reverse is the letter "M" entwined with a bar, and upon the bar there is a cross. Around the symbols are twelve stars, while beneath the "M" are two hearts, one crowned with thorns, the other pierced with a sword. Much prestige was gained by the medal after the sudden, and unexpected, conversion to Catholicism of Alphonse Ratisbonne while wearing it as he visited a church in Rome to arrange a funeral. Ratisbonne was a Jew, and he went on to found the Order of Our Lady of Sion to work for understanding between Jews and Christians. It also considerably gained in popularity after it became the badge, hung around the neck as the vision had directed, of the Association of the **Children of Mary**.

Missionary Union of the Clergy, a pious association founded in Parma, Italy, and formally approved by Pope Benedict XV in October 1916, to foster a missionary spirit among the clergy, and through them among the Catholic faithful at large. As part of the missionary zeal of the Church, it was placed under the direction of the cardinal who headed the Congregation for the Propagation of the Faith (more correctly known, since 1967, as the Congregation for the Evangelization of Peoples). Thanks to the encouragement of Pope Benedict XV the association quickly spread throughout the Church. There are three levels of membership, the ordinary and the perpetual being distinguished only by the amount of money which they donate to the society each year. In addition there are honorary members - bishops and cardinals. Members are expected to make themselves and those to whom they minister aware of the needs of the missions, and to encourage missionary vocations among the young.

Missionary Youth, Pious Union of, a society started in Turin in 1920 to foster missionary vocations, and to assist in other ways the work of the missions. The members undertake this task by prayer, by almsgiving and by spreading knowledge of the work of missionaries. The society began in Turin, in the first Oratory founded by St John Bosco, and the first members were students of the Salesian Congregation which he had founded.

Montserrat, a Benedictine monastery some thirty-eight miles from Barcelona in Spain, and a **shrine** to the **Virgin Mary**. The statue of her venerated there dates from the twelfth or thirteenth century. It is polychrome, but with black features - it is called *La Morenita*, or "the little dark one". The monastery began in the eleventh century, but was rebuilt in the nineteenth century. It was a centre of Catalan nationalism, and the black madonna is the **patron** of Catalonia, with a **feast** day on 27 April.

Motherhood of Mary, a **feast** sometimes also known as the Divine Maternity of Mary, was first approved for Portugal, at the request of King Joseph Emmanuel, in 1751 by Pope Benedict XIV, who himself composed the Mass. It was allocated to 11 October as it was thought - mistakenly - that the Council of Ephesus of 431 which defended Mary's title of Theotokos or "God-bearer" had ended on that date. To commemorate the fifteen-hundredth anniversary of the Council, Pope Pius XI made the feast a universal observance in the Catholic Church.

Mount Carmel, Our Lady of, a **feast** of the **Virgin Mary** celebrated on 16 July. It came into being as an observance of the Carmelites about the year 1380, soon after the Order had been formally established and approved. The feast was given official sanction by Pope Sixtus V in 1587, and it became the patronal feast of the Carmelites in 1600. It proved to be a particularly popular **devotion**, especially in Spanish territories, and spread quickly. In 1726 it became a feast of the whole Church, but in 1960 became an optional memorial. In December 1816 Bernardo O'Higgins dedicated to Mary under this title his "Army of the Andes" when he set out from Mendoza in Argentina in an attempt to free Chile from Spanish domination. Though he soon afterwards captured Santiago the Spanish forces remained in the south of the country, and threatened his hold on the Chilean capital. O'Higgins promised to proclaim Our Lady of Mount Carmel **patron** of an independent Chile should he decisively defeat the Spanish. This he did at Maipú in the outskirts of Santiago on 5 April 1818. He carried out his vow and built a **shrine** at Maipú, which has since become a major centre of devotion in the city.

music, patron saint of, a title now attributed to Saint Cecilia, a third-century virgin and martyr, who died because she refused to marry the pagan to whom she had been betrothed, having previously dedicated her life to God. Despite the fact that when her tomb was opened in 1599 her body was found to be incorrupt (it rapidly disintegrated, however, on exposure to the air), there is no evidence that such a martyr existed, and the story of the betrothal to Valerian dates from two centuries after her alleged martyrdom. In her spurious "Acts" it is said that "while the organs played" at her wedding she, in her heart, "sang only to God". The phrase "while the organs played" was originally taken to mean that she was herself playing the organ at the ceremony. In 1584 the Roman Academy of Music was put under her protection, but at least until the Middle Ages Pope St Gregory the Great (c. 540-604) had been regarded as the **patron** of music. John the Deacon, in his life of the Pope, attributes to him the founding of the "schola cantorum" in **Rome**, though this is very unlikely. It is equally unlikely that the Pope could have had any influence upon the type of music known now as Gregorian chant. The **feast** of St Cecilia is 22 November, that of Gregory the Great 3 September.

N

nails, holy, the nails with which Christ was fixed to his **cross**. It is unclear how many of these there would have been, but St Ambrose, writing much after the alleged finding of them suggests that only two were found by St Helena, mother of the Emperor Constantine. One legend relates that Helena threw a nail from the cross into the Adriatic to quell a storm, when she was returning from Jerusalem. Again according to legend Constantine, on receiving the nails from his mother, made one of them into a bit for his horse, put another into the helmet of the statue of himself which also contained wood from the cross, and forged a third into the imperial diadem. Gregory the Great, who served as emissary from the Bishop of Rome to Constantinople, is reported to have brought a fourth nail back with him when he returned to Rome in 585. It was placed in the church of Santa Croce in Gerusalemme, which had been built to house the relic of the cross, and it is there still venerated. Indeed, there are two nails venerated in Rome and three in Venice: over thirty different places claim to have these **relics** . Clearly the most that could be said for these is that they contain filings from the original nails. The nail which was put into the imperial diadem, it is claimed, still survived in the Iron Crown of Monza, which was used by the Lombard kings. The style is undoubtedly Byzantine, but later than Constantine. The nail which became a bit for Constantine's horse was preserved in the imperial treasury until, it seems, it was stolen at the time of the fourth crusade and taken to Carpentras, north-east of Avignon: a seal of the Bishop of Carpentras dating from 1226 depicts the relic. It does, however, have a rival. Milan also claims the bit, given, it is said, by the Emperor Theodosius to St Ambrose, but no record of this is earlier than the fifteenth century.

National Union of Italy for Transporting the Sick to Lourdes, Loreto, and the Sanctuaries of Italy, a society founded in Rome in 1904 and approved formally in June 1909, for the purpose of supporting the sick who are poor, and unable to pay their own way, who may wish to travel to the **shrines** of Lourdes and elsewhere.

Nativity of Mary, a **feast** of the **Virgin Mary** now celebrated on 8 September, though the day has varied in different countries. It seems likely that the feast originated in the East by assimilation to the feast of the **Nativity of Saint John the Baptist,** and came to Rome no later than the middle of the seventh century. Pope Sergius I (687-701) instituted a **procession** for this feast as he did for the other three major feasts of Mary then observed in Rome, though, unlike that for the **Assumption,** it did not long survive. By the end of the ninth century it was observed throughout the whole Church, and in the eleventh became a day on which all were required to attend Mass. In 1241 it was given an **octave,** and a century later a **vigil** was added. There is no clearly understood reason why Mary's nativity should be kept on 8 September, though it is ninth months after the **Immaculate Conception.**

Nativity of Saint John the Baptist, one of the oldest of the **feasts** of **saints,** dating from the fourth century and celebrated six months (24 June) before Christmas.

natural disasters, protectors against. St Agatha, a saint of Sicily, though of unknown date, is prayed to for protection against volcanic eruptions, possibly because she is also the **patron** of bell founders, and bells were rung to warn of the danger from an eruption; Emygidus (martyred 304) is the patron of the Italian town of Ascoli, and when in 1703 it escaped unharmed from a major earthquake, Emygidus was given credit, and became the protector against earthquakes; because St Florian is recorded as having been martyred by drowning in 304, he has since been recognized as an intercessor in time of flood; Francis Borgia (1510-72) was declared a patron of earthquakes by Benedict XIV in 1756, possibly because he was already acknowledged as a patron of Portugal, which had just suffered a major earthquake; so great was the reputation of St

Genevieve (c. 422-c. 500) as a miracle-worker that the people of Paris, of which she is patron, appealed to her in any instance of major disaster; similarly Gregory Thaumaturgus's (c. 213 - c. 270) reputation as a miracle-worker meant that he was appealed to in times of great danger, though specifically in time of flood because of a story that he halted a flood on the River Lycus.

Nine First Fridays, the belief that salvation has been promised to those who receive the eucharist on the first Friday of nine consecutive months. It arises from a promise of Christ in a vision to St Margaret Mary Alacocque (1647-90), and is associated with **devotion** to the **Sacred Heart** which St Margaret Mary had a great part in revitalising.

novena, a period of nine days of prayer to obtain some special intention or grace. There is no evidence that a nine-day period was of particular significance to the Jews, but it was to both the Greeks and Romans, who commemorated a death with nine days of mourning, and a **feast** on the ninth day. This practice, whether directly or indirectly, was carried over into Christianity in the form of nine days of masses after a death - some Christians left instructions in their wills that these masses should be said, and they became the rule for senior ecclesiastical dignitaries in the Middle Ages. As well as novenas for the dead, there seem to have been novenas of preparation: in Spain 18 December was for a time celebrated as the feast of the **Annunciation**, presumably because it was nine days before **Christmas**, and could be said to reflect the nine months in which the **Virgin Mary** carried Christ in her womb. Whatever the reason for it, the practice of celebrating nine **votive** masses of Mary before Christmas became widespread in Europe, and by the seventeenth century, possibly in imitation, religious orders were keeping a novena before the feast of their founder. Very much earlier - by about the year 1000 - novenas to certain **saints** had developed, those to whom people looked for **healing**, such as St Hubert, whose protection was sought by those who had been bitten by dogs and who consequently went in fear of rabies. However popular novenas came to be, it was not until the nineteenth century that **indulgences** came to be attached to them: nearly forty such are listed in the **Raccolta**.

Novena of Grace, a nine-day period of prayer in honour of the Jesuit St Francis Xavier, which had a particular reputation for bringing about the ends prayed for. Its origins lie in 1633 when a Fr Marcello Mastrilli, also a Jesuit, was seriously injured in an accident. He was urged by a vision of Francis Xavier that he should to go to the East as a missionary, and although dying, he made a vow to do so. In a second vision Francis Xavier told him he would be cured, and that he would die a martyr's death. This duly occurred in Japan in October 1637. The apparent efficacy of the intercession of Francis Xavier gave rise to the **novena**. Traditionally the Novena of Grace is celebrated so that it ends on 12 March, the day on which Xavier was canonized, and includes a visit to a Jesuit church or chapel. Those conditions are not required in order to obtain the **indulgence** which is now attached to this particular novena.

O

Oberammergau, a small town south of Munich where a play portraying the Passion of Christ is performed every ten years in fulfilment of a vow made in 1633. The mayor of Oberammergau and other community leaders undertook to present the play, the townspeople taking all the roles, were their town to be spared the plague - as it was. The regular performances now attract great crowds of visitors to the town.

Oblates of St Benedict, a form of association between lay people and individual monasteries, which has much in common with **confraternities** or **third orders**. The word "oblate" was used from the very beginning of Benedictine style monasticism to describe those boys whom their parents pledged to God by putting them in a monastery, to live out their lives in the service of the monks, or as monks themselves when of an age to enter. It is evident, however, that even from the seventh century there were devout people of both sexes who offered themselves to monasteries (the word "oblate" comes from the Latin *oblatio*, or "offering"), though the numbers do not appear to have been significant until the eleventh century. By that time it was not uncommon for lay people to associate themselves with a monastery, accepting in some degree the authority of the abbot and enjoying its spiritual privileges although not living within its walls. In that century Abbot William of Hirschau in Southern Germany, whose monastery seems to have been particularly effective in drawing laity to itself, drew up a rule for such people. Some who followed this rule remained outside the religious house, dressed in lay clothes, working for the good of the monastery, and enjoying some of its benefits. Others adopted a form of life more strictly religious in kind. This form of oblates flourished in the Middle Ages, but went into decline at the time of the French Revolution, then underwent a revival in the latter part of the nineteenth century, especially at Monte Cassino and Subiaco. The former statutes of the oblates were restored, and received the approval of the Holy see. Oblates do not take vows, nor any permanent obligation. They are not strictly speaking tertiaries, though very similar to them, because their relationship is an individual one to an individual monastic house. But they may not be members of a third order once they have been accepted as oblates. A **devotion** to the liturgy is encouraged among oblates, and, if at all possible, they are urged to say the divine office. Should they so wish they may be buried in their black **scapular** and tunic. A number of religious congregations have taken the name "oblate", in particular the now defunct Oblates of St Charles in England and the Oblates of Mary Immaculate.

octave, or eighth day, the renewed celebration on the eighth day after a **feast** of the feast itself, or even a celebration throughout the whole period of eight days. The first mention of such a custom in a Christian context is with the **dedication** of **basilicas** in Tyre and in **Jerusalem** in the fourth century, possibly in conscious imitation of the dedication of the Temple in Jerusalem. From then on octaves are more frequently mentioned, associated first of all with **Easter** and **Pentecost**, and then with **Christmas**. The linking of octaves to feasts of **saints** begins in the eighth century, and becomes more common in the ninth. Not all octaves were regarded as being of the same importance: Easter and Pentecost being in the first rank, a number of other feasts of Christ being put slightly lower, and those of saints (but oddly including the **Ascension**) lower still. In the 1969 reform of the **calendar**, however, only two octaves are left, those of Christmas and Easter.

Octave of Prayer for Christian Unity, sometimes called "A week of prayer", is a period from 18 January to 25 January devoted to prayer and events on the theme of ecumenism. The dates were chosen because they ran from the **feast** of St Peter's Chair at Rome (no longer in the Roman **calendar**) to the feast of the Conversion of St Paul. The first inspiration for this **octave** came from Paul Wattson in 1908. The Faith and Order Movement, eventually subsumed in the World

185

Council of Churches, from 1926 published suggestions for a similar octave to Wattson's, which was basically Roman Catholic, to be held around the time of **Pentecost**. Wattson's version was broadened in scope in 1935 through the plea of the Abbé Paul Couturier for a universal week of prayer for unity. From the mid 1950s the Faith and Order Commission of the World Council of Churches has been collaborating with a Roman Catholic ecumenical agency (Unité chrétienne in Lyons) in producing guidelines for the celebration of the octave. Responsibility for the Roman Catholic participation in drafting the proposed texts for each year has, since 1966, been borne by the Pontifical Council for Promoting Christian Unity.

October, the month in the **calendar** in which particular **devotion** is shown, as in **May**, to the **Virgin Mary**, but in this instance under the title of Our Lady of the **Rosary**. "October devotions" appear to have arisen naturally from the celebration of the **feast** of the rosary in that month, but in 1868 a Spanish Dominican obtained from Pope Pius IX an **indulgence** for all who attended such services. Pope Leo XIII in 1883 extended the custom of such services to all parish churches, to pray for the normalization of relations between the Holy See and the Kingdom of Italy, after the final disintegration of the papal states in 1870. Though the Lateran Pacts between Italy and the Holy See in 1929 brought an end to the obligation to hold such services, the custom continued.

Our Lady Health of the Sick, of St Joseph her Husband, and of St Camillus de Lellis, Archconfraternity of, a society begun in 1860 by Brother Ferdinand Vicary and established in the Roman church of St Mary Magdalen where, from the early seventeenth century there had hung a picture of the **Virgin Mary** under the title of **Health of the Sick**. The names of Saints Joseph and Camillus de Lellis were added as patrons of the sick. In 1866 it was raised to the status of an Archconfraternity. Members wear a **scapular** which has on the front pictures of the Virgin Mary and of Saints Joseph and Camillus de Lellis, and on the back a small red cross. Apart from the obligation to recite certain prayers, members are expected to visit the sick, and to encourage them to receive the sacraments of the Church.

Our Lady of Mount Carmel, Confraternity of, an association under the spiritual guidance of the Carmelite Order. The first **confraternity** of this name was founded at Florence in 1280. Members receive the **brown scapular,** which has to be blessed and handed to the member according to a specific ritual. Authority to bless the **scapular** can be obtained from the Apostolic Penitentiary, or from the heads of either branch of the Carmelites. Members of this association enjoy both the "privilege of a **happy death**" and the **Sabbatine Privilege.**

Our Lady of the Sacred Heart of Jesus, Archconfraternity of, an association under the spiritual guidance of the Missionaries of the **Sacred Heart.** The **confraternity** began in 1854 at the same time as the missionary congregation was founded, in the diocese of Bourges in France. In 1878 the Congregation acquired a ruined church in Rome, dedicated it to Our Lady of the Sacred Heart and, the following year, made it the seat of the association. Members are required only to say, morning and evening, the invocation "Our Lady of the Sacred Heart, pray for us", though they are also encouraged to offer each morning the day's activities to Our Lady, and to wear a **medal** of Our Lady of the Sacred Heart. The purpose of the association is to foster **devotion** to the **Blessed Virgin** under this title, praying to her in particular in the most difficult situations, both in secular and in spiritual matters.

P

Palm Sunday, the Sunday prior to **Easter**, and the one which begins the celebrations of **Holy Week**. Its origins are to be found at Jerusalem in the sixth century. By that time the practice had developed of assembling on the Mount of Olives and then, after the reading of the appropriate gospel, processing into the city. This practice spread throughout the East, whereas in some parts of the West - France and Spain - at the same period those preparing for baptism were taught the words of the creed and their ears were anointed. The gospel read to accompany this ritual was John 12:1-25, which recounts both the anointing of Jesus by Mary at Bethany, and the triumphal entry of Christ into Jerusalem. During the seventh and eighth centuries the people began in a small way to act out the words of the gospel narrative by bringing branches to church for this ceremony, and calling out Hosanna, though it was not until the ninth century, as far as is known, that **processions** with palm branches were incorporated into the liturgy. The processions seem to have become widespread from the tenth century onwards, though they are not attested in the papal liturgy until the eleventh century, and even then they were fairly modest - the pope distributing palms in a chapel of the **Lateran**, then processing swiftly to the **basilica**. Elsewhere, however, even in Rome itself, they were rather more splendid affairs. The people gathered outside the town. After the palms had been blessed, there was a procession to a specially erected cross and then onwards into the town. At the entrance to the town the procession would be greeted with the "gloria laus", and in some instances the bishop then had the privilege of freeing prisoners. After all had entered the church, the mass would be said, during which the gospel of the passion would be read. The Roman liturgy did not recognize this more ebullient form of celebrating Palm

Sunday until 1955, when a revised set of instructions for the first time formally included the congregation in the procession, and prescribed that the blessing should take place outside the Church building.

Palmar de Troya, the site in Spain of a supposed vision of the **Virgin Mary** to three children on 30 March 1968. Despite being denounced by the Archbishop of Seville, it continued to flourish, with right-wing messages of both a political nature and a religious one: in December 1974 the vision claimed that the Pope (Paul VI) was being drugged by those around him and was leading the Church astray, a story repeated throughout the following year. On 1 January 1976, the former Archbishop of Saigon ordained a number of priests and just over a week later, bishops, without authority either from the Archbishop of Seville, or the Pope. One, Clemente Dominguez who was blind, declared himself pope, and appointed a number of cardinals.

Pange, lingua, gloriosi corporis mysterium (= "Tell, my tongue, the mystery of the glorious body"), a **hymn** written by St Thomas Aquinas in the same metre, and with the same three opening words, as that written by Venantius Fortunatus (cf. the next entry). It was written for the institution of the **feast** of **Corpus Christi** by Pope Urban IV in 1264 - Thomas was asked to provide the office. This hymn is used at Vespers, and was also much used in Corpus Christi **processions** in the later Middle Ages and subsequently. It is also used at the procession on **Maundy Thursday**. The last two of the six stanzas, which begin with the words *Tantum ergo sacramentum*, are used at **Benediction**.

Pange, lingua, gloriosi lauream certaminis (= "Tell, my tongue, the victory gained in glorious conflict"), a **hymn** written by Venantius Fortunatus (c. 530-600) who was born near Ravenna but served for a long time as secretary to Queen Radegunde in her convent at Poitiers, and died shortly after being appointed bishop of that city. He also wrote *Vexilla regis prodeunt*. It was composed to mark the reception of a **relic** of the cross sent by the Emperor Justin II and his wife to Queen Radegunde. It is written in a metre which was the rhythm used by songs of the Roman legionaries. It is now used at

Matins and Lauds for **Passiontide**, and is also used at the Veneration of the Cross on **Good Friday**.

Paray-le-Monial, a **shrine** in France, some seventy-five miles north-west of Lyons, to St Margaret-Mary Alacoque who was responsible for the revival of **devotion** to the **Sacred Heart** of Christ in modern times. She was born at L'Hautecour in Burgundy in 1647, and after a childhood and youth of quite precocious piety, in 1671 joined the Order of the Visitation at Paray-le-Monial. From December 1673 until the middle of 1675 she enjoyed a series of visions of Christ in which he told her that love for his heart must be spread through her throughout the world. In the visions Christ also asked for an hour's prayer each Thursday in memory of the passion - **Holy Hour** - and the reception of communion on the **First Friday** of each month. In the final vision, Christ also asked for the establishment of what is now the **feast** of the Sacred Heart on the Friday after the **octave** of **Corpus Christi**. She confided the task she had been given to the Jesuit priest, Claude de la Colombière, who was her confessor for a time, and it was he as much as St Margaret Mary who actively promoted the devotion. When St Margaret Mary was put in charge of the convent's novices she had more opportunity to further her crusade, and the feast of the Sacred Heart began to be celebrated in the convent in 1685. A chapel to the Sacred Heart was built in 1687 and the devotion spread outwards to the convents of the Order. St Margaret Mary died on 17 October 1690 and was **canonized** on 13 May 1920.

pardon of Le Puy, a ceremony which first took place in 992 in the cathedral at Le Puy, France, occasioned by the approach of the millennium, and the fear which that induced.

Paris, Our Lady of, a **shrine** of the Virgin Mary dating back to 775, though its fame spread particularly after an incident in 885 when, according to a contemporary poet, Bishop Gozlin called upon the Virgin's aid against the Normans who were besieging the city. An arrow thereupon struck the Norman leader dead, and the ships, which had come up the Seine, fled. The relieved and grateful Parisians then carried a statue of the Virgin in triumphant procession.

Passing of St Joseph, Pious Union of, a society founded in Rome in February 1913 to encourage prayers for the dying, and also for those in **purgatory**.

Passion of the Lord, Sodality of, an association under the spiritual guidance of the Congregation of the Passion to further **devotion** to the person of Christ crucified. The origins of this **confraternity** date from the founder of the Passionists, St Paul of the Cross, himself, who proposed that in addition to those living in communities, there should be **tertiaries** or **oblates** attached to his Congregation. This was decreed in 1744, but the experiment was discontinued in 1775. A number of informal associations continued, however, and the first approval for them from the Holy See was granted in 1833, with full recognition in 1861. Two years later Pope Pius IX, at the request of the Superior General of the Passionists, allowed the Congregation to grant to appropriate members of these confraternities of the Passion the Passionist **scapular** and their badge. In 1867 a sodality of the Passion was established in a Passionist church in Rome which, in 1918, was declared to be an Archsodality by Pope Benedict XV. Membership is conferred by the reception of the scapular which they are then expected to wear about their necks, and the entry of the member's name in the book of the sodality. The sodality is divided into groups, each one of which is headed by a "zelator", who may be male or female whose task it is to see that the members maintain the spiritual discipline which is associated with the sodality. They are expected to undertake some mortification each Friday, and to meditate daily upon some aspect of the passion of Christ, as well as to serve the needs of the sick and the poor.

patron saint, a **saint** who, either by tradition or by conscious choice, is venerated by the clergy and people of a place, trade or pastime (St Hubert, for example, is the patron saint of **hunting**) as their special protector or intercessor in heaven. The notion of patron in Roman society, someone who extended to poorer or less influential *clientes* his protection and support, appears to have been carried over into the cult of the saints at least from the fourth century onwards, or even earlier if there is included in the broad category of saint those imprisoned for their faith in the mid third century. These men and women provided certificates for the less steadfast who had lapsed from Christianity during persecution so that they might be received back into the fold: their quasi-intercessory powers with the local church stemming, it would seem, from the holiness of their lives to which their imprisonment gave proof. In the early centuries the word "patron" was not as usual as titles such as "lord", "advocate", "protector", but it became established from the seventh century onwards. Patrons of places were chosen for a variety of reasons, though most commonly perhaps because the saint was born, lived or, more particularly, died in the locality, or because his or her **relics** were preserved there. Some were chosen as patrons of trades because of the manner in which they earned their own livelihood: Eligius or Eloi, bishop of Noyon and patron of metalworkers had himself been a highly accomplished goldsmith. Others were selected as protectors against natural calamities or other occasions of danger: Agatha, against volcanic eruptions, Roch against storms, Marina for protection in childbirth. Many of the stories upon which the selection of patron saints has been based are legendary - wholly so in the case of some of the best known, such as Saints Christopher, Catherine or Barbara, or, indeed, Hubert, cited above. The selection of patrons was first regulated by Pope Urban VIII in 1630, when he declared that they must be **canonized** (i.e., not of the rank of the Blessed), that they must be chosen by clergy and people with the approval of the bishop, and that the choice be confirmed by the Sacred Congregation of Rites. These prescriptions were included in the 1917 Code of Canon Law, and though new regulations were issued in March 1973, the general lines have remained unaltered except that, with the changing structure of the Roman Curia, confirmation is now required from the Congregation for Divine Worship. Attempts have been made, however, to ensure that the historical existence of patron saints can be verified, and where this is not possible, that they be changed. The practice of having protectors against particular eventualities is now officially frowned upon, but survives.

Peace and a Good Journey, Our Lady of, a **shrine** of the **Virgin Mary** at Antipolo, some fifteen miles east of Manila. The statue which is venerated there was brought to the Philippines from Mexico on 25

March 1626 by the newly-appointed Governor General, and was first placed in the Jesuit church in the capital, but six years later moved to Antipolo. In 1639 the church was set on fire, but the image survived, and was then hacked about the face with lances. It was taken for safety to Cavite where the statue was credited with protecting the port from attack by the Dutch in 1647. It was then taken several times on journeys to Mexico as a talisman for a safe passage, and eventually returned to Antipolo, where it is still venerated, especially on the Sundays of May and June. There is a considerable **devotion** to Mary under this title outside the Philippines, particularly in Spain.

Peace of San Miguel, Our Lady of, a **shrine** of the **Virgin Mary** in the city of San Miguel, El Salvador. Its statue was carried in procession in the town on 21 September 1787 when the region was threatened by a nearby volcanic eruption, and has since been regarded as a protection throughout the country's many troubles and during its Wars of Independence. The Infant on the statue's left arm carries an olive branch in the right hand.

Pellevoisin, a village near Châteauroux in central France, in which Estelle Faguette claimed to have witnessed fifteen **apparitions** of the **Virgin Mary** between February and December, 1876. Faguette was born in Chalons-sur-Marne in September 1846, but when she was fourteen her family moved to Paris. Her upbringing, especially while in Paris, was extremely pious and at the age of eighteen she entered a convent. Her stay there was fairly short, however, and she returned to her parents in September 1863, unable to walk without the help of crutches because of an accident in the convent. Although her leg improved, she was rarely in good health. Nonetheless, partly it seems through her piety, she obtained a position with the de la Rochefoucauld family and moved to their country residence at Pellevoisin. Her health continued to deteriorate, and she was moved to a small house in the village owned by the de la Rochefoucaulds, where her parents came from Paris to look after her. On 14 February 1876 a local doctor said she had only a few hours to live. That same night the apparitions began. According to Estelle's account, she first caught sight of the Devil "pulling faces at me", and then noticed the Virgin Mary who drove the Devil away. Mary told her she would suffer five more days in honour of Christ's **Five Wounds**, but on Saturday would be either dead or cured. The apparition told her "I want you to publish my glory", whereupon Estelle saw a slab of white marble. The apparitions were repeated for the next three nights. On the fifth night, however, she again saw the marble slab, this time with a golden heart in flames engraved on it, pierced by a sword, and crowned with roses. After this vision Estelle's health improved. In July the visions were renewed, in the course of which the Virgin communicated a secret to the visionary.

These apparitions occurred at the same time as the crowning of a statue of Our Lady of **Lourdes** by the Archbishop of Paris, to which she had been invited, but to which her employers had forbidden her to go. She was well enough to return to full-time work, and re-entered the de la Rochefoucauld household at the Château de Poiriers. On 9 September, however, she experienced a strong urge to return to the room in which her visions had occurred. In the afternoon the Virgin again appeared, this time holding out to her what appeared to be a **scapular** of the **Sacred Heart**. In subsequent appearances the Virgin lamented in particular the state of the Church in France. The final appearance was on 8 December 1876, the Feast of the **Immaculate Conception**. Estelle had been making a copy of the apparition's scapular: she now kissed the original scapular, was told to present the local bishop with the copy she had made, and to promote devotion to it. Only two days later she went to the Archbishop of Bourges, who was sympathetic and encouraged her propagation of the scapular devotion.

An Archconfraternity was established at Pellevoisin for that purpose, and a monastery, under the charge of Dominicans since 1893, was built round the house of the apparitions. This rapidly became a pilgrimage centre - the first pilgrims arrived within twelve months of Estelle's recovery. The main pilgrimage is led by the Archbishop of Bourges, and takes place on the first weekend of September, though groups continue to arrive throughout the year. Pilgrimages include enrolment into the scapular devotion. Estelle Faguette spent most of the rest of her life in and around Pellevoisin, though in January 1900 she travelled to Rome to meet Leo XIII, who four months later formally endorsed devotion to the Sacred Heart scapular. She died on 23 August 1929, and is buried at Pellevoisin.

Pentecost, or fiftieth day, is a Christian **feast** with obvious links with the Jewish "feast of weeks" (seven times seven days) which marked the conclusion of the harvest. At least in the Qumran community, and possibly elsewhere among Jews, Pentecost was regarded as the feast of renewing the covenant, and commemorating the giving of the law. It is not clear that the first- and early second-century Christians regarded the period between **Easter** and Pentecost as a time of rejoicing, but by the end of the second century that was certainly the case, and such penitential practices as **fasting** and kneeling for prayer during the season were forbidden.

Perpetual Rosary, Society of, a society founded in the first half of the seventeenth century by a Florentine Dominican, Fr T. Ricci, to ensure that the **Rosary** was said not only every day of the year, but every hour of the day. The **confraternity** spread quickly, but went into decline towards the end of the eighteenth century. It was revived by a French Dominican, Fr Augustin Chardon, in 1858, and his new constitution was approved by Pope Pius IX in April 1867. It is divided into divisions and sections, each with a "prefect" or, in some countries, a "zelator", in charge. The prefect of a division has to establish enough sections to cover every day of the month, while the prefect of the section has to find twenty-four people to cover each hour of the day or night. Each member is expected to fulfil his or her obligation by spending a full hour saying all fifteen decades of the Rosary.

Perpetual Succour and of St Alphonsus Liguori, Archsodality of Our Lady of, a society founded in May 1871 in recognition of the popular **devotion** of the people of Rome to a picture of the **Virgin Mary** under the title of "Perpetual Succour". This picture is believed to have been brought to Rome in 1499 by a Greek merchant fleeing the Turkish conquest. The church of St Matthew in which it was originally placed fell into disuse and in 1869 the **icon** was transferred to the church of St Alphonsus Liguori, where it promptly became known once again for its wonder-working. This church is in the charge of the Redemptorists, and they provide spiritual guidance for its members. Members wear the **medal** of Our Lady of **Perpetual Succour**, and are expected to have this picture displayed in their houses. They consecrate themselves to the Virgin Mary under this title when they join the **confraternity**, and repeat the **consecration** every month. The society was raised to the rank of an Archsodality in May 1876.

Perpetual Succour, Our Lady of, a title of the **Virgin Mary** (meaning "of constant help") derived from an **icon** of the fourteenth century which was probably painted in Crete (see previous entry). As a **feast** of Mary it began in 1876, celebrated in **Rome** 26 April, elsewhere on 27 June. Under this title Mary is the **patron** of Haiti.

Philomena, Saint, a supposed virgin and martyr, public **devotion** to whom was sanctioned by Pope Gregory XVI in 1835 after a number of miracles had been attributed to her intercession. A tomb was discovered in 1802 in the Roman catacomb of Priscilla which contained the bones of a fifteen-year old girl and a phial of blood. At the time this phial was believed to prove that the person had been martyred, and an inscription was taken to indicate that the person interred there was named Philomena. A very considerable cult developed around this presumed saint, fostered in particular by the Curé d'Ars, St **John Vianney**. The archaeological evidence for this being the tomb of a martyr, or that the bones found there were of the person first buried in the catacomb, was very weak indeed, and despite the widespread devotion, and use of her alleged name as a Christian name, her **feast** day - 10 August - was suppressed by the Holy See in 1960. See also **Work of St Philomena, Archsodality of**.

Piedramillera, a town in Navarre, Spain, where, on 11 May 1920, a small group of girls claimed to have seen the eyes of the figure of the crucified Christ move to look at them. This event mirrored that at **Limpias** just over a year earlier, and never achieved the celebrity of the earlier occurrence.

pigs of St Anthony, the St Anthony being Anthony of Egypt (251-356). About the year 1100 an Order of Hospitallers was founded bearing his name at La Motte where his **relics** were supposedly interred, a place which became a **shrine** to which **pilgrims** came seeking healing from ergotism, a skin disease. The Order became very popular throughout Western Europe, and their pigs, each equipped with a bell, were allowed to roam freely in towns to scavenge for food, the pigs themselves then providing income, or food, for the sick being cared for by the Hospitallers.

pilgrimage was at first associated with journeys to the Holy Land to visit the scenes of Christ's life, and the sites of his passion and death. As early as Origen (c. 185-254) Christians were eager to see the land which Christ knew and to walk in his footsteps. Such journeys to Palestine grew in popularity after the conversion of Constantine, and especially after the visit there of Constantine's mother, St Helena, in 326 when she was already some seventy years old. She founded basilicas on the Mount of Olives and at Bethlehem and, according to tradition, discovered the true **cross**. By the time that the (probably) Spanish nun Eseria visited Palestine in about 382 most of the places associated with Christ had been marked by churches, around which the liturgy of **Holy week** turned, thus enabling pilgrims to enter in spirit into the events of Christ's last days. The route which he reputedly took while carrying the cross, the Via Dolorosa (= "sorrowful road", see **Stations of the Cross**) was already marked out in the streets of Jerusalem by 1231. Apart from Palestine, Egypt was another favoured spot for pilgrimage until the fifth century, but later on, in the early Middle Ages, Rome became a major centre, though Saint Jerome's belief that pilgrimage was a form of self-isolation, a fleeing of the urban environment, was one which survived among Irish monks in particular and was handed on by them to Anglo-Saxon monks and to others. From the sixth century onwards pilgrimages of varying duration according to the heinousness of the offence committed were imposed by the Irish for serious (public) sins. At first pilgrimages were imposed as a form of penance without any specific **shrine** as the goal of the pilgrim. From the tenth century, however, a particular place came to be mentioned more frequently, Rome being the most common destination. Also in the tenth century the whole of the land route across Europe to Palestine fell into Christian hands, which made the journey safer, at least in theory. At about the same time northern Spain came under Christian control, thus opening up the route to Santiago. Along the way hospices were established to house the pilgrims, while other shrines, such as those to Saints Leonard, Eutrope and Giles were created in order to cash in on the piety of those travelling through France to the shrine of St James.

From being a religious remedy, pilgrimage gradually entered the civil code, becoming a form of banishment imposed by civil authorities for violent crimes. Impetus for this development may have come from the Inquisition which classified judicial pilgrimages into "minor" (the lesser shrines of France), "major" (the four great shrines of **Canterbury,** Santiago, Cologne and Rome), and "overseas" (i.e., to the Holy Land). The Inquisition tended to insist that the pilgrimages had to be carried out by the guilty party, but the civilly imposed judicial pilgrimages could be readily commuted for cash. This use of pilgrimages as punishment was a good deal less common in England than on the continent, but foreign pilgrims were nonetheless a common sight in medieval England as they were elsewhere in Europe because of the popularity of the English shrines.

The number of travellers to the shrines of Europe and Palestine was considerable, and those who profited from them apart, their presence was not always welcome in the communities through which they passed. Though pilgrimage was meant to be a penitential exercise - and indeed for some it was - many treated it as a form of tourism, and earned a poor reputation for pilgrims as a whole. Indeed, towards the end of the Middle Ages they were identifiable as a group, since a form of "uniform" was adopted, almost a religious habit. They carried long wooden staffs, wore a pouch or "scrip", usually of leather, at their waist, put on a tunic and a broad-brimmed hat, turned up at the front. The staff was often given to the pilgrim, and the clothes blessed, in a church, thus making of the setting out a religious ritual in itself, somewhat on the par with entry into a religious order. To indicate that the goal of the pilgrimage had been reached, a badge, eventually made of lead, was worn - the symbol of palms for those who had been to the Holy Land (hence the English word "palmer") and cockleshells for those who had been to Santiago.

By the end of the Middle Ages there were many who agreed with Luther that "pilgrimages give countless occasions to commit sin and despise God's commandments", though the ire of the reformers was directed at least as much at the **indulgences** attached to pilgrimages as to the pilgrimages themselves. The **relics** which drew crowds to shrines, and statues of the **saints** in the churches were other objects of scorn. Among Roman Catholics the practice of visiting shrines never wholly ceased, though journeys to the Holy Land became rarer, at least in part because of the troubled state of Europe from the sixteenth century onwards. In the nineteenth century, however, there was a considerable revival of interest among both Catholics and non- Catholics, not a little aided by the efforts of Thomas Cook to promote tourism, while the visions at **Lourdes** in the middle of the century began a major new movement of pilgrims from all parts of the world. At least in times of political stability, the Holy Land, Rome, Santiago and Lourdes are now visited regularly by Catholics and often by non-Catholics, while some of the smaller ancient local shrines such as **Walsingham** have received a new lease of life. It has indeed been calculated recently that there are 6,150 active shrines in Western Europe, with smaller numbers (973 and 330) in Latin America and North America respectively. The vast majority (nearly 66 percent) of shrines attracting pilgrims, at least in Europe, are dedicated to Mary, and half of all European shrines are to be found in Italy, France and Spain. There would seem to be about 150 million Christians taking part in pilgrimages each year, the vast majority of them Roman Catholics. Rome and Lourdes are each thought to attract more than four million visitors, while the one hundred and twenty-nine active shrines in the United States are visited by some seven million people annually.

Pillar, Our Lady of the, a **shrine** to the **Virgin Mary** near Zaragoza, Spain. Though there is no evidence for this **devotion** before the twelfth century, it has a special place in Spanish piety. According to the legend, St James had a vision while he was preaching of Mary carrying the infant Christ, while behind her came angels carrying a pillar. Mary asked for a church to be built in her honour at the site. The pillar, she said, was the symbol of the people's constancy. "Pilar" is a common female name in Spain. The **feast** is celebrated on 12 October.

Pio, Padre, a Franciscan (Capuchin) friar, born at Pietrelcina North East of Naples on 25 May 1887 and died on 23 September 1968. His family name was Forgione, and he was baptized with the name

Francesco: he took the name Pio at his religious profession after the Dominican Pope St Pius V. He was ordained to the priesthood on 10 August 1910. Six years later he was sent to the village of San Giovanni Rotondo in the Gargano region of Apulia, and there spent the remainder of his life. Soon after mass on 20 September 1918, in front of a large **crucifix** depicting Christ with very large nails in his hands, blood pouring from his wounds, and his face bespattered with blood, Padre Pio received the visible **stigmata** - he claimed to have received them invisibly, in other words, known only to himself, shortly before his ordination. The wounds were visible to others when he said mass, (he kept his hands covered at other times) and were through the palms of the hands as most crucifixes show them. It is reported, however, that the wounds in his feet caused him the greater pain. When his body was examined after his death there was no sign of them remaining. Padre Pio was credited with unusual powers of discernment, especially in the confessional, and also with the faculty of bilocation. The cell in which he spent his life as a friar at San Giovanni has been preserved as a **shrine**: he is buried in a marble tomb in the crypt of the church.

Pompeii, Our Lady of, a **shrine** to the **Virgin Mary** created in the 1880s in the valley of Pompeii, near Naples, by the Blessed Bartolo Longo. Longo was born on 11 February 1841 near Brindisi to a moderately wealthy and devout family. He went to study law at the University of Naples, during which time he was attracted to spiritualism, and himself became a medium, but in June 1865 was persuaded by a friend to consult a Dominican priest, who drew him back to the practice of Catholicism. In reparation for his past life he began to devote himself to evangelization, and work with the poor, walking around Naples with a large **rosary** wrapped around his arm. He went to live for a time in the house of a young widow, the Countess Marianna Farnararo, and in October 1872 undertook the management of her estates in the poverty-stricken and bandit-ridden neighbourhood of the ancient ruins of Pompeii. He started a **Confraternity of the Rosary**, whose purpose was the Christian burial of the dead. He organized a festival of the Rosary, and gave every household a rosary and a picture of the Virgin. In November 1873 he arranged a highly successful mission, after which he founded a Confraternity of the Madonna of the Rosary. The local bishop, impressed with Longo's work, recommended that he build a church. He began to collect money for this project, but first acquired a picture of the Madonna of the Rosary from a second-hand dealer in Naples. The image was a poor one, the picture itself dilapidated: he had it restored by a landscape painter and it was put on display two months later, on 13 February 1876. Miracles were reported immediately, which encouraged Longo to have further work done on the picture: the figure of St Rose was changed to St Catherine of Siena, the features of the Virgin were improved: in 1878 Longo published *The History, Miracles and Novena of the Virgin of the Holy Rosary of Pompeii*. In 1883, the year in which Pope Leo XIII wrote his first encyclical on the Rosary, the Pope granted a plenary **indulgence** to all who visited the shrine at Pompeii. The following year Longo launched a periodical, *The Rosary and the New Pompeii*, the printing of which provided much-needed work in the region. Miracles, regularly reported at the sanctuary, were fully reported in this journal, which achieved worldwide circulation. Meanwhile, however, there had been considerable gossip about the relationship between Longo and the Countess: on 1 April 1885 they married in the chapel, and presence, of the Cardinal Archbishop of Naples. The marriage was unconsummated: Longo had much earlier in life taken a vow of chastity. On 8 May 1886 the picture was solemnly crowned and then enthroned. On 5 May 1901 the pope created the sanctuary at Pompeii a pontifical basilica: on the same day a facade to the sanctuary was inaugurated, dedicated to Mary **Queen of Peace**. From the money donated to the sanctuary Longo established hospices for the poor, for delinquent boys and other similar causes. Amid charges of mishandling these funds, Longo surrendered them all to the Holy See. The charitable works continued under his inspiration, however, as did the expansion of the sanctuary: a campanile was inaugurated in May 1924. On 9 February 1924 the Countess died: Longo died at the age of 86 on 5 October 1926. He was beatified in 1980.

Pontifical and Royal Confraternity of Our Lady of Montserrat, a society which claims to go back at least to July 1223 when the "**Confraternity** of Our Lady of **Montserrat**" was established with the Archbishop of Tarragona and the Queen of Aragon as its first members. In 1821 the monastery was almost entirely destroyed and in 1835 the monks were dispersed, so the confraternity itself, which linked its members to the monks of Montserrat and fostered **devotion** to the **Virgin Mary** under that title, disappeared. It was resurrected in 1880, when the millennium of the finding of the statue of the Virgin was celebrated. Each parish which has a branch of this confraternity must have an altar, or at least a statue, dedicated to the Virgin under this title. Members wear a **medal** and are permitted on public occasions to carry the banner of Montserrat, a flag divided equally into red and gold.

Pontifical Work for Vocations to the Priesthood, an association established by Pope Pius XII in November 1941 to promote and foster vocations to the priesthood. St Pope Pius X had, in 1913, already recommended that sodalities be established throughout the world for this purpose. It is under the former Congregation for Seminaries and Universities, now called the Congregation for Catholic Education. It exists in particular to assist diocesan directors of vocations, and to produce material for their use, and it also promotes a sense of the dignity of the priestly state.

Pontifical Work for Vocations to the Religious Life, an association founded in February 1955 and put under the direction of the Congregation for Religious, whose purpose is to foster a true notion of the value of the religious life, promote vocations to it, and to engage in works of piety so that God may grant more vocations. Among these works of piety are **fasting** and **abstinence** on the **feast** of the **Assumption**, and the saying of special prayers for vocations.

Pontifical Work of the Holy Infancy, a society founded in 1843 by the Bishop of Nancy, France, Mgr Charles Forbin-Janson, under the inspiration of Pauline Jaricot, who became its first member. Its purpose is to work for the saving of those babies, in China and elsewhere, who had been abandoned by their parents. Through the donations of its members the babies were not only to be baptized, but then brought up in Christian institutions. This organization has received very considerable support from successive popes, beginning in 1856 when Pope Pius IX ordered that it be established in every diocese, and allotted it a Cardinal Protector. Responsibility for its governance now falls to the Congregation for the Evangelization of Peoples. Children may become members from the time of their baptism up to their thirteenth birthday. They are organized in groups of twelve, with a "zelator" in charge of each group, and by various means are instructed in the Church's missionary activity, especially to other children. Members are required to say the **Hail Mary** each day, and to add an invocation in which they pray for themselves, and for the children of non-Christian parents. They are also expected to make a monthly donation to the association.

Pontmain, a **shrine** of the **Virgin Mary** in Brittany (France), where it is claimed Mary appeared in the evening of 17 January 1871 to be seen by twelve-year-old Eugène Barbadette and then also by his ten-year-old brother Joseph. Though neither parent saw anything of the woman dressed in blue, the boys' mother immediately took it to be a vision of Mary. More children were brought, and some of them, too, claimed to see the vision. The parish priest, who was himself deeply devoted to Mary and was trying to encourage his parishioners in the same **devotion**, soon had the crowd praying. As they prayed the vision changed somewhat. An oval frame now surrounded the apparition, and there appeared beside her four candles, two at knee height, two at shoulder height. The vision promised "God will answer you in a short time", a phrase taken to be a reference to the Franco-Prussian War then drawing to its close. Approbation of the vision was granted by the ecclesiastical authorities in 1872, and a **basilica** was opened five years later.

prayer, attitudes of, the stances adopted by Christians while praying. The earliest form appears to have been taken over from Greek and Roman religion, and was to stand with palms upwards and arms outstretched either in front of the body, or, more commonly, held upwards. A variation on this was what is known as the "orans" position, where the arms are bent at the elbows but still held upwards. At least by the third century Christians were also holding their arms in such a way as to make the sign of the **cross**. This seems to have been particularly, though not only, practised by Celtic monks, who sometimes prayed lying on the floor with arms outstretched, and sometimes did so standing or kneeling. Standing or kneeling in this way could be extremely painful if continued for any length of time, and was therefore employed as a form of penance known as the "vigil of the cross". This stance lasted throughout the Middle Ages and down to modern times, at least in some religious orders. Two positions of prayer which died out after being in vogue in the Middle Ages were to hold the hands fairly close to the chest in a variation of the "orans" position, and to cross the arms across the chest. The most common modern form, in which the hands are placed flat against each other with the fingers pointing upwards, appears to date only from the ninth century and was not universal until the thirteenth. Its origin appears to have been the oath of loyalty made by a feudal subject to his lord, when he placed his hands between those of the lord in a manner which expressed humility and subjection, attitudes which were also appropriate in a Christian's approach to God. Whatever the position of the hands when praying, Christians, at least in the earliest years of the faith, stood facing the East, and churches were oriented (as the word itself indicates) in the same direction. This was a pagan custom before it was a Christian one, but as Christians thought of Christ as the "sun of righteousness" and other similar titles it transferred readily to the new faith and lasted certainly down to the late Middle Ages.

Precious Blood, a devotion to the blood of Christ which developed in the thirteenth century, associated possibly with relics brought back from the crusades such as that of the Holy Blood of **Hailes**. The Abbey of Fécamp, which also claimed a relic of Christ's blood, is generally thought to have been the place where the **litany** of the Precious Blood was written during the twelfth or thirteenth centuries, though it was not until the 1960s that the litany came to receive official approval by the Church. The devotion seems to have been spread through the widely-popular legend of the quest for the Holy Grail, the cup with which Joseph of Arimathea was reputed to have caught the blood which flowed from Christ's wounds as he hung upon the cross. Among the remoter origins of the **devotion** are the stress on the humanity of Christ, certainly well developed by the twelfth century, and eucharistic devotion of the kind that gave rise to the **feast** of **Corpus Christi** in the thirteenth century. It was encouraged by accounts of the **stigmata** of St Francis, with the emphasis on the **five wounds**, and it is later found particularly among Franciscan spiritual writers. The Franciscans later rather abandoned the cult, however, and it was taken up with more enthusiasm by the Dominicans. The Dominicans were great supporters of St Catherine of Siena, and it was she who gave clearest expression to the devotion in the Middle Ages. The earliest liturgical recognition came in 1582 – the grant of an office "For the Blood of Christ" to the diocese of Valencia, but the widest propagation of the cult would appear to have been in the eighteenth century with permission to celebrate the feast being granted to several dioceses, and the establishment of a **Confraternity of the Precious Blood** in the Roman church of St Nicholas in Carcere. In the nineteenth century St Gaspare de Bufalo founded the Missionaries of the Precious Blood and in 1822 won permission to celebrate the feast on the first **Sunday** of July: the feast was extended to the whole Church in 1849.

Precious Blood of Christ, of Our Lady of the Abandoned, and of the Agony, Pious Union of, an association founded in the diocese of Huesca, Spain to attend the last hours of those condemned to death. Active members of this **confraternity**, had to be at least thirty-three years old before they were permitted to spend time in a cell opposite that of the condemned person in order to convert him. The prior of the confraternity is first required to seek from the civil authority a commutation of the death penalty, and only if that fails - and after telling the condemned person of the attempt to save him - is he invited to be co-opted into the confraternity, signifying any readiness to do so by kissing a **crucifix**. Before the sentence is carried out there is **exposition** of the **Blessed Sacrament** for two hours to pray for the condemned prisoner. All members are expected to attend, for in addition to the "active" members there are honorary ones - priests and religious - and patrons, who may be both male and female, who support the work of the confraternity through almsgiving.

Precious Blood, Pious Union of, an association under the spiritual guidance of the Fathers of the Precious Blood, a Congregation founded by St Gaspare de Bufalo, who also founded, with Francisco

Albertini, this **confraternity** in December 1808. It became an Archconfraternity in 1815, the same year that Gaspare de Bufalo's Congregation came into being, though it was not until 1851 that the Archconfraternity came formally under the Congregation. The purpose of the association is to spread **devotion** to the Precious Blood. The names of members are written in the register of the association.

Premonstratensians, Third Order of, an association or **confraternity** of lay people under the spiritual governance of the Premonstratensian canons, or Norbertines as they are sometimes called. This **Third Order** takes its origins from an event in 1122 when the founder of the Premonstratensians, St Norbert, having refused to accept into his Order one of the most powerful of French noblemen, claiming that to do so would subvert the feudal structure of the country, nonetheless gave him a **scapular** of white wool as a sign of his union with the Order. Many other members of the nobility likewise joined, their names being inscribed in books kept for that purpose in every Norbertine house. In the sixteenth century the scapular was replaced with a medal worn around the neck, showing a host in a **monstrance**, indicative of the tertiaries' particular **devotion** to the Eucharist. They are also expected to display an especial devotion to the **Immaculate Conception**.

Presentation in the Temple, a **feast** celebrated on 2 February which originally commemorated the encounter between Christ and Simeon (Luke 2:25ff.), and was therefore known as the *Hypapante*, or "Meeting". It is very ancient: Egeria recounts it being observed in **Jerusalem** c. 386 by a solemn **procession** from the **basilica** of the Holy Sepulchre to that of the Resurrection. The gospel account puts the occasion forty days after Christ's birth, but as at that time the nativity was taken to be on 6 January, the Presentation/Purification was held on 14 February: when **Christmas** was fixed on 25 December it was moved back to its present date of 2 February. The procession with candles is also quite early, dating from the fifth century, and arises from Simeon's description of Christ as "the light for the revelation to the Gentiles". When the feast came to Rome in the second half of the seventh century it was still known as the *Hypapante*, though a hundred years later the name "Purification" - also of course mentioned in the gospel narrative (Luke 2:22) - came to be used in France and gradually gained ground elsewhere. The title "Presentation of the Lord" replaced the Purification in the reform of the **calendar** in 1969, thus restoring the primitive orientation of the festival. The practice of **blessing** candles on that day (hence the alternative name "Candlemas") no doubt stems from the carrying of lights in the procession which was an early addition to the liturgy. The blessing, however, did not come in until the tenth century, in Germany, and did not reach Rome for another two hundred or so years.

Presentation of Mary in the Temple, a **feast** in honour of the **Virgin Mary** which is inspired by a story in the second-century apocryphal gospel, the Protoevangelium of James. It is clearly inspired by the account in 1 Samuel 1:1-28 of the birth of Samuel. His barren mother vowed that she would dedicate her son to God, were she to give birth. Similarly, according to the legend, the parents of Mary, Anna and Joachim, were childless until after Anna's natural child-bearing age, but when Mary was born they promised to dedicate her in the Temple. When a church was dedicated to Mary in Jerusalem in 543 near the ruins of the Temple, the feast of the Presentation of Mary appears to have been established to mark the occasion: that is, at least, a possible explanation. Certainly the feast emerged in the East in the middle of the sixth century, and gradually became a major observance, held on 20 November. It seems to have come to the West by way of Greek monasteries of Southern Italy, and hence to England, where it appears in manuscripts from c. 1030, with the observance fixed for 21 November. Permission for it to be celebrated at the papal court in Avignon was granted in 1372, and it shortly afterwards spread to the rest of France. It was abolished as a universal observance by Pope Pius V (1562-72), but restored by Sixtus V in 1585. It is now, after the latest reform, only a memorial.

Priest Adorers, Pious Union of, a society conceived by St Pierre Julien Eymard (1811-68), who was also the founder of the Blessed Sacrament Fathers, under whose spiritual guidance it remains. The idea of such an organization came to the **saint** in 1857, but it was not until a year before his death that he drew up the first draft of its statutes, and not until 1878 that they were accepted. It was formally approved by Pope Leo XIII in 1881. From then on it grew quickly, both in numbers and in geographical extent. It exists both for the mutual assistance of its members, and to foster **devotion** to the eucharist. Members are expected to spend at least an hour a week before the tabernacle, to offer Mass annually for deceased members of the **confraternity**, to attend meetings arranged for the society by the diocesan director, and to make an annual donation to its expenses.

Priests of Good Will, Confraternity of, a society founded in Germany in the seventeenth century to foster the spiritual life of the clergy. Before they were allowed to join this **confraternity**, priests had to demonstrate their uprightness of life, and had once a year, in June, to report upon their constancy in living according to the rules of the confraternity as to dress, study and so on to their local director, or "definitor". Failure to do for two years would result in expulsion.

Priests' Eucharistic League, an association founded in Rome in December 1905 and created an Archassociation the following year. It is under the spiritual guidance of the Blessed Sacrament Fathers. Its purpose is to unite all those clergy who believed in, and wished to promote, the frequent, even daily, reception of the eucharist among those of whom they had the pastoral care.

prisoners, the release of, was achieved, it was believed, through invoking St Foy at her **shrine** of **Conques**, but other saints were also credited with special powers in this regard, including Saints Giles, James, Leonard and, rather later, Martial.

processions have formed part of religious ritual since time immemorial, and it is hardly surprising that they are to be found in Christianity from its first centuries: by the end of the second century there may have already been solemn funeral processions to cemeteries. In the Roman liturgy of the time of Pope Gregory the Great (c. 540-604, pope from 590) there were solemn processions to the stational churches with **candles** and processional crosses, during which the **litanies** were sung (so close was the link between processions and litanies that the former were regularly called *litaniae*). Some processions are part of the liturgy - regularly so in the Eastern rites, on certain days such as **Palm Sunday** in the Western. There were also commonly processions on other days, particularly on the **feast** of **Corpus Christi**. Usually, though not necessarily, processions have a penitential aspect in the Roman rite, and the former Roman ritual contained the structures for some dozen different occasions. Among these were of course Palm Sunday, Candlemas (now the **Presentation**) and Corpus Christi, but in addition were listed processions to obtain God's mercy in time of war or famine, for example, for fine weather or for rain, and for the translation of **relics**.

Protection of the Widowed Mother, Pious Union of, a society founded in the Jesuit church in Mendoza, Argentina, in December 1942 to assist, both spiritually and materially, those who had been widowed.

Pueri Cantores, Pious Union of, an association of boys' choirs (*pueri cantores* means "boy singers") which began in 1907 as "The Little Singers of the Wooden Cross". In France in 1939 a plan was formed to link all the choirs together in a form of federation. This plan was carried out in 1946, with about a hundred groups joining, most of them from French-speaking territories, though including Holland. The first international gathering was held in Paris the following year, with three thousand choristers involved. The purpose of the association is to promote liturgical music among boys and through them, as well as to build international ties and to foster the general education of the choristers.

purgatory, not itself a **devotion** (though there has been since the late sixteenth century a suggestion by some notable theologians that those in purgatory might be approached in prayer as intercessors before God), but a doctrine without which such Catholic devotions as **indulgences** and prayers for the dead would have no meaning. The belief that prayers for the dead are efficacious can be found in the Second Book of Maccabees (12:39-45), regarded by Catholics as canonical, and it constitutes a fairly constant tradition within the Christian Church, both East and West, until the Reformation. Though it has been argued that the word "purgatory" as such did not enter theological vocabulary until the second half of the twelfth century, the notion that there was a "place" where souls might be purged of the punishment due to sins - even though these had been forgiven - is much older.

Purification, until recently a **feast** of the **Virgin Mary** observed on 2 February. It has now, however, been replaced by the **Presentation in the Temple**, which is a feast of Christ rather than of Mary.

Q

Quarant' Ore, the (original) Italian name for the **devotion** known more commonly in England and the United States as the **Forty Hours**.

Queen and Mother of the Christian Family, Pious Union of Mary, the, a society founded in Naples in 1956 for the protection of the family through various means - by prayer, by reading, by almsgiving, by establishing workshops and so on. Members are of different degrees. The "beloved sons and daughters" (*Figli prediletti*) undertake to foster **devotion** to the **Virgin Mary** under this title of Queen and Mother of the Christian family, and to use, at least once a day, the **invocation** proper to the **confraternity**; "Husbands and Wives" promise to live Christian lives and give an example to others; ordinary members, auxiliaries and benefactors give money for the aims of the society. What funds are left over after the society's expenses have been met are given to the poor. Members are encouraged to consecrate themselves to the **Immaculate Heart of Mary** and to the **Sacred Heart**.

Queen of Peace, a title by which the **Virgin Mary** has been venerated in Toledo since the end of the eleventh century, when it was bestowed upon a recently-erected image of Mary in thanksgiving for the establishment of peace with the Moors. A **feast** was approved for local use only in 1658, but was spread by several religious orders, particularly in the wake of the First World War, when it was included in the **litany of Loreto**. The feast is observed on 9 July.

Queen of the Apostles, a title of the **Virgin Mary** which has only this century come to prominence. It is observed on the **Saturday** after the **Ascension**.

211

Queenship of Mary, a title of the **Virgin Mary** which has always been implied by the expression "Our Lady". A **feast** of the Queenship of Mary, however, was not established until 1954, to mark the centenary of the declaration of the dogma of the **Immaculate Conception**. It was then fixed for 31 May, but has since been transferred to 22 August, eight days (i.e., an **octave**, though it is not formally called such) after the **Assumption**. It is an obligatory memorial.

Quicumque Christum quæritis (= "All you who look for Christ", though it is better known in the translation "All ye who seek a comfort sure"), a **hymn** used at Vespers and Matins of the **feast** of the **Transfiguration**. It is formed from a much longer poem by Prudentius Aurelius Clemens (348-c. 410), who was born in Spain, and spent the years of his retirement composing Latin verse. He was perhaps the most outstanding of the early Christian poets.

Quinche, El, a **shrine** of the **Virgin Mary** some twenty-five miles from Quito, founded in 1586, which has become in the most popular **devotion** to Mary in the Ecuador.

Quinquagesima (= "fiftieth"), the **Sunday** before the first Sunday in **Lent**. The first Sunday in Lent was known as "Quadragesima", to mark the forty-day **fast** ("Quadragesima" = "forty"), but in the stricter discipline of monastic communities there seems to have been a wish to extend the fast forwards. The first evidence of its existence would seem to be the Council of Orleans in 511, and it had certainly made its way into Rome by the end of the second decade of the sixth century, or a very little later. By the middle of the same century a "Sexagesima" (= "sixtieth") had made its appearance, quite illogically, for the Sunday before Quinquagesima. Finally, at the beginning of the seventh century in Rome there was established "Septuagesima" (= "Seventieth"), possibly under the influence of Pope Gregory the Great (540-604). On that day the **alleluia** ceased to be used at mass until **Easter**. The use of Septuagesima remained limited to Rome, it seems, during the seventh century, and only spread when Roman liturgical books came to be used more widely in the course of the eighth century.

R

Raccolta (= "collection" or "harvest"), part of the Italian title of the book containing all the prayers and **devotions** to which **indulgences** have been granted. The first edition of this book was published privately in 1807, but the sixth edition contained a decree of the Sacred Congregation of Indulgences dated 30 November 1825 acknowledging as authentic all the indulgences recorded in it. The first English edition was a translation by Fr Ambrose St John of the Birmingham Oratory in 1856. This kept as its title *The Raccolta*, and the tradition has continued. The latest English edition, *The Raccolta or A Manual of Indulgences* was published "by authorization of the Holy See" by Benziger Brothers of New York in 1957. The latest summary of indulgences with the legislation affecting them, *Enchiridion Indulgentiarum: Normae et Concessiones* was published in 1986 by the Apostolic Penitentiary.

Ransom, Third Order of Our Lady of, an association or **confraternity** of lay people who pursue their Christian perfection under the governance, and in the spirituality, of the Order of Our Lady for the Ransom of Captives. The **Third Order** was established at the same time as the foundation of the Order itself (known familiarly as the Mercedarians from the Spanish form of the name, Our Lady of **Mercy**, or "de la Merced"), its members drawn from those who supported the Mercedarians' work by raising money to pay ransoms, or helped the sick and those on **pilgrimage**. There are records of individuals, including married couples, being received into the confraternity as early as 1234. Its constitutions were confirmed at a general chapter held in Barcelona in 1272. The Mercedarians, and the Third Order, had their greatest period of expansion in the sixteenth century, but have since declined in numbers. Members of the Third

Order wear a white **scapular**, and have a particular **devotion** to Our Lady of Mercy.

Raphael the Archangel, recorded in the Old Testament as the companion of Tobias, has been venerated since early Christian times, but was given a **feast** of his own only in 1921, which has since been removed from the **calendar**.

Regina caeli laetare ("O Queen of heaven rejoice"), a **hymn** or **prayer** to the **Virgin Mary** said or sung during **Eastertide**. According to a totally unreliable account found in the *Golden Legend* of Jacques de Voragine, composed between 1255 and 1266, Pope St Gregory the Great (d. 604) heard angels singing the verses as the picture of the Virgin, painted by St Luke, reached the bridge which crossed the Tiber during a **procession**. This story gained such popularity that it became the practice in Rome to sing the *Regina Caeli* at this point during processions. However, the hymn itself does not date from much before the year 1200, and is possibly slightly later. In the office used by Franciscans it had replaced the **Salve Regina** after Compline during Eastertide by the middle of the thirteenth century, and Pope Clement VI directed that it be sung in his household, then at Avignon, in 1350. It did not replace the **Angelus** as an Easter prayer until modern times: Pope Benedict XIV instructed that it should do so in 1743.

Regla, Our Lady of, a **shrine** of the **Virgin Mary** near Havanna which is said to owe its origins to a Peruvian, Manuel Antonio, who in 1690 built a small chapel to Mary. A sailor caught in a storm while voyaging to Havanna two years later, vowed to dedicate himself to the service of this shrine should his life be spared - which it was. He became a hermit and lived at the shrine until his death in 1743, thereby adding to its fame.

relics, literally the "remains" of **saints** which have been regarded as objects of **devotion** from early in Christian history. Traditionally, relics have been put into three categories. First-class relics are the bodies, or parts of the bodies - a bone, say, or a finger - of saints. Second-class relics include anything that a saint may have worn during his or her lifetime. The third-class relics consist of anything which has touched the body of a saint (see **brandea**). The remote origins of the cult of relics can be found in the narrative (the *Passion*) of the martyrdom of Bishop Polycarp of Smyrna in 155 or 156. After he had been burned to death his ashes were reverently gathered up by his congregation. The early devotion to the tombs of martyrs led, in the fourth century, to the division of the bodies of martyrs so that more communities might share in the power which it was presumed lay in the bones. In 415 the body of St Stephen, the Protomartyr, was discovered at Kefar Gamal not far from Jerusalem, and his remains were divided and dispatched to different parts of the Christian world. This practice was banned in Rome itself, a prohibition repeated in the last decade of the sixth century under Pope Gregory the Great, presumably because it was being violated. Rome did not, on the other hand, forbid the import of relics into the city, and they came especially from those areas of the Empire threatened by invasion. In the unsettled conditions of Italy in the eighth and, more particularly, ninth centuries, popes gave permission for the catacombs outside the walls to be opened and bodies of the supposed saints lying in them to be brought into the safety of the city. This was the occasion for much division of bodies, and the widespread distribution of relics. In addition, **pilgrims** either to Rome or to Jerusalem frequently brought back relics as mementoes of their adventures.

The cult of relics was powerfully reinforced by Charlemagne. Church law required that all altars should have relics enshrined within them, and those without them destroyed. Charlemagne used the solemn rituals associated with the transfer of relics to churches within newly christianized areas as a means of impressing the converted Saxons and Avars, and tying them more closely into his empire. He also extended the practice of taking ecclesiastical oaths on relics to the taking of all oaths.

From the ninth century onwards and throughout the Middle Ages the cult of relics became a central part of popular religion. It was a basic tenet of the people's faith that the saint was not dead, and that the presence of relics signified the physical, living presence of the saint in the place in which they were preserved. He or she was then expected to exercise protection over the church or monastery, and over the surrounding countryside. Pilgrims were attracted in the hope that the saint whose presence was verified by the relics would heal or work other miracles on their behalf, and a number of collections of these miracle stories survive, kept as witness to the power of their particular saint by the local clergy, who were not averse to theft as a means of obtaining the relics of someone whose presence in their particular monastery or church would both enhance its reputation and, through the offerings of pilgrims, improve its finances. The crusades increased the flow of relics - many of them distinctly dubious - into the West. The Church in the East never gave them so prominent a position in its worship, though their veneration was approved in 1084 by the Council of Constantinople.

In 1215 the Fourth Lateran Council forbade relics to be displayed outside their reliquaries, or sold. Though the high point of the cult of relics had been passed by the Reformation, it attracted some of the sharpest criticism of the reformers in part at least because it was by that time closely associated with **indulgences**. The Council of Trent, however, in its final session, while attempting to control abuses (including financial), condemned those who claimed that no veneration should be shown to relics. Possibly as a consequence of Trent's reassertion of the respect due to them, the cult of relics flourished again in the seventeenth century and into the nineteenth. The 1917 Code of Canon Law insisted that relics must be authenticated by a cardinal or the local bishop, and that the sale or fabrication or unauthorized distribution of them be punished by excommunication. There was little attention paid to them in the decrees of the Second Vatican Council beyond the statement in the Constitution on the Liturgy n. 111 that "It is traditional to honour the saints in the church, and to hold their authentic relics and pictures in veneration." Canon 1190 of the current Code simply states:

It is absolutely wrong to sell sacred relics. Distinguished relics, and others which are held in great veneration by the people, may not validly be in any way alienated nor transferred on a permanent basis, without the permission of the Apostolic See.

The recognition of the authenticity of relics is now the responsibility of the Congregation for the Causes of Saints. Responsibility for the veneration of them, however, falls to the Congregation for Divine Worship. It is now required that any relic used in the dedication of a church or altar must be recognizably part of a human body. Reliquaries should be closed, and, if offered for veneration, hold only one relic. They may be placed - preferably - in a crypt or an oratory, or beneath or behind the altar, but may not be placed upon the altar.

reliquaries, containers for the **relics** of **saints.** They date from the earliest Christian times, the earliest apparently being small *ampulae*, or jars, which contained either dust that had gathered on the martyrs' graves, or oil from the lamps which burned beside them. Rings containing relics, or pendants which hung about the neck, were also common. Later there developed reliquaries in the form of cloth purses, which in time came to be constructed of metal. Precious metal and gems were also used in more elaborate productions, sometimes in the form of a house or a church, or in the shape of the part of the saint's body which was enshrined within them, such as an arm, a leg, or a head. Occasionally an entire statue might be made to hold a small relic of the person depicted in the figure. The legislation of the Fourth Lateran Council of 1215, which required relics to be kept within reliquaries and not displayed outside them, encouraged the development of the reliquary. Relics of the **cross** are most frequently contained within reliquaries of a cruciform shape. A more recent development has been glass reliquaries in the form of the monstrance used to exhibit the sacred host. But this type is no longer officially approved.

reparation, not itself a **devotion,** but a concept which lies behind many of them, above all devotion to the **Sacred Heart.** God has redeemed the human race through his Son Jesus Christ, but many have rejected that act of love on God's part, or are at best ignorant of it. Those Christians who have remained loyal, and are conscious of their debt of gratitude to God, wish to "make up for" (reparation) the ingratitude of others. This conviction was nourished in particular by the **Good Friday** liturgy, and in particular the chant of the Re-proaches (the *Improperia*), which put into the mouth of God a complaint about the ingratitude of the people he had created and redeemed. It was an early aspect of the monastic vocation, especially in the East, that the penitential life of monks was a form of reparation for the sins of others, and the belief that a person could suffer, and somehow thereby placate God for the wrongs done by someone else, was encouraged by the development of the doctrine of **purgatory** and of **indulgences**.

The notion of reparation became closely linked with eucharistic devotion as it developed in the thirteenth century, culminating in the establishment of the **feast** of **Corpus Christi**, and in particular as a reaction to the rejection of this sacrament by unorthodox movements of the period. Four centuries later Catherine de Bar (Mother Mechtilda of the Blessed Sacrament) founded the Benedictines of Perpetual Adoration of the Blessed Sacrament to offer reparation for the indignities suffered by Christ in the Sacrament at the hands of the Huguenots during the French Wars of Religion. When the eucharistic devotion known as the **Forty Hours** arose in the sixteenth century, the Jesuits, among its chief propagators, saw it as a form of reparation for the license associated with the celebration of Carnival at the beginning of **Lent**. The Jesuits were also responsible for the spread of the notion of reparation in their use of the *Spiritual Exercises* of their founder, St Ignatius Loyola, which required the person making the *Exercises*, after reflecting on the Passion of Christ, to ask what Christ had done for him or her, and then to determine what he or she would do in return.

The definitive association of the concept of reparation with that of devotion to the Sacred Heart came with the apparitions of Christ to St Margaret Mary Alacocque at **Paray-le-Monial** in 1675, when Christ asked that a feast of the Sacred Heart be established as a "public apology" (*amende honorable*) for the indignities he had suffered in the Sacrament of the altar. This devotion was spread by many religious orders, and by the Jesuits in particular, and also through the establishment of associations of lay people, **confraternities**, with reparation as their main purpose. This movement gained strength, especially in France, as a consequence of the persecution of the Church during the Revolution, and in the turbulent years throughout the nineteenth century. It was in England, however, that the first full treatise on the concept of reparation was written: F.W. Faber's *All for Jesus*, published in London in 1853. In Ireland the "Pioneer Total Abstinence Association of the Sacred Heart", founded in 1898, undertook to make reparation for the sufferings inflicted upon the Sacred Heart by alcoholics.

Rocamadour, our Lady of, a **shrine** to the **Virgin Mary** in France. According to legend, the wooden statue of the Virgin had been carved by Saint Amadour, whose incorrupt body was discovered in 1166. Amadour, otherwise unknown, was identified in popular legend with the publican Zacchaeus of Luke's Gospel, 19:1-10, who was married to St Veronica, and who had been a friend of St Peter. Rocamadour, one of the major medieval shrines of France, owed much of its prominence to the enthusiasm of pilgrims *en route* to **Santiago de Compostela**, who flocked there, at least in part because of its reputation for miracles.

Rogazione Evangelica del Cuore di Gesù, **Pious Union of the**, a society started in the church of the **Sacred Heart** attached to an orphanage in Messina, Italy, in December 1900, whence it spread to the diocese of Trani, also to a church of the Sacred Heart. Its purpose is to pray for vocations to the priesthood, and to pray also for strength and good fortune for those already in the priesthood or religious life. To these intentions are added prayers for parents bringing up children, and for civil governors, as well as for all Christian people, that they might benefit from the work of the clergy.

Roncesvalles, on the French-Spanish border, some thirty miles north of Pamplona, and the scene of a famous defeat of Charlemagne's army by the Moors on 15 August 778. It was on the main route for pilgrims crossing into Spain *en route* for Santiago de Compostela. It became, however, a modest **shrine** in its own right in the ninth century after an abbot of the monastery there reported seeing a **apparition** of the **Virgin Mary**, accompanied by a deer and a choir of **angels**.

rosary a form of prayer made up of fifteen "decades" of ten **Hail Marys**, each decade being preceded by the recitation of the **Lord's Prayer** and completed by the **doxology**. These fifteen decades are divided into five joyful mysteries, recalling Christ's birth and early life, five sorrowful, recalling his Passion, and five glorious, commemorating the resurrection and concluding with the crowning of the **Virgin Mary** in heaven.

It is customary to say the Hail Marys while counting them off on beads, which traditionally number fifty of the one hundred and fifty Hail Marys which make up the complete recitation of the rosary. It is almost certainly in the one hundred and fifty repeated prayers that the origins of the **devotion** are to be found. The earliest prayer of the Church consisted of saying the one hundred and fifty psalms of David. These were of course to be found in the Old Testament, and in order to give them a more New Testament sense they were frequently introduced by an "antiphon" or followed by a prayer which put them into a Christian framework: a number of such texts survive from the fifth and sixth centuries, representing the practice in churches and monastic communities of that period. Lay people, so long as Latin was a common language, could join in, but when it ceased to be a living language and the laity were unable to join in the saying of the psalms, they seem to have replaced that form of devotion by the repetition of the Lord's Prayer and, when devotion to the Virgin Mary became a central part of Christian life in the twelfth century, by the Hail Mary.

The counting of the Lord's Prayer and later the Hail Marys on a piece of twine with knots in it was quite probably taken over from Islam, and by the middle of the thirteen century had become very common. Even the division into three groups of fifty prayers reflected a division of the psalter into three parts, which goes back at least to the fourth century. The first time the phrase "the psalter of Saint Mary" occurs, referring directly to the saying of a third of the whole rosary, is in the writings of a Dominican friar in the middle of the thirteenth century, though he was commenting on earlier writers. The location of these writers suggests that the devotion developed principally in the Rhineland, and it was there, too, that it was given its name, which meant a garland of roses for wearing on the head. An explicit comparison between such a garland and the recitation of the Marian psalter occurs in the rule of a Flemish beguinage of 1343. Much of the popularity of the devotion seems to be the consequence of its being taken up by members of the Carthusian Order, and passed from house to house, and from the Charterhouses themselves into families of friends and benefactors. From time to time apparitions of the Virgin encouraged its spread by hints as to the usefulness of the **indulgences** attached to saying it.

Though it seems that the early spread of the rosary owed a great deal to the Carthusians, it has been, traditionally, a form of prayer associated with the Dominicans, and indeed with their founder, St Dominic, himself. There is no real evidence to suggest that Dominic had anything to do with the propagation of the rosary, but one of its protagonists, and possibly the most effective, was a fifteenth-century Dominican, the Breton Alan de la Roche (c. 1428-75). It had been a Dominican practice, as it had been a Franciscan one, to establish **confraternities** linked to their houses, which shared in the spiritual benefits of the Order. Such confraternities always had certain prayers attached as an obligation of membership. Alan de la Roche was particularly devoted to the saying of the rosary, on which he preached and (posthumously) published books, and when he founded a confraternity of Our Lady and St Dominic at Douai, where he was stationed between 1464 and 1468, he made the saying of the "Psalter of the Virgin Mary" one of the obligations of membership. It was, however, not so much the confraternity at Douai that associated the Dominicans so strongly with the rosary, as that at Cologne founded by the Dominican Prior of Cologne, Jacobus Sprenger, one of the authors of the notorious work against witches, the *Malleus Maleficarum*. Sprenger, in imitation of de la Roche, imposed the rosary as an obligation of membership of his confraternity, and set about promoting his foundation by negotiating indulgences for it. A year after it began, he had five thousand members. A year later, it is claimed, there were ten times that number, and within four years five hundred similar confraternities, linked to that of Cologne, had been established. The Master General of the Order was soon involved, granting licenses to friars to establish confraternities in Florence and elsewhere.

The use of the word "mysteries" as a term for the fifteen decades seems to have first been used in 1480 in the statutes of the confraternity established in Venice, which divided them up into joyful, sorrowful and glorious, and in 1481 in those of the confraternity at Florence. The manuals produced for these confraternities in Germany, Italy and then across Europe played a considerable part, especially through the woodcuts which illustrated them, in promoting the devotion.

They frequently portrayed Mary and Jesus handing the rosary to distinguished individuals or, following the teaching of de la Roche, giving the rosary to St Dominic. The practice of attaching themes for meditation while the rosary was being said had been popularized by the Carthusians, and had been taken up in the preaching and writing of Alan de la Roche. The choice of the themes (and to some extent how many there were) remained variable for a long time, but the present division had appeared by the end of the fifteenth century.

Though there may have been nothing in the origins of the rosary to link it to the Dominican Order, the Rosary Confraternities developed under its aegis until it had a quasi-monopoly over their establishment, and to some extent over the devotion itself: it was, for instance, a Master General of the Dominicans who in 1671 issued a summary of all the indulgences surrounding it. The principal confraternity, to which all others who wished to share in the indulgences attached to Rosary confraternities had to be linked, was based at the Dominican church of Santa Maria sopra Minerva in Rome. It was at that church that the paraliturgical method of saying the rosary developed, with the people either alternating with a priest, or reciting the Hail Mary with half the congregation saying the first part, and the other half reciting the remainder - a practice, incidentally, which is said to have helped the wording of the second part of the Hail Mary to become fixed. In the early years of the seventeenth century the **Hail Holy Queen** and the **litany of Loreto** were added at Santa Maria Minerva, and all churches of the Order were instructed to organize the saying of the Rosary three times a week according to the manner it was said in Rome. Alongside this public form of saying the Rosary, however, others were developed of a less formal kind. Timoteo Ricci O.P. is credited with establishing the "**Perpetual Rosary**" in 1629 when he persuaded a Dominican house in Bologna to allot every hour in the year to one of its members, who undertook to say the rosary during that period. The occasion for this proposal was an epidemic in the city, and the prayers were to be said for the dying, for the conversion of sinners, and for peace. Another similar initiative was that of Pauline Jaricot in 1826 when she established the **Living Rosary**, which linked the saying of the rosary with raising funds for the missionary activity of the Church. Jaricot's association only came under Dominican auspices forty years after its foundation.

The visions at **Lourdes**, where the Virgin Mary appeared holding a rosary in her hands, gave new impetus to the devotion in the second half of the nineteenth century, as did the writings of Pope Leo XIII who published no less than twelve encyclicals on it. New forms of the devotion, such as the Month of the Rosary and the Rosary Crusade, have ensured that it remains the most popular of all forms of private prayer in the Catholic Church.

Rosary, Our Lady of, a **feast** originally celebrated on different days by the different **confraternities** of the **Rosary** set up in the second half of the fifteenth, and throughout the sixteenth century by members of the Dominican Order. On 7 October 1571 the combined fleets of the Christian powers defeated the Turkish navy in a naval engagement which became known as the battle of Lepanto. The date was, by chance, the first Sunday of the month, and a day which had long been especially celebrated by the Rosary confraternities, and the victory was attributed to Our Lady of the Rosary. At the request of a Spaniard who had fought in the battle, Pius V granted a feast of Our Lady of **Victory** to a confraternity in Barcelona in March 1572: it was to be kept on the first Sunday of October. In April of the following year Pope Gregory XIII allowed the feast to be celebrated in any church which had a Rosary confraternity. Its observance gradually spread and it became a feast of the whole Church in 1716 in thanksgiving for another victory over the Turks at Peterwardein by Prince Eugene of Savoie-Carignan. The date was eventually (1913) fixed not for the first Sunday but for the date of the battle of Lepanto, 7 October. Under the same title there is also a **shrine** of the **Virgin Mary** in Lima, Peru, which goes back, according to tradition, to the founding of the city, and contains the oldest statue venerated in the country, said to have been the gift of the Emperor Charles V.

Our Lady of the Rosary is also venerated at a **shrine** at Piat, North of Lucon in the Philippines, where a statue of Mary has been venerated since 1604. **Devotion** spread, however, because of an event during a drought in 1624. Two priests interpreted this as a punishment for the sins of their parishioners, and recommended penitence and a procession to the shrine which, in the case of one parish, was half-a-dozen miles away. The people of this parish prepared with fervour, and made their confessions before going to

223

communion and setting out on the journey. But before midnight rain fell, putting an end to the drought. When, the following day, they reached Piat they discovered that no rain had yet fallen there: the people of the other parish had not yet confessed their sins.

Rosary, Queen of, a **shrine** of the **Virgin Mary** on Flores, one of the islands that constitute Indonesia. According to tradition, in 1550 a statue of Mary was washed into the Straits of Malacca after a flood had destroyed the church in which it had been venerated. The statue floated along looking for someone to accept it, but finding no one until it came ashore on Flores. There a local princess, walking by the sea, heard singing and saw a radiant white lady step on to the shore. The princess, whose name was Resino, ran for her father, and both went to the figure to ask her name. The statue did not speak, but bending down wrote "Renja Rosario", Queen of the **Rosary**, in the sand. Since neither father nor daughter were literate, they filled out the tracings with stones to preserve them, and when, six months later, a missionary landed on the island, he was able to read the title under which the Virgin wished there to be honoured.

Rural Life Conference, National Catholic, a society founded in the diocese of Desmoines in the United States to work for the salvation and sanctification of those who work in the countryside.

S

Sabbatine Privilege is a promise, clearly derived from that attached to the wearing of the brown scapular by members of the Confraternity of Our Lady of Mount Carmel, that those who wore the scapular would be freed from purgatory on the Saturday (hence "sabbatine") after their death. Saturday was apparently chosen as the day of release because it is the day of the week dedicated to the Virgin Mary. Traditionally it was believed that this privilege was revealed to Pope John XXII in 1322 by the Virgin Mary herself, and was thereafter incorporated into a papal bull. This bull of John XXII was mentioned by Pope Clement VII in 1530, and then regularly by popes in the sixteenth and seventeenth century, though Carmelite writers themselves had referred to it from the second half of the fifteenth century. The question of the historicity of the bull was raised in the sixteenth century, and it was hotly debated, especially between Carmelites and Jesuits, in the seventeenth. No evidence of John's bull in which the Sabbatine Privilege is mentioned can be found in papal registers, and there is every reason to doubt its existence. In so far as the text of it has survived in other documents, it bears a clear relationship to the vision of Simon Stock, recounting the gift of the brown scapular to the Carmelite Order. The terms of the privilege were described by the Holy Office in 1613 as follows: "Through her continuous intercessions, pious suffrages, merits and special protection the Most Blessed Virgin [of Mount Carmel], especially on Saturday, the day dedicated to her by the Church, will help after their death the brethren [i.e., the Carmelites] and members of the Sodality who die in charity. In life they must have worn the habit, observed chastity according to their state, and have recited the Little Office. If they do not know how to recite it, they are to observe the fasts of the Church and to abstain from meat on Wednesdays and Saturdays, except for the feast of Christmas". The addition of these conditions prevent the Sabbatine Privilege from becoming a purely mechanical application of the doctrine of **indulgences**. The Sabbatine Privilege was confirmed by Pope Pius XI in 1922.

Sacred Heart, a **devotion** to Christ in which the heart is understood as a symbol of his love for human beings. It first appears explicitly in the thirteen century, particularly in the writings which recount the revelations made to (St) Gertrude (c. 1256-1302) of the Benedictine monastery of Helfta in Saxony. She received the **stigmata**, and her own heart was pierced by a light from the heart of Christ. In the case of Gertrude, and of other nuns of her monastery, the devotion was linked closely to the passion of Christ, and in particular to the wound made by the lance in his side. After Gertrude a number of mystics and spiritual writers wrote of Christ's heart, usually but not invariably associating it with his wounds, and with that made by the lance in his side, but without apparently developing a devotion to the heart of Christ as such - there is only one prayer, dating from the fourteenth century, directed to Christ's heart as such which became widely known, though many local or private ones have survived. Possibly under the influence of the life of Christ by Ludolph the Carthusian (c. 1295-1378), which made special mention of Christ's heart, devotion to the heart began to be disseminated among Carthusian writers in particular. The best known of these was Jan Gereecht (Lanspergius, 1489-1539), who, in his "Quiver of divine love" (*Pharetra divini amoris*), recommended the monks of the Charterhouse of Cologne to have in their cells a picture of the heart of Christ. This image appears to have displayed a heart wounded by the lance, surrounded by representations of the hands and feet, similar, in other words, to that associated with the devotion to the **Five Wounds**. In the sixteenth century, therefore, this devotion had not strayed far outside the Rhineland where it had been first conceived, though from Germany it seems to have passed to a number of devout religious of a variety of Orders, and to the Society of Jesus, whose members carried it to missionary countries. It was a Jesuit, Fr Druzbicki (1590-1662) who composed the first office of the Sacred Heart.

In 1617 there was founded at Poitiers in France the Benedictines of Our Lady of Calvary. The founder, Fr Joseph of Paris (1577-1638) imposed upon the nuns a number of devout practices such as the "Exercise of the Five Wounds" and the "Exercise of the Compassion of the Blessed Virgin" which were forms of contemplation centred on the heart of Christ, though approached through the Passion. More directly, St John Eudes (1601-80) required the priests of the congregation he founded, the Congregation of Jesus and Mary, and the nuns, the Sisters of Our Lady of Charity, to exercise devotion to the Sacred Heart, and all their churches and chapels were to be dedicated to it. He was the first to establish a liturgy of the Sacred Heart (the office of Druzbicki had been for private devotion only). He composed both an office and a mass which he had approved by the Bishop of Rouen then by other bishops throughout France. In 1670 he produced a mass for the Sacred Heart of Jesus (he had already written one for the Heart of Mary). The use of the mass spread slowly, and was only formally approved by Rome in 1861, but within John Eudes' lifetime a number of **confraternities** of the Sacred Heart had received papal recognition. The real impetus to the spread of the devotion, however, came from the nun of the Visitation of **Paray-le-Monial**, St Margaret Mary Alacocque (1648-90). This story is told under the entry for Paray, from which town it spread throughout France and elsewhere, partly through the commitment of the Visitation nuns themselves, and partly through the work of the Jesuits who had been associated with Margaret Mary. In the final revelation, Christ had told Mary that he wished a **feast** of the Sacred Heart to be established in **reparation** on the Friday after the **octave** of **Corpus Christi**. On 19 May 1693 Pope Innocent XII granted a plenary **indulgence** to anyone who went to communion in a church of the Visitation on the Friday designated in the revelation, and four years later the Duchess of York, exiled claimant to the title of Queen of England, petitioned the Pope for the feast to be established. The request was turned down, but the Pope sanctioned the celebration of a mass of the Five Wounds in churches of the Visitation. Meanwhile the number of confraternities dedicated to the Sacred Heart was notably increasing.

The mass and the office of the Sacred Heart were eventually approved for Poland and for the Roman Archconfraternity of the Sacred Heart at the beginning of 1765, and a new version of both was given approval in May of the same year. It was not until the beginning of the next century, however, that the devotion became widespread, in the aftermath of the Napoleonic War. Religious orders were founded under that title, many more confraternities were established, the first "month of the Sacred Heart" was observed in 1833. In August 1856 the mass of the feast was prescribed for the whole Church, and its celebration was twice raised in rank, first in 1889 and then in 1929. In 1875, to mark the two-hundredth centenary of the visions at Paray-le-Monial, Pope Pius IX exhorted all Catholics to consecrate themselves to the Sacred Heart, and his successor, Pope Leo XIII, encouraged all Catholics to dedicate the entire world to the Sacred Heart on 11 June 1899. Pius X required this consecration to be renewed annually, and in 1925 Pius XI laid down that this consecration be made on the feast of **Christ the King**.

Sacred Heart, Archconfraternity of, an association founded in 1797 in Rome in honour of the Sacred Heart, and raised to the level of an Archconfraternity in 1803. This was only one of the very many such **confraternities** which came into being after the death of St Margaret Mary Alacocque, but it is the one to which all others are to be linked to enjoy the spiritual benefits of membership, such as **indulgences**. Members are required to celebrate the **feast** of the **Sacred Heart** with particular solemnity, and to attend all other religious celebrations in its honour throughout the year. Apart from other prayers, they are expected to say the **invocation**, "Sweet Heart of Jesus, make me love thee more and more".

Sacred Heart for the Freedom of the Roman Pontiff and the Salvation of Humankind, Archconfraternity of the, an association founded at the basilica of the Sacré Coeur on Montmartre in 1876 by the Cardinal of Paris, Archbishop Guibert, at the suggestion of Pope Pius IX. It became an Archconfraternity the following year. The basilica was built as an act of national penitence and reparation after France's disastrous defeat by Prussia in 1870, and the **confraternity** was established to channel that **devotion**. Members are divided into three classes: simple members, who are required to pray for their country each day; members of adoration who not only say the prescribed prayers but are expected to pray before a **crucifix** or a statue of the **Sacred Heart** for half an hour once a week, or at least once a month; and apostles, whose task it is in addition to spread the devotion. As the confraternity was founded shortly after the loss of the papal states and the confinement of the pope in the Vatican, the first intention of the prayers of members was for the pope's liberty, and for the salvation of the human race. They are then to ask for God's protection for the Church, the pope, and for priests and religious; next for themselves, their families and their servants; to do battle against the impiety of the age and to make reparation for injuries to religion, to the rights of the Church and of the Holy see.

Sacred Heart of Jesus, Archconfraternity of Perpetual Devotion to, an association established in Rome by the city's Cardinal Vicar in 1891, and the same year raised to the rank of an Archconfraternity. As with other similar **confraternities**, members undertake to foster particular **devotion** to the **Sacred Heart**, but in this case the devotion is very highly structured on a three-week cycle, the first titled "of honour", the second "of **reparation**" and the third "of prayer". Each day of each of the weeks is dedicated to praying for a particular intention, and members are expected to use particular invocations to the Sacred Heart.

Sacred Heart of Jesus, National Archconfraternity of, an association formally established by the Archbishop of Malines on 11 June 1905 in Koekelberg, Brussels, in the basilica built by the Belgian people in honour of the **Sacred Heart**, and shortly afterwards raised to the rank of an Archconfraternity by Pope St Pius X. The members of this **confraternity** foster the same desires as those for which the basilica was built, namely to pray for the continued safety of the kingdom of Belgium, and that **devotion** to the Sacred Heart might be more widely spread among the people of that country. There are several ranks of members. Simple associates are required to say some particular prayers each day, together with a number of invocations. Adorers of the Sacred Heart, are required to do the same but add to that an hour once a month spent before the tabernacle, either publicly or privately. Then there are group memberships for schools or parishes, for example, whose members choose a day in which they will spend an hour before the tabernacle, and another group membership for religious communities which are required to spend a day a year similarly praying.

Sacred Heart of Jesus, Pious Union of Our Lady of the, a society founded in the parish church of Averbode, in the diocese of Malines, Belgium, in 1877 and created an Archsodality in 1885. It exists to foster **devotion** to the **Virgin Mary** under this title. Members of the **confraternity** are expected to wear the **medal**, appropriately blessed and to use the invocation "Our Lady of the Sacred Heart, pray for us" morning and evening. They are also required to contribute to the expenses of the society.

Sacred Heart of Mary, Pious Union of, a society founded in the church of St Eustachius in Rome at the beginning of the nineteenth century, and formally recognised in 1806. The purpose of this **confraternity** was originally to instruct boys in **devotion** to the **Virgin Mary**, but afterwards was dedicated simply to fostering devotion to her, and begging for her protection. Other societies with the same name had been established earlier than that in St Eustachius, the earliest in 1669.

Sacristans, Organists, and Lay Servants of the Church, Brotherhood of, a society founded originally in Avila, Spain, in September 1955 for the sanctification of its members, and their instruction in their tasks. Membership is divided into two groups - the "active" members, who still perform functions in their respective churches, and "honorary", who are now retired from such duties. They are required to make a retreat at least once every four years, to spend at least three hours a week in study of Latin, the liturgy or sacred music, and to make a small donation each month to the **confraternity**. On joining it, members are invested with a **medal**, which shows rays coming out from the tabernacle, and touching a number of objects associated with the liturgy, together with the motto taken from the Book of Psalms, "Zeal for your house consumes me".

Sacristans, Pious Union of, a society founded originally in the cathedral of Vienna, Austria, by the Cardinal Archbishop, Thomas

Innitzer, for the training both in their spiritual lives and in their official duties of those who looked after churches. Among their obligations is the daily recitation either of the prayer written especially for them, or of the **rosary**.

sailors, patron saint of, is traditionally St Erasmus or Elmo, bishop of Formiae, who died in the persecution of Diocletian c. 300. His **relics** were translated to the port of Gaeta in 842 after Formiae had been attacked by Saracens, and **devotion** to him appears to have spread from there to Naples and to other sea ports. Quite what caused sailors to invoke him is unclear, though it is usually suggested that the fact he continued to preach despite nearly being struck by a thunderbolt may have encouraged them to do so: they had considerable reason to fear such storms. The lights which sometimes appeared at mastheads as a consequence of these storms were therefore called "St Elmo's fire". His symbol came to be a windlass, which may have been the reason for his being invoked as **patron saint** of **childbirth**. His **feast** is kept on 2 June. Another patron of all connected with the sea is Francis of Paola (1416-1507), the founder of the Franciscan Minim Friars. Many of his miracles were associated with the sea, but in particular one in 1464 when he was refused a passage to Sicily across the Straits of Messina. He laid his cloak on the water, tied one end of it to his staff to form a rudimentary mast and sail, and travelled over on his cloak with his companions. His feast is celebrated on 2 April. The fourth-century St Nicholas of Bari, Bishop of Myra, is also sometimes invoked as patron of sea-farers on the basis of a story in his legendary life which recounts that he once appeared to some sailors caught in a storm at sea, and guided them safely to port. St Nicholas' feast is 6 December.

Saintes-Maries-de-la-Mer, a town on the Mediterranean coast of France where, it is said, two Marys - the mother of Cleophas and the mother of James and John - together with Lazarus and his two sisters, and a black servant called Sarah as well as a number of others arrived shortly after the death of Christ. The two Marys and Sarah stayed by the sea, while the remainder of the group preached the gospel in Provence. The church has long been a centre of **pilgrimage**, especially for gypsies, who have taken Sarah as their **patron saint**.

saints, men and women of renowned holiness of life, whose fame has made them objects of public, and official, worship within the Church. That, at least, is the situation nowadays, but has not always been so. The history of **canonization** (and beatification) is treated elsewhere. Here it is enough to note that this procedure for "making saints" is a late medieval development, and the numbers who have been given the title "saint" under this system are still only a small proportion of the total number of those Christians who have been so named. Christian saints differ in at least one essential particular from the holy men and women of other religions. At least within the Catholic tradition of Christianity they have been thought of as intercessors in heaven (the "Church triumphant") for those still on earth (the "Church militant"), or for those in **purgatory** (the "Church suffering"). In such a scheme of things there is no final boundary between the living and the dead: the **feast** day on which saints were (and are) celebrated is more often than not the day of their death, the *dies natalis* or birthday, which commemorates not the dying but the birth into heaven. Their privileged place in heaven allowed them to be protectors or **patrons** of Christians still on earth: the protection was given in return for loyalty in the form of **devotion** to the saint's memory. Among the saints one has to distinguish between martyrs who died for their religious convictions, and confessors who did not. At first confessors were those who suffered imprisonment or torture without actually being put to death but the term later came to have a much wider connotation and simply distinguished martyrs from other holy persons. Both terms "martyr" and "confessor" have the same meaning: "witness".

Devotion was, understandably, first evident in the case of martyrs. It has been suggested that the earliest form of cult was at the level of the family, and concentrated on tombs of the martyrs, but that this was quickly taken over by bishops to prevent such pieties proving a threat to unity within the local church. Certainly bishops played a large part in developing the cult, and instead of being a threat to unity the local martyr and his or her **shrine** became a focus of unity as the Christian community placed itself under the saint's protection - thereby breaking traditional relationships of patronage - and organized liturgies and, possibly more important as a social bonding, **pilgrimages** to the shrines.

After the era of persecution was over and there were no more martyrs in the strict sense, the concept of holy man (those recognized as saints are predominantly male) was extended to the local bishop and, perhaps more importantly, to ascetics whose desert existence was another form of martyrdom. In the first instance these ascetics were solitaries, and their independence of social structures as men set apart made them alternative patrons for Christian communities in their neighbourhood. This category of saintly ascetic first developed in the Eastern part of the Christian world but quickly came West. In that transition, however, significant changes were made. While the Eastern saints had been predominantly solitaries, in the West they became monks living in community; they were, more often than not, priests rather than laymen; they worked miracles; and they associated an ascetic life with one of active evangelizing. Thus sanctity in the West became distinctly clerical, whereas, although some distinguished bishops were given the title, in the East it remained much more independent of Church structures.

This division between notions of sanctity in East and West had long-term consequences. While in the East the Emperor in Constantinople remained a powerful figure, in the West the Roman Empire devolved into a number of separate kingdoms in which the bishops were powerful figures, alternative foci of power to that of local magnates. The bishops exercised their authority by a concern for the weak and powerless in society, and thus established one of the major characteristics by which sanctity has come to be judged in the West: the performance of works of charity towards the poor, the sick and the imprisoned. This did not necessarily mean that the powerful clerics were at odds with the powerful magnates. Occasionally they were, perhaps frequently were, but the ideal for both side was that government of society was a common task, with the cleric - bishop, abbot or abbess - allied with the secular ruler. This meant that these ranks of churchmen and churchwomen were naturally drawn from the same class as the civil rulers, with the consequence that in the early Middle Ages at least the saintly bishop, abbot or abbess was frequently aristocratic or of royal blood. The converse of this was that, from the Carolingian time onwards, kings were increasingly seen to fall into the same category, a process hastened by a coronation ritual which appeared to place those who underwent it in a quasi-priestly class. The notion of royal saints became particularly important in those regions of Europe and just beyond where Christianity was a relatively new arrival. The ruling families gained legitimacy from their saintly royal protectors.

These were developments of the ninth, tenth and eleventh centuries, and in the tenth and eleventh at least they went side by side with a renewal of religious life by the reform of the monasteries and the emergence of "congregations" or groups of monasteries following a similar understanding of the Rule of Saint Benedict. It was one of the functions of the stricter interpretation of the Rule to make those who followed it into saints, and the monastic community was therefore the place where sanctity could be found. This meant that the virtues required for monastic living - poverty, celibacy and obedience - became closely linked to the ideal of sanctity as it was generally understood. Yet this form of monastic sanctity had an important element in common with the sanctity of bishops and, more particularly perhaps, those of noble families whose assigned task in life it was to govern either Church or State. Theirs was a sanctity which lay in the minute observance of the tasks of one's state, whether monastic or royal. The fulfilment of duty was the criterion, and personal piety was of less significance.

In the late eleventh century, however, there was a major change in the understanding of monastic life which was eventually to be reflected even in lay attitudes to holiness. In the first period of monastic reform, with its stress on the obedience owed to the Rule, monks had been seen as "soldiers for Christ", battling away against the powers of evil on behalf of the rest of sinful humankind. In the later period there came much more of a stress on personal, rather than on liturgical, devotion, and monks were seen, as they had been in the early years of monasticism, as penitents, performing acts of asceticism in **reparation** for their own sins, and for those of the world. Religious life in this sense was interpreted as a freely-chosen following of Christ: there was little or no suggestion that holiness was attached to status. This was, perhaps, an understandable outcome of the eleventh-century clash between Church and State known generically as the Investiture Contest: monarchs were no longer sacred figures by virtue of their office.

But if saintly virtues were now more personal than institutional then some authority was needed to pronounce upon them: **canonization** began, though people (including an increasing number of laity) whose merits were well-known in the localities in which they had lived or worked continued to be recognized as saints and given local cults which sometimes reached wider audiences. Canonization, however, was one aspect of the increasing centralization (and bureaucratization) of the Church which was going on in the High Middle Ages. This phenomenon produced a reaction on the margins, and particularly perhaps among those most institutionally marginalized of Christians, women. In the late thirteenth and throughout the fourteenth centuries there were a large number of holy women visionaries, whose prophecies and calls for reform of the highest levels of the Church attracted attention both from the ordinary faithful, and from those to whom the words of rebuke were directed. The response to this apparent threat was to incorporate it into the official structures through formal recognition of the seers' holiness, and then by replacing it during the late fourteenth and fifteenth centuries with a more institutionally-friendly band of preacher-saints. These preachers were concerned not merely to improve the morals of individuals: they saw it as part of their task to improve the society in which they lived by creating structures to look after the poor (the *monti della pietà*) the sick (hospices) and so on: a return, in other words, to an earlier ideal of sanctity.

The notion of saints as heavenly protectors or intercessors was, of course, one of the fundamentals of Catholic devotion which was attacked in the sixteenth-century Reformation. Much scorn was poured, by humanists as well as reformers, upon the myths which surrounded many of those who received popular veneration, and the Church took two important steps to counter the criticisms. First of all the procedures for canonization were more strictly organized and put under one of the new "congregations" into which the papal curia (or bureaucracy) was divided. Secondly, a Jesuit, Jean Bolland (1596-1665) began work on critical editions of the sources for saints' lives, working in accordance with the **calendar** of the Church's year. The first volume, the *Acta Sanctorum* for January, appeared in 1643: Bolland's successors, who are known as Bollandists, have now reached a preliminary volume for the saints of the month of November. The Protestant attack on saints occasioned a long hiatus in the series of papal canonizations: when they began again the selection reflected a desire to honour men and women (but still predominantly men) whose lives expressed the values of the Counter-Reformation, founders of the reforming, and actively apostolic at least in the case of the male ones, religious orders; reforming churchmen; and missionaries. That the traditional pattern by which sanctity was recognized was still in operation is evident from the kinds of people in these categories: above all male, clerical, and well-connected - though with the papacy playing so active a role in the selection of saints, some of the connections were papal rather than directly noble.

The same sort of criteria have operated down to the present day. The number of saints canonized under the rules operated first by the Sacred Congregation of Rites and now by the Sacred Congregation for the Causes of Saints has not been large, though Pope John Paul II has speeded up the process considerably, canonizing almost as many as all his predecessors put together. Among them, however, are large numbers of martyrs all canonized together, which rather skews the figures. There is a conscious effort on the part of the Congregation to attempt to redress the balance of saints by bringing forward more women and more lay people, but the processes are, for the most part, so long drawn-out that any changes take a long time to make any impact on the statistics of sanctity. In any case, the changes may be ill-considered. They are based upon the premise that the Church needs more female, and lay, role-models. No doubt lives of saints (hagiography) are written as if saints are thought of as role-models, but that is by no means obvious. There is a very distinct difference between the sort of person selected by a clerical bureaucracy for canonization, and the sort of person to whom there is popular devotion. The first represents virtues as understood by the Church - obedience to authority, chastity in whatever state of life he or she lived - whereas the figures which seem to appeal to the people at large, while not rejecting those virtues, display rather an independent spirit and a penchant, if not for the miraculous at least for the remarkable. Thee is a sense in which the ascetic or solitary figure of the early Church, as someone set apart, still appeals to the devotional life of Christians.

Salvation, Pious Union of Our Lady of, a society founded in Paris in January 1872 with the title of "Notre-Dame de Salut" to work for the salvation of France through prayer and through the Christianisation of the working class. Members of the **confraternity** pursue this end by saying the **Lord's Prayer** and by adding to it the invocation "Our Lady of Salvation, pray for us and save France". They are also expected to be open in their profession of Christianity, to engaged in some apostolic work in their diocese, and to donate a little money each year. To foster the Christian spirit members encourage **pilgrimages**, particularly to Rome, **Lourdes** and to the Holy Land.

Sand, Our Lady of the, a title of a wooden statue of the **Virgin Mary** venerated at Roermond in Holland. According to tradition a Polish nobleman called Wendelin, who had come to the region of the Roer River to seek tranquillity, found the statue beside an oak tree, itself close to a spring to which Wendelin had come to water the sheep he was tending. A chapel was in existence on the banks of the Roer from early in the fifteenth century. The church which now houses the statue in a niche above the altar dates from the end of the nineteenth century. Through a grating in the floor of the church it is possible to see the spring Wendelin found, and **water** from the spring is piped to pilgrims outside the chapel.

Saturday, as a day celebrated in honour of the **Virgin Mary**, goes back at least to the time of Alcuin (c. 735-804), who inserted a mass for Mary on that day into his collection of **votive** masses. Hitherto, and indeed for some time afterwards, the day had been observed, along with Friday, as a time of **abstinence** and prayer in memory of Christ's time in the tomb. It may be that when, in the tenth century, attention focused on Mary, it was a means of joining the Church's grief with that of Christ's mother. Whatever the reason, by the beginning of the eleventh century the custom of having a mass in honour of Mary on Saturdays except in **Lent** and on **feast** days was widely practised, and it became an accepted part of the liturgical week in the reforms introduced under Pius V (1566-72). The popularity of this form of **devotion** to Mary was undoubtedly enhanced by the **Sabbatine Privilege**.

Scala Coeli, an **indulgence** so called because it was associated with the church of St Mary at Scala Coeli in Rome. According to legend, St Bernard of Clairvaux, when saying a requiem mass in this church, had a vision of the souls for whom he was praying going up to heaven by means of a ladder (the *scala coeli*). Masses said at this church were given a special indulgence which could be applied to masses said in other, specially named, churches outside Rome - including, by the sixteenth century, some in England.

Scala Sancta, or "Holy Stair" near the **Lateran Basilica** in Rome, which lead up to the "Sancta Sanctorum", a chapel which is the only remaining part of the old Lateran palace which was otherwise almost entirely destroyed by fire in 1308. Up to the time when Pope Sixtus V (1585-90) began the restoration of the Lateran the steps were known as the *Scala Pilati* or "Stair of Pilate" because it was believed that these steps had, in their original location, been those up which Christ had walked into the Praetorium for judgement by Pilate. Tradition claims that these, like so many other **relics of the passion**, had been brought to Rome by St Helena, the Mother of Constantine, after her visit to the Holy Land in 327. They consist of twenty-eight steps of white marble. They have been much worn, and are now encased in wood, though **pilgrims** can see the original stair through some gaps which have been intentionally left. It is the practice for pilgrims to ascend the stairs on their knees, a custom introduced in 850 by Pope St Leo IV, and one to which Pope Pius VII (1800-23) attached an **indulgence**. The last time a pope performed this particular **devotion** was on 12 September 1870 when Pope Pius IX did so shortly before Rome, the last remaining part of the once extensive papal states, fell to the Piedmontese army.

scapular, a form of **devotion**, particularly to the **Virgin Mary**, which is traditionally attributed to an **apparition** of Mary received by St Simon Stock, the Prior General of the Carmelites who died in 1265. In origin the scapular was a narrow form of cloak reaching almost to the feet worn over the shoulders (hence the name, derived from the Latin *scapulae* meaning "shoulders") and hanging down front and back over the habit. Its use is enjoined for monks engaged in manual labour by the Rule of St Benedict. In the case of the Carmelites, however, it seems that "scapular" was used interchangeably with "habit" by the end of the thirteenth century. The promise made to St Simon Stock by Mary does not appear in any written source until the mid-fourteenth century. According to the earliest account, Mary appeared surrounded by angels, holding out the scapular and saying that anyone who died wearing the scapular would be saved. The story clearly refers not to all Christians but to members of the Carmelite Order, though there is no doubt that the scapular devotion among the laity dates from this narrative. It occurs in the life of St Simon contained in a catalogue of **saints** of the Carmelite Order, and although dated a century or so after the event it recounts, it must reflect an older tradition. How much older it is impossible to determine, and although there appears to have been a **confraternity** in Florence dedicated to **Our Lady of Mount Carmel** as early as 1280, there is no sure evidence of the use of the scapular by the laity in the thirteenth century. Carmelite authors began to speak of the scapular being worn by lay people from the early fifteenth century onwards. A work by a Belgian Carmelite, Arnold Bostius, in 1479, entitled "On the patronage and protection of the Blessed Virgin Mary" attributed the promise of eternal salvation to all those wearing the scapular to the doctrine of Mary as the **Mediatrix of All Graces**. Membership of the confraternity placed an obligation on its members to live their lives in imitation of Mary's virtues. This book was popularised by a Flemish Carmelite, John Paleonydor, and his work, *Fasciculus Tripartitus*, first printed in 1495 was regularly reprinted during the sixteenth and seventeenth centuries, which were the heyday of the confraternity of Our Lady of Mount Carmel. The confraternity's popularity, however, can be attributed as much to the promotion by popes during this period of the **Sabbatine Privilege** as to the scapular itself. The full-scale scapular was clearly not a practical item of clothing for lay people to wear constantly. It became very much smaller, a symbolic item rather than the real thing, and St Pius X agreed that a medal might be worn or carried in place of the small piece of cloth. This devotion to the "Brown Scapular" has been regularly encouraged by popes down to modern times, and is the origin of scapular devotions in general. There are, however, several other such forms of piety, sometimes derived from the habits of particular religious orders. Thus the black scapular of Our Lady of **Sorrows** was inspired by the habit of the **Servites,** and the white scapular of Our Lady of **Ransom** from that of the Mercedarians. There is also a blue scapular and several white scapulars, those of the **Immaculate Heart of Mary,** approved in 1877, of Our Lady of **Good Counsel,** approved in 1893 and of the **Sacred Hearts of Jesus and Mary,** approved in 1900. Members of the Confraternity of Our Lady **Health of the Sick** approved in 1860 wear a white scapular.

scourge, or instrument of flagellation used by the soldiers on Christ just before his crucifixion. An object claiming to be this implement is preserved in the abbey at Subiaco, but there survives no account of how it reached there.

seamstresses of Madrid have placed themselves under the **patronage** of St Anthony of Padua, and at a church dedicated to him in the Spanish capital young women, but especially seamstresses, prayed to him on his **feast** day that they might find someone to marry, dropping pins into the font for **holy-water.**

Servants of the Churches, Pious Sodality of, a society founded by a Jesuit missionary to the southern Slavs, Fr Vincent Basile, in the nineteenth century, and which was approved by Pope Pius IX. The **patron** of the association is St John Berchmans, a statue of whom, it is recommended, be kept in the sacristy of those churches where this society is established. The society's purpose was to ensure the proper decorum of those who in any way looked after the churches.

Servants of the Holy Spirit, Archconfraternity of, an association founded in 1877 in the church of Our Lady of the Angels, London, and created an Archconfraternity two years later, under the direction of the Oblates of St Charles, a Congregation of priests which no longer exists. The purpose of the **confraternity** was to honour particularly the Third Person of the Trinity, an obligation which the members carried out through a variety of means, such as keeping a **novena** before the **feast** of **Pentecost** and, if they were priests, saying daily either the *Veni Creator Spiritus* or the *Veni Sancte Spiritus.*

Servites, Third Order of, an association or **confraternity** of lay men and women who strive for Christian perfection under the spiritual guidance of members of the Order of the Servants of Mary. They are distinguished from other **Third Orders** by a **devotion** to Our Lady of **Sorrows**. The origin of the Servite Order itself seems to have been as a form of confraternity, the Laudesi, at Florence among merchants and noble families of the city. In 1240 seven men of this group, some of them married, adopted a form of life based upon the Rule of St Augustine. Some of their associates, and others who later joined them, appear to have continued in the lay state though a rule for them was not approved until 1424, under Pope Martin V. Members of the Third Order wear a black **scapular**.

Seven Sorrows of the Blessed Virgin Mary, Confraternity of, a society which traces its origins to the foundation of the Servite Order in Florence in the thirteenth century. The first **confraternity**, it is claimed, was established in the Servite church in Florence in 1266, but it was not until the very end of the sixteenth century that it began to spread, and in 1607 Pope Paul V granted the head of the Servites permission to erect the society in any church of the Order: there was one set up in the church of St Marcellus in Rome in 1615. In 1628 Pope Urban VIII gave the Prior General of the Servites authority to establish this confraternity in any church, provided the appropriate religious authorities approved. When the confraternity is erected in a church, a particular chapel, or the altar of Our Lady of **Sorrows** if there is one, is designated as that at which members carry out their particular **devotions**. Members are inducted by the imposition of a **scapular** made of black wool, which has received the approved **blessing**.

Seven Words, Confraternity of, an association or **confraternity** founded in the Church of St Michael, Valladolid, Spain, in 1929 to honour the Passion of Christ, specifically through attending the **procession** to the Holy Sepulchre during **Holy Week**. There are different grades of membership, determined in part by the amount of money which members donate to the confraternity's purposes; there is also a women and girls' section, whose task it is to decorate the church during Holy Week, and particularly the **altar** at which the

241

confraternity carries out its particular **devotions**. Membership is strictly controlled, and aspirants have to be recommended as well as provide evidence of their willingness to undertake its obligations and of their probity of life.

shrine, a holy place or building where a much-venerated sacred image or **relics** are kept, to which an especial **indulgence** has been attached, or where **apparitions** have occurred. It has come to mean a place which is the focus of **devotion** and of **pilgrimage**, sometimes specially constructed, such as the National Shrine of the Immaculate Conception in Washington, D.C., or the many "grottoes" containing images of the **Virgin Mary** in the grounds of convents, churches and so on, or sometimes arising naturally on the spot where, for example, a martyrdom occurred. The word derives from the Latin *scrinium*, meaning a chest in which books and papers were held - and later the bones of saints for veneration. In the Roman Catholic Church's official Latin usage, the word now used is *sanctuarium*, "sanctuary". Although ecclesiastical authorities had from time to time issued ordinances about the establishment and conduct of shrines, there was no mention made of them in the 1917 Code of Canon Law. The 1983 Code, however, devotes five canons to the subject, defining a shrine as "a church or other sacred place which, with the approval of the local Ordinary [i.e., the local bishop], is by reason of special devotion frequented by the faithful as pilgrims" (canon 1230). The number of Christian shrines which still attract pilgrims has recently (1987) been calculated at 330 for North America, 973 for Latin America and no less that 6,150 for Western Europe. A detailed study of the active European shrines reveals that no less than sixty-five per cent are dedicated to Mary, compared with only seven and a half per cent to Christ who is far outdone by shrines dedicated to male saints, nearly twenty per cent of the total. Of the shrines identified, Italy, France and Spain (in that order) account for more than half the locations.

Shroud of Turin, a supposed **relic** of Christ, the shroud in which Christ's body was wrapped at his burial. There have been a number of claimants for this title of Christ's winding sheet. There was one at Compiègne which survived eight hundred years, only to be destroyed at the French Revolution and another at the Cistercian abbey of Cadouin from 1117, a trophy of the crusades, which managed to survive the French Revolution only to be discovered to be, in 1934, arabic cloth of the tenth century embroidered with pious Islamic inscriptions. The Turin shroud, though more famous, does not have as old a history as these. It is first recorded in the town of Lirey (France) in the middle of the fourteenth century when it was given to the church there by Geoffrey de Charney. How he came by it is uncertain. His family wanted to put it on exhibition, but the local bishop objected, claiming that the image of Christ upon it had been painted on. There was considerable controversy, but the family's wishes finally prevailed and the shroud continued to be put on exhibition. In 1453 it became the property of the House of Savoy, who took it first to Chambéry and then, in 1578, to Turin. The history of the relic was not very different from others until 1898 when a lawyer of Turin, Secondo Pia, took a photograph of the shroud and, while developing it, saw not a negative - as one would have supposed - but a positive image of a man bearing wounds very similar to those which Christ was known to have suffered. Indeed, they revealed details which might not have been expected, such as, for example the fact that the nails went through the wrists and not through the palms of the hands, as Christ is generally portrayed. In the late 1960s and through the 1970s there were a number of tests made of the shroud which seemed to indicate that it was indeed from the first century of the Christian era, and a miraculous image of someone who very likely was Jesus. In 1980 Umberto II of Italy bequeathed the relic to the pope, and since then it has been subjected to further tests, which suggest that the shroud is medieval in origin.

Silent Night, a **Christmas** carol or **hymn**, written in 1818 by Josef Mohr, then assistant priest at Oberndorf, just North of Salzburg in Austria, and set to music by the village organist and school teacher, Franz Gruber. At the time the hymn was composed Mohr was thirty-one years old and Gruber twenty-six.

Siluva, Our Lady of, a **devotion** to the Virgin Mary in the province of Siluva, Lithuania. According to legend, the province had been almost wholly converted to Protestantism, and the churches destroyed. Some years after this a number of shepherds saw a vision of a woman holding a child in her arms and weeping. She asked them why they worked that particular piece of land whereon had once stood a church in which her son had been adored. People came from round about, and when they began to dig the land they found a statue of the Virgin, a remarkable event which hastened the return of the province to Catholicism.

Sint Josef, zorg!, Pious Union of, a society founded in Holland in March 1936 to bring together all members of religious orders under the protection of St Joseph (the title, which is used as a prayer, means "St Joseph, care for us") for mutual support both in temporal matters and spiritual, and to combat Communism. It began in the house of the Redemptorists in Zenderen, in the Archdiocese of Utrecht, but spread into Belgium, France and Germany.

Slavery of Love, Holy, a form of **devotion** to the **Virgin Mary** which owes its more recent manifestation to the writings of St Louis Marie Grignion de Montfort (1673-1716), though the expression "slave of the mother of God" goes back at least as far as St Ildephonsus of Toledo (607-69). In medieval spiritual writing it became quite common. At the end of the sixteenth century there appeared at Alcalá de Henares (Spain) the first of several **confraternities** which carried the title "Confraternity of the Holy Slavery", or something similar: "The Slaves of the Exiled Holy Virgin" was established, again in Spain, at Valladolid in 1612 by a Benedictine. A member of the Alcalá confraternity, Simon de Rojas, went on to set up his own, "The Confraternity of the Slaves of the *Ave Maria*", which was approved by Rome in 1616. It was spread by Trinitarian houses (Rojas was a Trinitarian) throughout Spain, and into Belgium, then part of the Spanish Empire, by an Augustinian friend of Rojas, Bartolomé de los Rios. Pierre de Bérulle (1575-1629), the founder of the Oratorians in France, incorporated the notion of holy slavery into his own very influential spiritual teaching, and it was through this that it reached de Montfort. As mother of Christ, de Montfort argued, Mary was also mother to all human beings; as the one who consented to the Incarnation she became Co-Redemptrix with Christ. Both attributes gave her dominion over the souls of all humankind.

On these grounds he proposed an act of total consecration of the individual, body and soul, material wealth and spiritual virtue, as a slave to Mary. This doctrine he propounded in a *Treatise of True Devotion to the Blessed Virgin* (hence his doctrine is frequently called "the True Devotion"), but his manuscript was put into a trunk and lost until 1842, when it was discovered in the Mother House of the order he founded, the Montfort Fathers. It was examined, and declared free from error, in 1853. Pope St Pius X (1835-1914, pope from 1903) endowed those who recited de Montfort's formula of consecration with a plenary **indulgence**, and gave further indulgences to the Confraternity of the Queen of All Hearts founded to further the consecration: in 1913 he erected it an Archconfraternity.

Snow, Our Lady of the, a **feast** celebrated on 5 August which commemorates the **dedication** of the **basilica** of Santa **Maria Maggiore**. According to a legend dating, it would seem , from the ninth century, a Roman called John wanted to give all his money to the **Virgin Mary**, and asked her to show him how this was to be done. As a consequence of his prayer, snow fell on the Esquiline Hill during August, Rome's hottest month, and both John and Pope Liberius were informed in a dream that on the exact spot covered by the snow, the church dedicated to Mary was to be built. The story became very popular, though the feast itself does not seem to have been widely celebrated outside Rome until the fourteenth century, when it was extended to the whole of Rome and to some other dioceses. It became particularly popular in France, and was created a feast of the universal Church in 1568. It is now, in the revised **calendar**, an optional memorial.

Sodalities of Our Lady, an association under the spiritual guidance of the Society of Jesus, and known now as the Christian Life Movement. The first members of the Society had founded apostolic groups of laymen, and so had individual Jesuits in different cities across Europe. Credit for forming what became the "Marian Congregations", however, is usually ascribed to a Jesuit from Liège, Jean Leunis, who taught at the Jesuit "Roman College", the predecessor of the Gregorian University. In the Autumn of 1563 he gathered a group of his best students for prayer and discussion. Their particular

devotion was to the **Virgin Mary** under the title of the **Annunciation** - this was to be the dedication of the church attached to the College, which was at that time being built. The purpose was to foster not only the spiritual life, but the active Christian life, of its members.

In ten years, largely due to the commitment of the earliest members, sodalities existed in twenty-two cities across Europe. In December 1584, little more than a fortnight after the death of Fr Leunis, Pope Gregory XIII designated the first sodality at the Roman College the "primary" sodality, to which all others had to be linked to enjoy the same spiritual privileges. The growth of the movement was such, however, that there had developed distinct branches - in 1569, for example, it was divided into sodalities for those in high school and sodalities for those at university, or studying theology, and there were further subdivisions. The sodality at the Roman College was therefore the first (*prima*) of the primaries (*primaria*), and it is this *prima primaria* to which all others now existing are linked.

Sodalities for women were allowed to affiliate to the sodality at the Roman College in 1751. It was common practice to structure sodalities according to trade or profession - one sodality for lawyers, for instance, and another for servants. In the seventeenth century the sodalities were extremely influential, but their success rose and fell with the fortunes of the Society of Jesus, and they suffered much from Jansenist opposition. At the time of the suppression of the Society in 1773 there were some 2,500 sodalities. Though the sodalities themselves were not suppressed, they did not fare well, and after the restoration of the Society in 1814 grew only slowly. They eventually reached, however, the proportions of a mass movement with, at its height, some 80,000 individual sodalities associated with the *Prima Primaria*. The earliest sodalities had been very selective in their entry requirements, creating an elite society. This aspect disappeared in the nineteenth and twentieth centuries. In 1910 the Jesuit General began to establish national offices for the sodalities, with Jesuits in charge of promoting them, and it was a natural extension to form, in 1953, with the encouragement of Pope Pius XII who was himself a member, a world federation.

Solemnity of Mary, the title restored to the **feast** which marks 1 January, a day which was until 1969 more widely known as the

Circumcision. As *Natale Sanctae Mariae* (= "Anniversary of St Mary") it was the first feast of the **Virgin Mary** celebrated in Rome, beginning, apparently, in the early years of the seventh century.

Sorrows of Our Lady, Seven, a **devotion** to the **Virgin Mary** which seems to have begun in the twelfth century, though it did not become widespread until the fourteenth with the veneration of Mary at the foot of the **cross**, and of other sorrows. During the following century the number of these sorrows or sufferings varied - sometimes five but usually more, up indeed to 150. Even when the number was fixed at seven, the sorrows were not always identical, though in the form in which they have survived they are found first in a late fourteenth-century collection of the Chancellor Philippe de Maizières, who died in 1405. These are the prophecy of Simeon, the flight into Egypt, losing Jesus in the Temple, meeting him on the way to Calvary, at the foot of the cross, the descent from the cross, and the burial. These themes were quickly developed into a form of Divine Office, in which the person saying it asks for her help through her sufferings during the Passion. The devotion was fostered by a Confraternity of Our Lady of the Seven Sorrows established by Jean de Coudenberg: its statutes were approved in 1497. The Archduke Philippe le Beau became a member in 1492, and the **confraternity** continued to attract support from the nobility - the future Emperor Charles V enrolled in 1511. The Feast of the Seven Sorrows was first celebrated in Mainz in 1423 as **reparation** for the injuries inflicted on Marian images by the Hussites. There was a feast of the Sorrows at **Bruges** by the end of the fifteenth century, whence it spread to France. In 1668, when the Servites were first granted permission for the feast of the Seven Sorrows (some times called Seven Dolours) of Mary, the date was fixed for the third Sunday in September, that is, the one following the **Exaltation of the Cross**. When it first entered the **calendar** in 1727 it was to be observed on the Friday before **Palm Sunday**. The feast of the Seven Sorrows, as distinct from the feast of Our Lady of Sorrows, was made an observance of the whole Church by Pius VII in 1814 as an act of thanksgiving after his return to Rome from captivity in France. The date was changed to 15 September in 1913. Our Lady of Sorrows now has the rank of obligatory memorial.

At Quito in Ecuador, in the Jesuit boarding school of St Gabriel on 20 April 1906, a picture of Our Lady of Sorrows attached to the wall of the refectory was observed to open and shut its eyes - an event seen by a large number of the pupils and their teachers. A great number of miracles were attributed to the intercession of this lithograph, and its fame so spread throughout the country that devotion to Mary under this title became a major cult in Ecuador.

Soul of my Saviour, a popular **hymn** based upon the **prayer** which begins *Anima Christi.*

Souls in Purgatory, Pious Union for the, a society founded in the Basilica of St Nicholas of Tolentino in March 1884 by the Bishop of Macerata and Tolentino to assist the souls in **Purgatory** by the prayers of the members. It is under the guidance of the Augustinian Friars in whose charge of the Basilica was at the time. Members are required to pray daily for the souls in Purgatory and to offer a mass once a year at least for them. They are also expected to wear, or to keep at home, the **medal** of St Nicholas of Tolentino with, on its reverse face, a representation of souls in Purgatory.

Stabat mater dolorosa (= "The sorrowful mother is standing"), one of the greatest and best-known hymns of the Roman liturgy. It occurs both in the office, divided up between Vespers, Matins and Lauds, and it is also used as a **sequence** of the mass of the **feast** of the **Seven Sorrows** of the **Virgin Mary**. It was added to the liturgy as a sequence only in 1727, though it had been used in other ways since the later Middle Ages. Its authorship is disputed. The most likely candidate is Jacopone da Todi (c. 1230-1306), a lawyer who became a Franciscan, and a skilled poet. Other possible authors include St Gregory, St Bernard and St Bonaventure, but the earliest records suggest Jacopone, and the sentiment of the poem, which prays that one might suffer with Mary as she suffered alongside her son, is Franciscan. There are several English translations, the best known perhaps being "At the cross her station keeping".

Star of the Sea, a title of the **Virgin Mary** under which she has long been an object of **devotion**. It is believed to have arisen through a misunderstanding of the of the Vulgate text of Isaiah 40:15. St Jerome translated the Hebrew *mâr* as *stilla*, which in Latin means a drop. The Hebrew name of Mary, *mâryâm*, was taken to mean "drop of the sea" and then, later, when *stilla* was in turn misread as *stella*, "star of the sea". As a result of this mistaken etymology, Mary became the **patron** of **sailors**. The **hymn** *Ave Maris Stella*, which presents Mary as the Gate of Heaven, also has her guiding travellers into port. The hymn is known from ninth-century manuscripts, but in all probability was written earlier. From then onwards this image of star of the sea became a common one in Western devotion. There is a statue of the Virgin Mary venerated under this title in Maastricht in Holland. According to legend a boat found itself unable to leave its berth on the River Meuse which runs through the town, and when the captain examined his cargo he found a statue dating from the fifteenth century in the hold. He left it in the nearest church - and was then able to set sail. This statue is carried in procession twice a year, on the Monday after Easter and on the Sunday closest to the **Feast** of the **Assumption**.

station, a Latin term which seems to have arisen from the military meaning of sentry-duty, particularly for night duty. Hence it entered the Christian vocabulary because **vigils** were kept at night beside the tombs of martyrs. These vigils were frequently marked by **fasting**, so *statio* in early use appears to have had that connotation. But as vigils often ended in some liturgical celebration, the word was transferred to that event. So "Station at St Lawrence's" as an instruction meant that the people were to gather for a solemn liturgy at the church dedicated to St Lawrence. But these liturgies were accompanied by **processions**, and in medieval times the term was applied to stopping points along these processional routes. St Gregory the Great is traditionally said to have assigned churches to the station days, and in these the liturgy was kept with particular solemnity. **Indulgences** came to be attached to these churches, giving them especial prominence on the **pilgrim** route. The most important of these stational churches are **Maria Maggiore**, for the first **Sunday** of **Advent**, and for the first and third masses of **Christmas** Day; the **Lateran** for **Holy Saturday**, and Santa Sabina for the ceremony of the ashes on **Ash Wednesday**.

Station of Honour of the Sacred Heart of Jesus, Archconfraternity of, an association begun in 1863 by the nuns of the Visitation Order, and formally constituted an Archconfraternity first for France and Belgium in 1878, and eventually in 1903 as an Archconfraternity for the rest of the world. Members of the **confraternity** choose an hour of the day - their "station" - at which time, though without laying aside whatever they are doing, they spend an hour mentally adoring Christ in the **Blessed Sacrament**. They are also urged to come together once a month for Mass and communion. They make this prayer in **reparation** for the neglect of Christ in the eucharist.

stations of the cross, also known as the **way of the cross**, a title which has been used by a number of **confraternities** for one of the older and most popular **devotions** of the Church. It recapitulates, by means of pictures or other images, the route taken by Christ on the way to his crucifixion. The antiquity of the devotion depends upon what exactly constitutes the practice of the **stations**. If in essence it is the recapitulation of some of those holy places of **Jerusalem** which were specifically linked to the last hours of Christ, then there were a number of building in Europe which attempted to do so, the earliest being the fifth-century church of San Stefano in Bologna - though that would seem to have been an isolated case. After **pilgrimage** to the Holy Land became more common in the Middle Ages, such buildings, with perhaps altars dedicated to various incidents in the gospel story, became more common in the fourteenth and fifteenth centuries. At about the same period it is recorded of the German mystic Henry Suso (c. 1295-1366) that he followed Christ step by step in his imagination as he meditated upon the passion, making as it were a spiritual pilgrimage along the way of the cross.

It is about the same period that accounts of pilgrimages to Jerusalem begin to contain references to some of the sites on the *Via dolorosa*, the route supposedly taken by Christ on his way to Calvary. In the account of 1480 by Felix Fabri there is a story that the **Virgin Mary** until her death followed the same stages of the Jerusalem pilgrimage as did the fifteenth-century pilgrims themselves, a route, it has been suggested, dictated partly by the location of the **shrines** known from the fourth century, partly by the requirements of the Turkish authorities of the city, and partly by the Franciscan friars, who acted as guides to the holy places, wishing to get their charges out of Jerusalem as quickly as possible so as not to disturb their working relationship with the Turks. By the time of Felix Fabri's narrative several of the incidents which go to make up the modern stations of the cross were already established: there is the beginning of the journey, set in the Church of the Holy Sepulchre, and the end of it on Calvary; there is the story of the **veil** of Veronica, of Simon of Cyrene being forced to assist in carrying the cross; a fall by Christ under the weight of the cross, and the incident with the women of the city. William Wey, an English pilgrim who went to Jerusalem in 1458 and again four years later, uses the word "stations" for the sites he visits in that city, and does not use it for other sites in the Holy Land at large, or even in the neighbourhood of Jerusalem, which he also visited.

By the end of the fifteenth century, therefore, some of the incidents of the *Via dolorosa* had been identified and apparently called "stations". Martin Ketzel, who went on pilgrimage about 1468, and repeated the journey sometime later because he had forgotten the exact details of distance between the beginning of the journey and the end, had a series of carvings made before the end of the century and set up in Nuremberg. There were seven of them, set apart the correct number of paces by his reckoning. They were (1) Jesus meets his mother - who faints; (2) Simon of Cyrene; (3) women of Jerusalem; (4) Veronica; (5) Christ falling; (6) Christ on the ground under the cross; (7) Christ taken down from the cross and laid in the arms of Mary. They were popularly known as "the seven falls". This series of stations was frequently copied in the sixteenth century, though the scenes depicted varied from set to set. It was quite common in some illustrated versions to begin the account of Jesus's "falls" long before the condemnation by Pilate, which was the start of the Ketzel series of carvings, and of the modern stations.

Credit for the version of the stations as they are now known seems to go to Jan van Paesschen, Prior of the Carmelites at Malines, whose book *The Spiritual Pilgrimage* was published in Louvain in 1563, the author himself having died about twenty years earlier. This took as its structure a year-long pilgrimage to the Holy Land and back, assigning meditations for each day and describing the scene observed on that day. While the reader is (mentally) in Jerusalem, Paesschen

251

takes him or her along the way of the cross, listing the stations in the order they have now come down to us. He adds details about the distances from one station to the next, details taken not from the route in Jerusalem but from the statues erected in Louvain in 1505 in imitation of Ketzel's. Van Paesschen's work was used by Adrichomius in a book on *Jerusalem at the Time of Christ*, published in 1584. Adrichomius's version seems to have enjoyed much greater popularity than the original. Neither author had been to Jerusalem, and their accounts did not coincide with the pilgrimage along the route to Calvary as demonstrated to pilgrims by the Franciscans who looked after the holy places. In the sixteenth century they produced their own careful guidebooks, but by the seventeenth the influence of Adrimochius was growing, and they adapted their traditional account to that of Adrimochius.

From the fourteenth century onwards **indulgences** had been attached to pilgrimage to the holy places in Jerusalem, and in 1731 Pope Clement XII decreed that those who devoutly made the stations of the cross would gain the same indulgences as if they had themselves visited the holy places. This "communication" of indulgences greatly assisted in the spread of the stations as a popular devotion, under the auspices of the Franciscans. It was in particular the work of the Franciscan St Leonard of Port Maurice (1676-1751) to make them better known: it is claimed he established them in nearly six hundred places in Italy. Pope Benedict XIV erected them in the Roman Coliseum. They did not reach England much before the middle of the nineteenth century, and entered the United States at the same period. The form of prayer which became common was taken from the writings of St Alphonsus Liguori, and a stanza of the hymn *Stabat mater* was commonly sung. The only significant requirement to complete the devotion and obtain the indulgences attached, however, was to meditate upon the passion of Christ, and to walk from one station to another while doing so.

Steeple, Our Lady of the, a **devotion** to the **Virgin Mary** which, it is claimed, goes back to the mid ninth century when a priest turned part of the palace of Diocletian at Spalato in the former Yugoslavia into a chapel in honour of Mary and of Pope St Gregory the Great. Some time later, outside the chapel but on the wall of the palace, a steeple was built, which gives the sanctuary its name.

stigmata, the impression upon an individual of the **Five Wounds** of Christ - in the hands, in the feet, and in the side - though some stigmatists have also displayed marks of the crown of thorns upon their heads. It is debatable whether the stigmata of St Francis of Assisi, which he received in 1224, two years before his death, were the first on record. On the other hand they are certainly the earliest for which there is clear evidence, even though very few people saw them, and they are the only ones which the Church has recognised: until the recent reform of the **calendar**, the "Impression of the Stigmata" was a **feast**, celebrated on 17 September. If there were any stigmatist before St Francis, they were few: since that time there have been very many, almost, but not quite, all of them being Catholics. The marks of the wounds are frequently accompanied by bleeding on certain days, Fridays in particular, and with pain. There are also claimed to be other phenomena such as "inedia" (i.e., not eating), which is not uncommon among stigmatists, some of whom claim to live on nothing more than the eucharistic host. This has proved to be more difficult to establish than the stigmata themselves. Recent commentators have tended to explain the stigmata as being caused by a form of hysteria. It has been shown, for example, that a number of stigmatists have replicated in their bodies the wounds displayed on particular crucifixes, and since the **shroud** of Turin has indicated that the wounds may not have been in Christ's hands but in his wrists, at least in one instance the wounds of a stigmatist have appeared in his wrists.

Stille Omgang ("the silent circuit"), an association established in 1881 in the chapel of the Beguinage in Amsterdam. It commemorates a miracle reputed to have taken place in 1345 when a man on the point of death received communion, but shortly afterwards vomited into a basin. No remains of the host were noticed in the basin, and the contents were thrown on the fire. The next day, however, one of the women who were looking after the sick man saw the sacred host in the fire, entirely unharmed. It was taken from the flames and wrapped in linen and eventually placed in a special chapel, known

253

as the Oratory of the Holy Place. This chapel was closed in 1538, and devotion was transferred to the chapel of the Beguinage in 1607. The journey which had been taken by the host through the streets of Amsterdam was recalled in an annual **procession** which followed the same route. It was made silently at night, and became known as the "night journey". The **confraternity** was formed to promote devotion to the Blessed Sacrament and to maintain and encourage the procession and to act as stewards during it.

striking the breast, a manner of indicating sorrow for one's failings. The usage goes back to the earliest Church, and is attested to by Saints Jerome and Augustine among others. In the liturgy of the mass as it was celebrated until the mid-1960s it was the practice to strike the breast three times during the *Confiteor* (= "I confess"), the *Agnus Dei* (= "The Lamb of God") and the *Domine, non sum dignus* (= "Lord I am not worthy") which was said just before receiving communion. The priest also struck his breast once during the canon of the mass at the words "*Nobis quoque peccatoribus*" (= "and to us also, sinners"). These customs would appear to have died out, though striking the breast is still recognised as a sign of repentance.

Sub tuum præsidium, (= "We fly to thy patronage [or protection], O holy Mother of God ..."): a **prayer** to the **Virgin Mary** which is the first one known whose text has survived. It is still in use. The date of its composition is uncertain, but is not later than the fourth century. The oldest version to be found is a Greek text, but written on an Egyptian papyrus, and constitutes the earliest documentary evidence so far discovered to the existence of a **cult** of Mary. The prayer in this form emphasises Mary's title of Mother of God - though it well pre-dates the Council of Ephesus where that title was dogmatically defined - her unique sanctity, and the power of her mediation before God. It is probable that the prayer formed part of the liturgy, and possibly the liturgy of Egyptian Christianity in the first instance.

Sunday, the major celebration of the Christian week as a memorial of **Easter.** It seems very likely that the choice of this day as the holy day of the Christians dates back to Apostolic times, though the interpretation of the crucial passage in Acts 20 of Paul preaching on the first day of the week, depends upon which method of reckoning time is used. The Jews reckoned a day from sunset to sunset, the Romans, as is now common, from midnight to midnight, but the Greeks from dawn to dawn.

Suyapa, Our Lady of, more correctly Our Lady of the Conception of Suyapa, a **shrine** of the **Virgin Mary** in Honduras, where since 1925 she has been the official **patron** of the country. The cult under this title began in February 1747 by some Indians who had to sleep by the roadside when returning from work one Saturday. As one of them lay down to sleep his hand encountered something hard in the soil which, when he dug it out the following morning, he found to be a small statue of the Virgin, standing upon a golden globe. It quickly became a particular object of **devotion** to the indigenous inhabitants, who built a small church to house it.

Sveta Gora, a **shrine** of the **Virgin Mary** in the former Yugoslavia. A church had existed on the site since at least the middle of the fourteenth century, but was destroyed by the Turks. In 1539 the Virgin appeared to a young shepherdess, Urska Ferligojeva, instructing her to build a chapel on the spot. A church was finally consecrated on 12 October 1544, and the image honoured there is one produced in accord with the description of the Virgin given by Urska Ferligojeva.

Svete Visarje, a **shrine** of the **Virgin Mary** to which the Slovak people are particularly devoted although geographically it now falls in Italy. It is situated in the Alps at a considerable height and, according to legend, came into being in 1360 when a shepherd, seeking his flock on the mountainside, found them gathered around a bush in which he found a statue of the Virgin. A group of people undertook to build a chapel on the spot, and in the course of the work one of them who was blind recovered his sight. The original church was completely destroyed in the First World War, but has been reconstructed. It is at such an altitude that it is impossible to visit in the winter, and the miraculous statue is taken down into the valley to Zabnice for veneration during the snows.

Syrian Priests, Pious Union of, a society founded by the Syrian patriarch Cardinal Ignatius Gabriel I Tappouni in June 1933 with its seat in Beirut to foster mutual support among the Syrian-rite clergy, and especially to give assistance to those who are ill or otherwise in need.

T

Te Deum laudamus (= "We praise you O God"), a **hymn** used in the Roman Catholic Church in the Office of Matins on Sundays except those of the penitential seasons, and also used on **feast** days. It is similarly used in the Church of England. It is thought to date from the late fourth or early fifth century and has sometimes been ascribed to St Ambrose or to St Augustine though it is now thought it was composed by St Niceta (335-415), Bishop of Remesiana, a town in the former Yugoslavia. He was of particular importance as a writer because his town lay on the borders between the Eastern and the Western Church, and he drew inspiration from both: the *Te Deum* is said to reflect Greek models. Because it is a work of such power and majesty, the hymn is often used at times of particularly solemn celebration, though at line 20 the tone of the hymn changes from one of praise to one of supplication in phrases taken from the psalms. There are various endings known to the hymn, and the present version of the last seven lines is not part of the original text.

Telgte, a **shrine** of the Mother of **Sorrows** near Münster, Germany. There, a wooden statue of the Virgin, which is said to have appeared one day in a lime tree on the outskirts of the town, is venerated. **Pilgrimage** seems to have begun towards the end of the fourteenth century, the most important solemnity being celebrated the day after **Pentecost**. The Westphalian family of von Galen is particularly associated with the shrine.

tertiary, a member of a **Third Order**

Thérèse of the Child Jesus, Pious Union of, a society founded in the Carmelite church in Rome on 1 October 1925 to foster the **devotion**

of its members, to pray for priestly, and particularly missionary, vocations and to support Catholic Action, and to spread the cult of St Thérèse. Members are expected to model their lives upon the virtues of their **patron**, to give alms, and to wear the **medal** of St Thérèse, which they are given on joining.

Third Order, an association or **confraternity** whose members live their lives in their own homes but seek Christian perfection under the governance, and in the spirit, of a particular religious order, according to regulations approved by the Holy See. There are nine Third Orders, of which the first to be formally constituted, and the best known, is that of St Francis, which was founded in 1221, though the Benedictine **oblates** could claim a longer history. Membership of a Third Order reflects the practice for membership of a religious order as such: there is a noviceship or year of spiritual training, followed by a "profession" and clothing in the **habit** of the order. Any superior of the Order to which the Third Order is attached may admit members, and this right to grant admission may be delegated to others, including to the diocesan clergy. The obligations which follow from the "profession" vary according to the statutes of each. They commonly include the saying of particular prayers and the wearing of the habit. Though this habit should be worn constantly, it can be replaced by a small **scapular** and girdle or belt indicative of the Order, and these in turn may be replaced by the wearing of a **medal**. The spiritual privileges and **indulgences** which a tertiary enjoys through membership normally require that the habit, or at least the medal, be worn. It is usually the right of a tertiary to be buried in the habit, and from a church associated with the Order of which he or she is a member.

Thirty-Three, Our Lady of the, a **devotion** to the **Virgin Mary** in Uruguay, dating from 1825 when the country was under the domination of Brazil. On 19 April that year thirty-three insurrectionists arrived from Buenos Aires with the intention of liberating their country. Their leader, Juan Antonio Lavalleja, established his headquarters in the city of Florida, where the parish church was dedicated to Our Lady of **Luján**. On 14 June the group prayed for Mary's protection in the church, and on 25 August signed Uruguay's

Declaration of Independence in the parochial office. After the success of the insurrection, the victory was attributed to the intercession of "Our Lady of the Thirty-Three".

Thorns, Our Lady of the, a title of an image of the **Virgin Mary** venerated in the diocese of Parma, at Sissa.

Three Hours Devotion, a form of service originally devised in Lima by a Peruvian Jesuit Alonso Messia (1665-1732), apparently at least in part as a consequence of the Lima earthquake of 1687. There was a preliminary shock of the quake on 1 April, which happened to be in Easter week that year, and it was afterwards reported that a statue of the Virgin Mary was found weeping. After the major quake, which occurred on 20 October, the statue was venerated with great solemnity. In subsequent years a form of religious service was held on the eight days before 20 October, closing with a service in the church to which Messia was attached and where the statue of "Our Lady of the Warning" was kept. This service, though it was not associated with **Good Friday** as was the Three Hours devotion, had some of its elements. Messia also had a small **confraternity** in his church, among whose devotions were those both to the statue of the Virgin, and to a **crucifix** known as the "Christ of Contrition". The earliest accounts of the Three Hours as led by Fr Messia indicate that it began at midday on Good Friday; that it was at first a private affair of Messia and some others; that it took place in Messia's church before a crucifix; and that it was at first a form of meditation, with little input from the priest except at the beginning. The meditations were built upon the "Seven Words" or phrases which the Gospels record that Christ spoke from the cross: Messia wrote short sermons upon each of them, which have survived. From Peru the practice seems to have spread first to Spain and then to Rome, where its celebration was not confined to the Gesù, the Jesuit church, though the Jesuits were undoubtedly chiefly responsible for spreading the devotion throughout Europe.

Three Marys and the Disciples of Saint John, Pious Union of, an association founded in Palencia, Spain, to carry out, and to encourage, **devotion** to the Blessed Sacrament. The "three Marys" are those

259

who stood, alongside St John, on Calvary when all the rest of Christ's followers had abandoned him. The significance of the title, therefore, is that members of this **confraternity** bind themselves to pray before the tabernacle in the place of those who fail to do so. Members are divided into two classes. The "contemplatives" undertake to attend mass daily, and make other visits to churches each day, making reparation in their prayers for those who forsake Christ in the tabernacle. The "active" members spread devotion to the Sacrament and to the **Sacred Heart** by running Sunday schools and evening classes, establishing libraries, writing pamphlets and so on. Female members are called "Marys", and male ones "disciples of St John". Both groups can contain contemplative and active members, but the ideal is to assign to each tabernacle three active "Marys", the leader of whom is called "the first Mary", and as many contemplative ones as possible. The same is true of the male section of the confraternity, except that the leader is called "the first disciple". It falls to these two to run the confraternity in each parish, under the parish priest. Members are given a medal, after having given sufficient evidence of their devotion, and are expected to wear it at Mass.

title, the board which, according to the Gospel writers, was put at the head of Christ's **cross** and listing in Hebrew, Greek and Latin the charge against him: "Jesus of Nazareth, King of the Jews". The board would have been white - it was also called an *album* - and the accusation would have been added either carved or written in red or in black. St Ambrose claimed at the end of the fourth century that it was found still attached to the cross and given to St Helena, Constantine's mother. However, when the (probably Spanish) abbess Etheria or Egeria was in Jerusalem shortly before Ambrose was writing, she claims to have seen not only the cross but also the title placed in front of the Bishop for veneration on **Good Friday**. It has been suggested that both accounts are correct, and that what Etheria saw was only part of the title, while the other part had been sent to the Roman church of Santa Croce in Gerusalemme, built to house a **relic** of the cross. That in Santa Croce seems to have been forgotten during the Middle Ages, to be found again on 1 February 1492 when it was rediscovered during building works. It was immediately placed in a glass case, and can still be seen in a chapel of Santa Croce. It is some nine inches long by five wide and apparently at one time white, though the colour has faded to grey. Only the Greek and Latin text are present - taken to be an indication that Etheria saw only a part of the title, that containing the Hebrew inscription. The Greek inscription is no more than the Latin transliterated into clumsy Greek letters, reading from right to left in the Hebrew fashion. However doubtful the authenticity of the title may be, no other place claims such a relic, an unusual circumstance when, for example, over thirty places claim to have one of the **nails** with which Christ was fixed to the cross.

Tomb, The Opening of Mary's, the principal Marian **feast** of the Christian calendar in Egypt, which is shared by Christians and Moslems alike, and occurs on 22 August, and was customarily preceded by a long fast.

tongue of St Anthony, a **relic** of St Anthony of Padua (1195-1231), a Franciscan friar renowned for his skill in preaching. His remains were removed to a new **shrine** in Padua in 1263, in the presence of St Bonaventure, then superior of the Franciscans. His body was found to have decayed, except for his tongue. His relics are still to be found in Padua.

Transfiguration, a **feast** celebrated on 6 August thought originally to have commemorated the **dedication** of the **basilica** on Mount Tabor, traditionally the site of the transfiguration of Christ as recounted in the synoptic Gospels. It was believed in the East that this event took place forty days before the crucifixion, and was therefore linked, not to passiontide which would have been impracticable, but to the feast of the **Exaltation of the Cross**, already fixed for 14 September. Forty days before that gives the 6 August date. Although observed in some Eastern rites from as early as the fifth century, it was not until the middle of the ninth that it came to the West, and until the eleventh before it was celebrated in the papal liturgy. Peter the Venerable (c. 1092-1156), the eighth Abbot of Cluny, was a great protagonist of the feast, and it is likely that it was his enthusiasm which spread the feast throughout the Cluniac congregation and gave it wider dissemination. Even so, it was not until 1457 that Pope Callistus III formally included it in the Roman **calendar** as a thank-offering for the victory of Christian troops over the Turks near Belgrade on 6 August 1456. In the East it is still observed as one of the most important feasts of the year, much more so than in the West.

translation, a term which, in ecclesiastical usage, can have a variety of meanings. It was used, for example, of the transference of a **feast** to a new date, when it clashed with a more important celebration. It was also used to describe the transfer of a cleric to another, usually more important, post. More commonly, however, at least in the Church's **calendar**, was the movement of a body of a **saint**, or of his or her **relics**, to another location. This happened for a number of reasons. A person's body might be moved to a more prominent position in the church in which it had been buried when he or she was "raised to the altars", that is to say, formally recognized by competent authority (until the thirteenth century this usually meant the local bishop, see **canonization**) as a saint. But it was applied to things other than the entire body - relics in the more general sense - or of objects associated with the saint. Perhaps the best known example of this was the alleged finding of some of the relics of the passion, and more particularly the **cross**, by St Helena, the mother of the Emperor Constantine. The classical account of this was contained in the *Panegyric on the Death of Theodosius* by St Ambrose, Bishop of Milan, at the end of the fourth century, and it supplied the standard form of accounts of translations: the search for the relic; its finding and authentication by the working of a miracle; problems involved in moving it from the place where it had been found; and finally the joyful welcome accorded to the relic when it reached the place to which it was being translated. (The best-known example of a translation narrative, at least in the British Isles, is that of St Swithin, Bishop of Winchester from 852 until his death in 862. At his own request he was buried outside the church, but when his remains were translated to a **shrine** within the cathedral in 971, the event was the occasion for many miracles, not least a continuous downpour, which led to the saying that if it rains on St Swithin's Day - 2 July - it will rain for forty days afterwards.)

travel, patron saints of, St Bona (c. 1156-1207) was declared **patron** of flight attendants because of her own extensive travels; Christopher is the traditional patron of travellers because of the medieval legend that he carried Christ over a river: there is no evidence of his existence apart from these stories, and he has been removed from the Roman **calendar**; Francis de Paola (c. 1416-1517) is associated with those who make their living by the sea, and who travel on it because, in 1464, being refused passage from Italy to Sicily, he spread out his cloak on the water, and crossed on that; because **Joseph** safely guided the **Virgin Mary** and Jesus into exile, and then back home again, he has been invoked as a patron of travellers in general; Joseph of Cupertino (1603- 63) had a remarkable reputation for levitation - hence he has become a patron of those who fly; for obvious reasons, Mary is invoked by those who fly both under her title of Our Lady of **Loreto**, and because of the Assumption; Nicholas of Myra, the fourth-century Bishop who became "Santa Claus", was, according to the legends about him, a considerable **pilgrim** in his early life, and was therefore invoked by travellers; Raphael the Archangel accompanied Tobias on his journey, according to the Old Testament, and hence becomes one of the patrons of travellers.

Trinitarians, Third Order of, or, more correctly, the **Third Order** of the Most Holy Trinity for the Redemption of Captives, is an association or **confraternity** whose members pursue Christian perfection in the spirit, and under the guidance, of members of the Trinitarian Order. Its members are expected to show a particular **devotion** to, and propagate the cult of, the Blessed Trinity. The parent Order was founded at the end of the twelfth century to ransom Christian slaves from non-Christian masters, and it seems to have had associated with it from the earliest times a number of lay people who undertook to collect alms for that purpose. No formal rule for them seems to have existed until towards the end of the sixteenth century, though papal documents appear to refer to there being tertiaries of the Trinitarians from the early years of the thirteenth century. Members of the Third Order are vested upon completing their noviceship with a white **scapular** which has upon it a red and blue cross. They also take vows of chastity and obedience, which they are required to observe according to their status in life.

Trinity Sunday, a **feast** in honour of the Holy Trinity, now celebrated on the **Sunday** after **Pentecost**. The earliest hint of such an observance goes back to the seventh-century Gelasian Sacramentary, which had a preface assigned to the Sunday after Pentecost which encapsulated the theology of the Trinity. About the year 800 Alcuin (c. 735-804), the Yorkshire-born monk who became religious adviser to Charlemagne, composed a series of masses for each day of the week, the first of them being a mass in honour of the Trinity. Alcuin's collection proved very popular, and this disseminated the celebration of the mass. Its usage within the monastic congregations of Cluny (1030) and later Cîteaux (1271) added to its popularity, but Rome was hesitant, the popes arguing that the Trinity was honoured in every mass, and especially in the **doxology**. It was not until 1334 that Pope John XXII included it as an obligatory celebration in the Roman **calendar**, and fixed the day of its observance as the first Sunday after Pentecost. Until that time it had in some places been celebrated on the last Sunday before **Advent**.

Triumph, Our Lady of the, a **shrine** of the **Virgin Mary** in Cuzco, Peru, otherwise known as Our Lady of the **Descent**.

tunic, holy, supposedly the seamless robe of which Christ was divested before his crucifixion, and now venerated in a special chapel of the basilica at Trier in Germany. On the staircases which lead to the **shrine** are statues of the Emperor Constantine and his mother St Helena: according to one tradition it was Helena who brought the relic to Trier. Another version has it that the tunic, together with a nail used at the crucifixion and a knife used at the Last Supper, were sent to the city by Pope Sylvester, Bishop of Rome in the early fourth century. Whatever the date of its arrival, the tunic or coat has been in Trier at least since the beginning of the twelfth century, though removed for a time during the Napoleonic Wars. Because whatever was there at first has been so covered with other cloths with which its fibres have mingled over the centuries, efforts to identify the cloth of the tunic have been unsuccessful. It seems possible that the outer wrappings at least came from the East, perhaps from fifth-century Constantinople. The tunic was rarely displayed - a number of times in the sixteenth century, very occasionally afterwards and twice in the nineteenth and twice in the twentieth centuries, the last time in 1959. There is also a tunic at Argenteuil near Paris, attested from 1156, which tradition claims was given to Charlemagne by the Empress Irene of Constantinople, and by him to his daughter who was abbess of a convent at Argenteuil. There it remained until 1793 when it was given into the parish priest's safe-keeping. He, however, cut it up into several pieces and hid them. It was put back together again two years later, and the reddish-brown **relic** has occasionally been put on display. In December 1983 an extremist group seized the Argenteuil tunic and held it to ransom, demanding money be paid to the Polish union movement, Solidarity, and three members of the group released from prison. The relic was returned two months later, and put on display at Easter.

U

Ubi caritas et amor (= "Where there is charity and love"), a **hymn** of unusual metre - there is a very clear-cut caesura after every eighth syllable of each line - which was written during the Carolingian era, and has sometimes been attributed to Rufinus of Aquileia. It appears to have been composed for the weekly **mandatum** (washing of the feet) which took place in monastic communities, and from that was transferred to the mandatum performed on **Maundy Thursday**.

Union of Reparation, a pious union or **confraternity** founded 1935 in the church of the Sisters of the Most Holy Name of Jesus at Elvaux in the Belgian diocese of Liège. Its purpose is to honour Christ in the Blessed Sacrament, and to give thanks for graces received to the **Sacred Heart** of Christ on behalf of those who fail to do so. To this end members instruct themselves and others in eucharistic doctrine.

V

Valle, Our Lady of, a popular image of the **Virgin Mary** in the church of the Holy Spirit on the island of Margarita in Venezuela.

Valley, Our Lady of (Catamarca, Northern Argentina), a **shrine** of the **Virgin Mary** dating from the seventeenth century. According to tradition, the statue of the Virgin had been brought to the region, possibly by Franciscans, and hidden in a cave when they were attacked by Indians. It was found there at the end of the sixteenth century. The **feast** is celebrated on the third Saturday after Easter.

Vassals of Christ the King, Mexican National Association of, a society founded in June 1924 in the basilica of the city of León, Mexico, to promote the kingship of Christ among Mexican families, and to atone for the suffering caused to the pope by Mexicans. Membership of this **confraternity** is open to everyone from the time of their first communion onwards. They are given a blessed **medal** of **Christ the King** which they are expected to wear at mass and other religious functions, and commit themselves by a form of consecration "to work until death to extend [Christ's] sovereignty in my homeland, always beneath the mantle of my most holy Mother of **Guadalupe,** Queen of Mexicans". Members are also expected to support financially the religious services held by the association. The eleventh of every month is kept as a day of particular **devotion** because it was on 11 January 1923 that Christ was declared King of Mexico.

veil of Veronica, a cloth claiming to be that with which Saint Veronica wiped the face of Christ as he carried his cross to Calvary, and upon which his image was left. It has been preserved as a **relic**

at St Peter's in Rome possibly since as long ago as the beginning of the eighth century, though any image which may have been upon the cloth has disappeared. The woman who performed this act is known as "Veronica", though there is no reference either to her, or to the act of wiping Christ's face, until the fourth or fifth-century *Acts of Pilate*, where her name is given as the woman who had the issue of blood (Matthew 9:20-22). The *Death of Pilate* (a work which is later still) contains the story of her wiping Christ's face. It has been suggested that the name "Veronica" simply means "vera eikon" or "true image", the supposed name of the saint being derived from the relic. This is quite plausible for, although she is referred to in the Latin text of the *Acts of Pilate* as Veronica, in the earlier Greek version she is called "Berenike", or "Victory bringer". Veronica having been invented, she subsequently had a varied career. According to some stories she came to Rome with the relic, cured the Emperor Tiberius with it, and then left it to Pope Clement. Other accounts have her marrying the Zacchaeus who climbed the sycamore tree to see Christ, travelling with him to France where he changed his name to Amadour (of **Rocamadour**) and settled down to be a hermit, while she evangelized France. As the **stations of the cross** developed in Jerusalem, a house came to be indicated as having been hers, and she found her way into the **calendar** of the church of Milan, though it was removed towards the end of the sixteenth century. In Milan her **feast** was celebrated on 4 February, elsewhere on 12 July.

Veni, creator spiritus (= "Come creator spirit", though better known as the **hymn** "Come Holy Ghost, Creator come" among Roman Catholics, and "Come, Holy Ghost, our souls inspire" among Anglicans) is used at **Pentecost** at Vespers and Terce, but is also sung on many other occasions such as, since the eleventh century, at the ordination of priests and bishops, the dedication of churches, at votive masses of the Holy Spirit and on other occasions when the Holy Spirit is particularly invoked - for instance at the start of the academic year. On the basis that no manuscript earlier than the tenth century is known to include the hymn, it is generally thought it was composed in the ninth century, possibly by Rabanus Maurus (776?-856), Abbot of Fulda and Archbishop of Mainz.

Veni, sancte Spiritus (= "Come, Holy Spirit"), a sequence, that is a **hymn** sung on certain **feasts** immediately before the reading of the gospel, in this case the feast of **Pentecost**. It came into universal use, replacing another sequence, in the liturgical reforms which followed the Council of Trent. In the Middle Ages it was known as "the golden sequence". The manuscript evidence suggests that it first came into prominence in France, in about the year 1200, and the style points in the same direction. Such evidence of authorship as exists, and it is not much, attributes the hymn to Stephen Langton, Archbishop of Canterbury. He was in Paris at the appropriate date, and was called from there to Rome in 1206, before becoming Cardinal Archbishop of Canterbury the following year. He died in 1228.

Verdun, the Virgin of, a popular **pilgrimage** site in Uruguay near Minas in the department of Lavalleja where a statue of the **Virgin Mary** has been built on the summit of the range of hills that surround the town.

Vexilla regis prodeunt (= "The banners of the king appear" though there is a well-known English translation by the nineteenth- century **hymn**-writer John Mason Neale which begins "The royal banners forward go"), is a hymn which celebrates Christ's triumph on the **cross**. It was written by Venantius Fortunatus (c. 530- 600) who was born near Ravenna but served for a long time as secretary to Queen Radegunde in her convent at Poitiers, and died shortly after being appointed bishop of that city. He also wrote *Pange, lingua, gloriosi lauream certaminis* to mark the reception of a **relic** of the cross sent the Emperor Justin II and his wife to Queen Radegunde. It is now used during the last two weeks of **Lent** (Passiontide), and also for the **feasts** of the **Finding of the Cross** and the **Exaltation of the Cross**. It was also at one time used for the **procession** on **Good Friday**.

Victimae paschali laudes (= "Let Christians offer a sacrifice of praise to the paschal victim"), the sequence used during **Easter** week. It is traditionally ascribed to Wipo (died c. 1050), chaplain to Conrad II, and a hymn-writer of Burgundy. It is unusual in its form, being half way between the original prose forms of sequences, and the full metrical form as in the *Lauda, Sion*, for example. It is composed as four pairs of strophes and antistrophes, which would have been sung by one choir responding to another.

Victory, Our Lady of, a **feast** originally established in honour of the **Virgin Mary** in 1571 in thanksgiving for the victory of Don John of Austria over the Turkish fleet at the battle of Lepanto. But because the victory had been attributed to the recitation of the **rosary**, two years later the feast was changed to that of Our Lady of the Rosary.

vigil, literally a "watching", which in Catholic usage came to signify the eve of certain important **feasts**. It had its origins, however, in the early Christian practice of beginning the celebration of Sundays, of Easter, and of some other major occasions, on the evening before, and carrying it on until the Mass at dawn. This practice either died out entirely as in the case of the Saturday vigil for every Sunday, or was moved back to the previous day, so that, for example, the vigil of **Easter** was celebrated until 1955 in the morning of Holy Saturday. In the pre-1970 **calendar** the vigil remained simply as a way of beginning a major feast on the previous evening: no overnight services were entailed.

Vincent de Paul Society, an organization founded by the remarkable Antoine Frédéric Ozanam (1813-53) a scholar, particularly of medieval Italian poetry, and a political liberal. He began this work in Paris in 1833, though his first intention was to instruct young men in the Catholic faith to help them to counter attacks on the Church. He soon came to the conclusion, however, that the best way to demonstrate this Catholic commitment was through works of charity. It was for this reason that he chose St Vincent de Paul, a **saint** renowned for his works of mercy, as the **patron**. Ten years after its foundation, his organization had a thousand members in Paris, assisting some two thousand poor families each week. At its height the Society had twenty thousand groups throughout the world: this is excluding the women's groups, first created in Bologna in 1856 and living by the same rules, while remaining distinct. The purpose of the Society is to study Catholicism, to put it into practice with works of charity, and to provide each other with mutual support. The sanctification of its members is part of the purpose, as it is in any **confraternity** (though the Society is not technically a confraternity), and every weekly meeting of the Society includes both prayers and some spiritual reading and instruction, as well as reporting on tasks undertaken during the week, and allotting new ones. There are several ranks of membership. The basic one is obviously that of active members, but those who have moved to a place where no group exists can remain as "corresponding members" of their previous group. There are also "subscribing members" who support the work by their almsgiving, and honorary members who also give money and may be present at certain meetings and other religious gatherings, but do not strictly speaking belong to the Society, and have no vote at any meeting they may attend.

Virgin Mary, Blessed, the mother of Christ who, according to Catholic tradition, remained a virgin before, during and after the birth of her son. For this belief it is difficult to find evidence in the New Testament which, at least on the face of it, treats **Joseph** as her husband and indicates that Jesus had other brothers. Though Mary, according to the Gospel of St John, was standing beside the **cross** of Christ as he was dying, she plays no part in the resurrection stories, and in so far as there are stories about Mary in the Gospels, Christ's attitude to his mother is ambivalent. She is not mentioned - except once, and that obliquely - in the letters attributed to St Paul, and the first time she reappears in Christian writing is in St Ignatius of Antioch, martyred early in the second century. Ignatius was concerned to stress against the gnostics that Jesus was a true human being, and did so by emphasizing the reality of his birth. The gnostic literature made much play with the notion that Christ's birth was painless, the event astonishing Mary herself. The apocryphal *Protoevangelium of James* which purports to narrate the birth of Christ and what happened afterwards in considerable, and miraculous, detail, makes much of the fact that Mary was a virgin after, as well as before, the birth. This second-century text also tells a number of stories about Mary herself: she was born when her parents Joachim and Anna were very old; she lived in the Temple in Jerusalem from the age of three to that of twelve; Joseph was chosen as her husband because he was already old, and so on. Such stories, intended to exalt

271

Mary, moved her from the realm of this world and put her into a supernatural context which detracted from the reality of Christ's human nature. The picturesque stories in the *Protoevangelium* have proved a fertile source of inspiration for artists. None of this had anything directly to do with **devotion** to Mary, but laid the basis for it. For example, a great deal was later to be made in devotional writing and in **hymns** of the play upon the word "Ave" (the first word in Latin of the **angel**'s greeting to Mary, "*Hail*, full of grace"), and the name of the first woman, Eve, in Latin "Eva". Attention was drawn for the first time to the parallelism between Mary and Eve by Justin Martyr (though he was writing in Greek) in the second half of the second century.

While it is important to keep theological discussion and devotional practice distinct, there is at least some indication that devotion to Mary was in existence by the third century. According to the fourth-century Gregory of Nyssa, whose mother had known the third-century Gregory Thaumaturgus (= "the Wonderworker"), one of the older Gregory's books had been given him in a vision by St John, accompanied and encouraged by Mary. This is the first known instance of a Marian **apparition**. Early in the fourth century, and therefore possibly in use at the end of the third, is a **prayer** to Mary known as the *Sub tuum præsidium*. The **feast** of the Church's year which afterwards became the **Purification** came to be celebrated in Jerusalem in the fourth century. In its earlier guise it commemorated "the Encounter" between Christ and Simeon in the Temple, and was kept on 14 February. Though clearly this was a feast of Christ, Mary is very much part of the gospel story, for Simeon addressed her, telling her that a sword would pierce her soul (cf. Luke 2:34-5). At the same time, and also in the East, the development of monastic life with its glorification of the virtue of chastity meant that the virginity of Mary came to be taken as the model for Christians, and Gregory of Nazianzen (329-89) records the prayer to Mary made by a virgin being tempted by the devil.

Increasingly through the fourth century, because of the Arian heresy which, in the eyes of the orthodox, denied Christ's divinity, Mary was honoured as "Theotokos" or God-bearer. By stressing that Christ was both God and truly born of Mary the unity of Christ as God and man was preserved. Thus, though the debate may have seemed to be about Mary, it was essentially about her son. This struggle against the Arians was not confined to the East but encompassed the whole Church, and in the West no one was more committed to this conflict, perhaps, than St Ambrose (c. 339-97). For him and for his congregation in Milan the battle was almost as physical as it was intellectual. In the West there was a particular problem: Mary could not be called "Mother of God" because such a title had potent pagan connotations. Nevertheless, Ambrose wrote a great deal about Mary, particularly in the context of virginity, arguing that Christ would have chosen for his mother only someone who was both physically and morally pure. She was therefore sinless. Neither in Ambrose nor in St Augustine of Hippo can it be said, however, that there is evidence of belief in the **Immaculate Conception** (the belief that Mary was, from the first moment of her conception, preserved without stain of original sin). While that attribute cannot be found in Ambrose, at least one other title of Mary which was to become much-used was formulated by him: she was not only the mother of Christ: she was also the mother of the Church.

The debate about the title "Theotokos" reached its apogee in the early fifth century, and culminated in the Council of Ephesus of 431 which affirmed the validity of the term as applied to Mary. Again, though the Council seemed to be about Mary, what was at issue was the unity of the divine and human natures of Christ in one person. The fundamental issue was christological. Nonetheless, the Council was followed by a great outburst of devotion to Mary. It is possible that there was one church dedicated to Mary before Ephesus - in the valley of Josaphat - but afterwards there was scarcely a major city without one, the most famous being that of Santa **Maria Maggiore** in Rome. The writing of hymns in honour of Mary also flourished. Jacob of Sarug (c. 451-521), a Syrian poet, in his long *Ode on the Blessed Virgin Mary*, developed some themes which were not to become common until the Middle Ages: she represents the Church; she is Mother of Mercy; she is the Virgin of Sorrows. Jacob of Sarug is also claimed, with some reason, as an early witness to a belief in the **Immaculate Conception**, though he clearly does not believe in the bodily **Assumption** of Mary. In the West the hymns of Venantius Fortunatus (c. 530-c. 600) display a new tenderness towards Mary, as well as exalting her role as mother of the Creator.

In the early sixth century there was another development which was to have long-term consequences for Marian devotion. Little is known about Oecumenius, sometimes called "the Philosopher", except that he is thought to have been a disciple of the heretical Severus of Antioch, and that he died in 538. Severus was a great protagonist of the glories of Mary, and in this Oecumenius certainly followed him. He wrote the first full commentary on the Book of Revelation, and in doing so identified the woman clothed with the sun of Revelation 12 as Mary, whereas earlier writers had interpreted this figure as representing the Church. Oecumenius was not quite the first to take this step: a disciple of St Augustine's had at least hinted at it earlier. In the later Greek work, however, the identification is complete and unequivocal: moreover the sun with which she is clothed is Christ himself, while the stars around the woman's head in the apocalyptic vision represent the twelve apostles.

About this time, too, there began to emerge liturgical **feasts** in honour of Mary, though it seems likely that one of them, the "Commemoration of Mary", would have been in the Eastern **calendar** even before the Council of Ephesus. This feast was kept originally on the **Sunday** before **Christmas**, though in Antioch and Gaul (France) in the sixth century it was being observed on 18 January, and elsewhere on 15 August. This latter date was that of the Jerusalem church, and it was the date on which, in about 600, the feast was ordered to be kept by the Emperor Maurice. By this time it was associated with what has become known as the **Assumption** of the Virgin, though in its earlier form it was the "Passing" or the **"Dormition"** (= "falling asleep") of the Virgin. An account dating from the end of the fifth century tells how Mary was forewarned of her approaching death by an angel; how she gathered all the apostles (including St Paul) together around her deathbed; how an attack was made on her funeral procession by Jews who were blinded by the act, and how the hand of one of them stuck to the bier; and how, finally, the Jews were converted by these events. Three days after her burial angels took her body to paradise. These legends, much illustrated in the East in particular, indicate that there was already belief in the Assumption of Mary by the end of the fifth century, through how widespread it was there is no means of knowing. It was not until the middle of the seventh century that the 15 August feast reached

Rome, where it was seen as a commemoration of Mary's death, as other feasts were celebrated commemorating the deaths of **saints**.

The feast of 15 August was not the first Marian celebration to be introduced to Rome. The Purification was earlier, sometime in the first part of the seventh century, though that was originally a feast of Christ, as was the **Annunciation**, established shortly after the Assumption. Finally, the **Nativity of Mary** was introduced towards the end of the same century. Rome was in general much more restrained in what was allowed to be said, or celebrated, publicly about Mary. Gaul and Spain were more open to influences from the East, though even they kept aloof from some of the more exuberant claims made for Mary. St Germanus (c. 634-c. 733), the Patriarch of Constantinople, claimed unlimited power for Mary as an intercessor with God, because Christ always obeyed his mother, and because she turns the anger of God away from sinners. The fundamental conception is that Mary has authority over God, an idea of which much came to be made in the Middle Ages.

Ambrose Autpert, who died in 784 as abbot of a monastery in Southern Italy, though he had been born in Southern France, may have read the Greeks in translation, perhaps even Germanus himself. He was the first Western theologian to write sermons specifically in praise of Mary - at least, none are known earlier than his. He calls Mary the Queen of Heaven, a title hitherto unused in the West though known in the East, and attributes to her the salvation achieved by Christ, because she was his mother. But because Christ is the brother of all Christians, then Mary is their mother also: an idea which is new in Autpert, and not something imported from the East. The power of Mary as an intercessor is one of Autpert's themes, and one which was given a considerable boost in the West when Autpert's contemporary Paul the Deacon (c. 720-c. 800) translated the Theophilus legend into Latin. This story tells how Theophilus sells his soul to the Devil, but repents and asks Mary to win forgiveness for him, which she does, forcing the Devil to return the contract. Not only is the story, the origin of the Faust legend, important in itself for reinforcing the role of Mary, but the text calls her the "redemption of captives" and the "refuge of sinners", titles later applied to her in the **litany of Loreto**. More significantly still, perhaps, she is called in the text the

mediatrix between God and human beings. The hymn *Ave Maris stella* may also be by Paul the Deacon. It most probably dates from the end of the eighth century, though the earliest manuscripts are from the ninth: from then on the image of **Star of the Sea** also becomes a common one in devotional literature.

One development, found in Simon Metaphrastes in the second half of the tenth century in the East, is the picture of Christ in the arms of his grieving mother, an image to become familiar as the *pietà*. In the West there was a growing number of stories of visions and healings performed by Mary. Odo, Abbot of Cluny, gave Mary the name of Mother of Mercy as the result of an apparition, reported to him by a robber turned monk, in which the Virgin revealed herself under this title. By the twelfth century the doctrine of the Assumption was very firmly on the theological agenda in the West, and that of the Immaculate Conception was beginning to be discussed - the latter by Eadmer in particular. Eadmer (c. 1055-c. 1124), a Saxon monk, was the biographer of St Anselm, Archbishop of Canterbury, who had been a close friend. He wrote a treatise on the conception of the Virgin, possibly for the introduction of a feast of that name in the Abbey at Bury St Edmunds, which explicitly argued that Mary had been preserved from original sin. This was also the period of the development of some of the best known Marian hymns and prayers, such as the *Salve Regina*, the *Alma Redemptoris Mater*, the **Hail Mary**, and of the **Little Office of Our Lady**, in which the Hail Mary was much used. The origins of the **rosary** are also dated to about this time.

There was a great deal of theological debate about Mary in the twelfth century, very largely inspired by St Bernard (1090-1153), the Abbot of Clairvaux who, though emphasizing the power of Mary as an intercessor, was distinctly careful about what he said concerning the Assumption, and made clear his opposition to the doctrine of the Immaculate Conception. On the other hand he brought a new tenderness to descriptions of the relationship of Christ and his mother. Some of his followers turned that tenderness into something almost sensual, confusing the two images of mother and spouse. Richard of St Laurent, writing in praise of Mary around the middle of the thirteenth century, devoted a whole book of his treatise to her beauty, by far the greater number of the pages being concerned with her physical, rather than with her spiritual, beauty. Richard presents Mary as Mother of Mercy, almost directly in conflict with her son, who is concerned with justice and vengeance. He also attributed to her the virtue of omnipotence. The treatise enjoyed a great vogue, however, because it was until the middle of the twentieth century thought to have been the work of the great Dominican, Albert the Great (c. 1200-80). Albert's own writings on Mary, on the other hand, were much more restrained, though he presented her as mediatrix, and upheld the doctrine of the Assumption - though not of the Immaculate Conception. In that he was followed by his disciple Thomas Aquinas (c. 1225-74), though Thomas was rather more restrained on the notion of Mary as mediatrix. The Franciscans - though not Thomas Aquinas's contemporary St Bonaventure - rather adopted the doctrine of the Immaculate Conception as their own. This was true of no one more so than Duns Scotus (c. 1264-1308), the first of the great medieval theologians to do so, following in the footsteps of his fellow-Franciscan William of Ware, under whom he had studied at Oxford. With the Franciscans and Dominicans ranged on opposite sides of the debate about the Immaculate Conception, the other orders of friars tended to take sides with the Franciscans on this issue, though they each had their own especial interest in Marian theology. The Dominicans meantime were fostering devotion to the **Angelus**, while Servites had a particular devotion to the **Seven Sorrows** of the Virgin, destined to become a major force in Marian piety.

The last few paragraphs have concentrated on the development of Marian devotion in the West. This is not because there was a dearth of writing about Mary in the East. Quite the contrary. But the high place in Christian piety which Mary came to hold in the West had been granted to her much earlier in the East. There was another important difference. In the Eastern Church there never developed a doctrine of original sin along the lines that were sketched out by St Augustine at the end of the fourth and beginning of the fifth centuries. Because there was no such doctrine, the debate about Mary's Immaculate Conception did not take place.

The common opinion that the Reformation occasioned a major break in the tradition of Marian devotion is generally overstated, at

277

least as far as the first wave of Reformers were concerned. It is true that their praise of her was restrained, at least in comparison with that of the medieval scholastics. But this indicated a rejection of the more extravagant language about her rather than any disrespect for her status: Luther, for example, appears to have believed in the Immaculate Conception at least until a few years before his death, and Bullinger in the Assumption. The Church of England retained many of the feasts of Mary in its calendar. On the other hand a belief in the value of the intercession of **saints** - among whom, of course, Mary is to be numbered - with God is not part of the reformed tradition.

In response to this more circumspect approach the Counter Reformation Church continued to exalt the glories of Mary. The Society of Jesus was prominent in this renewed devotion, though the language of Peter Canisius (1521-97) or that of the great systematic theologian Francisco Suarez (1548-1617) was much more circumspect than many of the writers of the Middle Ages. The Jesuits also promoted the Rosary as a form of devotion, and their form of "Third Order", the **sodality**, was dedicated to Mary. The restraint shown by members of the Society, however, was not universally imitated. In France, for example, particularly in the writings of Jean-Jacques Olier (1608-57), much more extravagant expressions of devotion to Mary are to be found. Olier's commitment to Mary is perhaps understandable - he had been cured of blindness during a **pilgrimage** to **Loreto** - but verges on the unorthodox. He believed that the most important period of Christ's life was that spent in Mary's womb, and attributes to her a part in the redemption because she made satisfaction for the sins of humankind. Because she played this part, according to Olier, she was given by Christ authority over his merits. Olier's views were important in the growth of Marian devotion because in the middle of the seventeenth century he founded the seminary of Saint-Sulpice in Paris, whose priests followed his spirituality, and were sent to found seminaries similar to Saint-Sulpice elsewhere in France, and overseas. The most extreme example of this French school of Marian devotion are the writings of St Louis Marie Grignion de Montfort (1673-1716), and in particular his *True Devotion to the Blessed Virgin*, but as this manuscript had been in all probability known to only a small group in his lifetime, and was lost shortly after his death, his influence can be evaluated only in the context of the period after which his book was rediscovered - which did not happen until 1842. It was then translated into English by F.W. Faber, and published in London in 1863.

The eighteenth century saw a distinct decline in Marian devotion, though in 1750 St Alphonsus Liguori (1696-1787) published his treatise on *The Glories of Mary*, which was an uncritical survey of teaching on Mary over the centuries, bolstered by the evidence of miracles and private revelations as well as by quotation from earlier authors. For St Alphonsus, Mary was omnipotent - though made so by her son. Despite its extravagances it became a popular book among Catholics. He compiled this book in an age of religious scepticism, but after the scepticism of the eighteenth century, the nineteenth tended to go to the other extreme and lean towards credulity. There were a series of Marian and other visions, which were widely reported, in particular that of the **miraculous medal**. A large number of religious congregations of both sexes were founded in the nineteenth century, and dedicated to Mary. There was renewed interest in the doctrine of the Immaculate Conception, which Pope Pius IX declared to be a dogma of the Catholic faith on 8 December 1854. This was promptly followed by yet another series of visions, at **Lourdes** in France, where Mary revealed herself to be the Immaculate Conception. Reports of such visions continue unabated into the last decade of the twentieth century, though throughout much of the Catholic Church Marian devotion went into decline after the Second Vatican Council (1962-5). The Council was held only a dozen years after Pope Pius XII, who had a great personal devotion to Mary, had declared the bodily Assumption of Mary to be a dogma of faith (1 November 1950). The wish of many of the fathers attending the Council was that there should be a separate document issued on the place of Mary in the Church, but eventually it was decided, at least in part as an ecumenical gesture to those non-Roman Catholic Christians who did not sympathize with the role Mary played in the devotional life of Catholics, to include Mary as a section within the Dogmatic Constitution on the Church. Both the apparent demotion of Mary at Vatican II and ecumenical considerations led to a reduction in Marian devotion, in **novenas**, the saying of the rosary and so on, but it has clearly been part of the policy of Pope John Paul

II, who placed an "M" upon his coat of arms and makes a point of visiting Marian **shrines** wherever his extensive travels take him, to restore a sense of devotion to Mary in the Church.

While it is not difficult, given the great quantity of writing about Mary that has taken place over almost two millennia, to recount the history of this devotion, it is much more problematic to account for it. When one recalls the relatively small part Christ's mother plays in the Gospels, it is difficult to see how it has come into being. Theologians have been careful to distinguish the veneration which ought to be paid to Mary and to the saints from the **adoration** owed to God, but though that is the theory, in popular practice the distinction has not always been clear. Some theologians and historians of religion writing from a feminist perspective regard Mary as a symbol by which women have been manipulated to accept a role in the Church subordinate to that of men. Others have drawn attention to the apparent association of Marian devotion and in particular of recent Marian apparitions with a right-wing religious or political stance. There is a degree of truth in such charges, but the devotional life of the Church, and the art of both Eastern Christendom and Western, would have been a great deal poorer were it not for the reverence shown to Mary, overstated though it may frequently have been.

Virgin Mary, relics of: these presented similar difficulties to the idea of relics of Christ as the belief grew that she had been bodily assumed into heaven. In the early twelfth century, however, the bishop of Coutances in France claimed to have some strands of her hair, and other hair relics then appeared elsewhere - at Laón, Astorga (Spain), **Maria Maggiore** in Rome and at other sites. On the other hand a tunic which had belonged to Mary was claimed by the bishops of Verdun as early as the tenth century, and by the following century tunics were venerated at Munchmunster, Regensburg and Trier. Phials of the Virgin's breast-milk are also to be found from the eleventh century onwards, again at Santa Maria Maggiore, Oviedo, Munchmunster and Chartres.

Visitation of Mary, a **feast** of the **Virgin Mary** which was taken over from the Byzantine rite which read the gospel account of Mary's visit to St Elizabeth (Luke 1:30ff.) on 2 July. This was developed by the Franciscans into a Marian feast observed on that day, though when it spread slowly beyond the Franciscans, it came to be kept on a number of different dates. It was made a feast of the whole Church by Pope Urban VI in 1389, in order to seek Mary's intercession in resolving the schism of the Church which had existed since 1309. Urban's efforts to extend the feast were not particularly successful - it only became a festival universally observed after the Council of Basel which in 1441 provided it with a special mass. In the reform of the **calendar** of 1969 the date of the feast was changed to 31 May, so that it falls, as it does in the story from St Luke, between the **Annunciation** and the **Nativity of John the Baptist**.

Volto Santo of Lucca in Italy is a life-size crucifix ("volto santo" = "holy face") which was brought to the town in 782, according to one version of the legend, to save it from destruction during the period of iconoclasm in the Byzantine Empire. Another version has it that it was painted by Nicodemus with the assistance of angels, placed in a boat after it had lain hidden for centuries, and allowed to drift out to sea. When it eventually made landfall it was put into an ox-cart, and the cart sent driverless on its way, finally to arrive in Lucca. Because that town was on the **pilgrim**-route to Rome for travellers from some parts of Northern Europe, the Volto Santo achieved considerable fame in the Middle Ages. It is still venerated and carried in **procession** through the town on 13 September, the **feast** which commemorates its **translation** to the town.

W

Walsingham, Holy House of, a **shrine** in Norfolk, England, supposedly in existence since 1061 when a noblewoman and Lady of the
Manor, Richeldis de Faverches, was instructed in a series of three
visions of the **Virgin Mary** to build in her village an exact copy of the
house in Nazareth in which the **Annunciation** had taken place. She
gave instructions that this be done, but the night following was
awakened by the sound of singing and went out to see angels leaving
the house, which they had both completed and moved to a new
location. Where Richeldis had seen the vision, two springs of water
appeared. These events made of Walsingham one of the four great
shrines of medieval Europe, alongside Rome, Santiago and Jerusalem. The site of the Holy House, a wooden structure which was
burned down at the Reformation, has been identified as lying within
the grounds of the fourteenth-century Priory of Augustinian Canons, in pre-Reformation times the guardians of the shrine. This
priory was originally founded in 1153, after a visit to the Holy Land
by Geoffrey. On the other hand the only evidence for the early (1061)
date for the beginnings of the shrine are a manuscript note in a book,
and an English ballad, both dating from the late fifteenth century.
There is, in other words, no clear proof of the foundation in 1061, and
it seems quite likely that the Holy House was established in the mid-
twelfth century, after Geoffrey had visited the Holy Land. Nonetheless, the shrine is considerably older than that of the similar house at
Loreto, and **devotion** to it was revived through the efforts of a Miss
Charlotte Boyd who, in 1863, acquired what is known as the "Slipper
Chapel". The meaning of this name is uncertain, though it may
reflect the pilgrim practice of taking off one's shoes at this place and
making the last stage of the journey barefoot - the Slipper Chapel lies
a mile South of Walsingham at Houghton St Giles. Miss Boyd, who

became a Roman Catholic while buying the building, made it over to Benedictine monks, and the first formal **pilgrimage** since Reformation times occurred in 1897. A quarter of a century later the Anglican parish priest, Alfred Hope Patten, revived the idea of a pilgrimage centre for members of the Church of England, and funds were raised to build a church on what was then thought -incorrectly - to have been the original site of the Holy House. A cloister was added which encompasses the Holy Well, an Anglo- Saxon well uncovered when the foundations were being dug for the new Anglican shrine. Its waters are drunk by pilgrims. In recent years much of the devotion to the Holy House and to **Our Lady of Walsingham** has crossed denominational boundaries.

Walsingham, Our Lady of, a statue of the **Virgin Mary**, associated with **Walsingham's Holy House** (see above). The medieval original, of uncertain date and provenance, was destroyed at the Reformation but reproductions of it can be found, based upon the image to be found on surviving **pilgrimage badges**. It shows the Virgin seated, in a high-backed chair, with a lily in the right hand and the Child Jesus on her left knee.

washing of the altar, a ceremony carried out at the papal **altar** in Rome on **Maundy Thursday**, when it is solemnly washed by dignitaries of the Church using wine and water. As a practice in some parts of the Church, the ceremony goes back at least to the seventh century. Its popularity owes much to the reforms instituted by the monastery of Cluny, and came to Rome in the early eleventh century.

water or wine, with which the **shrine** of a **saint** had been washed was regarded during the eleventh and twelfth centuries as a particularly effective medicine. In other instances **relics** were dipped into the liquid, which was then drunk by the sick, worn around the neck in small phials, or used to anoint diseased limbs, the lids of blind eyes and so on. See also **holy water**.

water, Gregorian, an especially prepared mixture of **water**, salt, ashes and wine which have all been previously blessed separately and are then blessed together in a solemn manner with a hymn to

283

water included, and used in the ceremony of the dedication of a church. Although the name comes from Gregory the Great, Pope from 590 to 604, who was thought to have been the compiler of the "Gregorian Sacramentary" which contains this ritual, it does not go back as far, though it was in use by the eighth century.

water of St Vincent Ferrer, a formula of **blessing** for **water** restricted to Dominican friars. The water is then given to the sick. St Vincent Ferrer (c. 1350-1419) was a Dominican who achieved considerable fame not only for his preaching but for his reputation as a healer.

water, salt and bread in honour of St Hubert, a **blessing** restricted to the diocese of Cologne, but one which is given to animals as well as to humans, to protect them from the bite of rabid animals.

Way of the Cross, Pious Union of the Living, an association created in 1901 under the spiritual guidance of the Franciscans simply as a means of encouraging **devotion** to the **Stations of the Cross**. The **confraternity** can be established in any church or chapel where the Stations have been erected, but must consist of at least fourteen members. To obtain the **indulgences** attached to the confraternity, a member may make the Stations on his or her own, holding in his hand a **crucifix** which has been blessed by a priest in authority in the confraternity, or someone properly delegated to do so.

Way of the Cross, Pious Union of the Perpetual, a spiritual association under the spiritual guidance of the Franciscans, which was originally founded by them in their church in Bordeaux, but the seat of which was later transferred to Rome. Membership of this **confraternity** is on two levels: those who undertake to make the **Stations of the Cross** once a week, and those who say they will do so once a month, on a particular day assigned to them. The ideal is not to make the Stations individually but in groups, and on two particular days in the year, on Passion Sunday and on the first **Sunday** in November, members gather to make the Stations with especial solemnity. As well as fostering **devotion** to the Stations of the Cross, members pray for the conversion of sinners, make reparation for injuries against Christ, and pray for the triumph of the Church.

weather, patron saints of, include Magnus of Fussen (died 772), who was invoked against the danger of hail to the harvest and lightning to the farmers, though this latter seems to have arisen because he was recorded as having driven vermin from the fields with a **blessing** and was in consequence prayed to by farmers, who extended his protection to all the dangers they found themselves in; St Vitus (died c. 300), is said to have been saved from martyrdom by a great tempest - hence he was invoked against danger from lightning and storms.

weekdays, in liturgical terms known as *feria II, feria III* and so on, only the Lord's day, *dies Dominica*, being given a name of its own: the others were simply numbered from it apart from Saturday which retained the Jewish name of "Sabbath" (*sabbatum*). The pagan names were not taken over into the Church's **calendar** presumably because they were derived from pagan gods. Jews fasted on Tuesdays and Thursdays: Christians fasted on Wednesdays and Fridays. To be different from Judaism may have been one motive for the choice of day, but Friday, *feria VI*, was kept in memory of Christ's death, and it was proposed by Tertullian that Wednesday was also a **fast** because it was on that day of the week that Judas betrayed Christ. From the fourth century to the eleventh in some parts of the Western Church, including Rome, **Saturday** was also kept as a fast day, though in the eleventh century it was commuted to a day of **abstinence**. From the ninth or tenth centuries the **hymns** at Vespers have day by day recalled the various days of creation, but on the whole the development of special significance to the days of the week within the mass was a later development. In the early Middle Ages it was not the custom to say mass daily, and when it was celebrated it was commonly a votive mass. The English monk Alcuin (c. 735-804), however, allotted certain themes to certain days of the week - he had the votive mass of the **Virgin Mary** on Saturday, for example, and on **Friday** naturally enough that of the Passion of Christ - and such customs have survived down to modern times (though not the medieval practice of offering mass for those in **purgatory** on a Monday, on the grounds that they had been given a day off suffering on Sunday). So in a Roman missal printed before the liturgical changes which began in the mid-1950s, the votive masses were assigned as follows: Monday, it being the day nearest to Sunday,

Mass of the Trinity; Tuesday, Mass of the **angels**; Wednesday, Mass of the apostles, with that of St **Joseph** being added in 1920; Thursday, Mass either of the Holy Spirit or after the development of the **feast** of **Corpus Christi** in the thirteenth century, the eucharist: Christ the eternal high priest was added in 1935; Friday, of the **cross** or of the passion; Saturday, as was said earlier, was celebrated in honour of Mary.

wells, holy, a **devotion** which is pre-Christian and is to be found in very many of the world's religions, to springs of water and their tutelary deities or spirits. In Christian times these spirits have been converted into **saints**, or, frequently, into the **Virgin Mary**. Springs are still associated with the presence of the divine: witness the miraculous waters of the spring at **Lourdes**, for example. In Britain the best-known example is that of **Saint Winefride's Well** at Holywell in Wales.

Winefride's Well, Saint, a shrine located at Clwyd, in North Wales. The miraculous powers of the spring water have been attested at least from the twelfth century, when the life of St Winefride was written at Shrewsbury, an abbey which housed her supposed **relics**. According to the legend, Winefride was the niece of St Beuno, a Welsh abbot (who also had a **holy well**). When about the year 634 she was beheaded by a rejected suitor, Prince Caradoc, a fountain sprang up where her head hit the earth. Beuno then raised her to life again, and she became abbess of a convent at the place still known as Holywell. The written *Life* almost certainly reflects earlier traditions, so it is uncertain when **devotion** to the shrine began, but it lasted throughout the Middle Ages and survived the Reformation. It is still alive today, though in 1917 mining activity diverted the original spring of water and another one had to be introduced. During medieval times it was, for example, visited by King Henry V, who came there to give thanks after his victory at Agincourt. The present chapel was probably built by Lady Margaret Beaufort, the mother of King Henry VII. Pilgrims bathe in the water three times, in memory of Beuno's promise that Winefride would grant their requests, if not at the first time of asking, then at the second or third.

Work of St Philomena, Archsodality of the, a society founded in 1885 and raised to the rank of an Archsodality the following year. Its members were to pray to God through the intercession of St **Philomena**, that those who had left the Christian path might return to it, that there might be more vocations to the priesthood, and that the clergy might grow in perfection. There were three classes of members: those who simply recited the statutory prayers, those who bought and read the **confraternity**'s periodical (*The Messenger of St Philomena*) and supported it financially, and those who wore the girdle of St Philomena, a belt of red and white with two knots at one end to symbolize the Saint's double title as virgin and martyr. As well as the prayer, "Saint Philomena pray for us", members were encouraged also to pray to St **John Vianney**, who had a particular **devotion** to the saint.

Y

Youth of St Anthony, Pious Union of, a society founded in Spain at the beginning of the twentieth century, and under the spiritual guidance of the Franciscans, whose Minister General is its head. Its purpose is to seek the protection of St Anthony of Padua for children. Members are divided into three classes: there is the adult group, who have care of the children; then the children themselves are divided into two groups, those who have received their first communion, and those who still desire to do so.

APPENDIX

The calendar of the Latin (Roman) Rite of the Catholic Church changed very considerably in 1969. On the left-hand side of Table 1 are listed the fixed liturgical celebrations as they were in the mid 1950s, before any major alterations occurred. On the right-hand side are listed the festivals as published in the Roman Missal of 1970. As can easily be seen, the 1970 calendar is vastly more straightforward with only four ranks of celebration. The pre-1970 calendar was rather more complicated than it has been possible to show. On very many days in the year - including Christmas Day - at least one other saint was commemorated in addition to the celebration noted here. There were, moreover, several ranks of "Octaves", though the Table distinguishes between only two. If the "Optional Memorials" are omitted from the post-1970 list it can be seen that there are relatively few obligatory liturgical celebrations.

Table 2 lists the moveable feasts of the Western Church. A number of these depend for their precise date upon the date of Easter Sunday, and this in turn depends upon the lunar calendar: it falls on the first Sunday following the full moon after the Spring Equinox in the Northern Hemisphere.

TABLE 1

Jan	Feast	Rank	Feast	Rank
1	Circumcision of the Lord and the Octave of Christmas	Double of 2nd class	Solemnity of the Mother of God and Octave of Christmas	Solemnity
2	Octave of S. Stephen	Simple	Ss. Basil and Gregory	Memorial
3	Octave of S. John the Apostle	Simple		
4	Octave of the Holy Innocents	Simple		
5	Vigil of the Epiphany	Semi Double		
6	Epiphany	Double of 1st Class with privileged Octave	Epiphany	Solemnity
7	Of the Octave	Semi Double	S. Raymund of Peñafort	Optional Memorial
8	Of the Octave	Semi Double		
9	Of the Octave	Semi Double		
10	Of the Octave	Semi Double		
11	Of the Octave	Semi Double		
12	Of the Octave	Semi Double		
13	Octave of the Epiphany	Greater Double	S. Hilary	Optional Memorial
14	S. Hilary	Double		
15	S. Paul, the First Hermit	Double		
16	S. Marcellus	Semi Double		
17	S. Anthony, Abbot	Double	S. Anthony, Abbot	Memorial
18	Peter's Chair at Rome	Greater Double		
19	Ss. Marius, Martha et al.	Double		
20	Ss. Fabian and Sebastian	Double	Ss. Fabian and Sebastian	Optional Memorial
21	S. Agnes	Double	S. Agnes	Memorial

Jan	Feast	Rank	Feast	Rank
22	Ss. Vincent and Anastasius	Semi Double	S. Vincent	Optional Memorial
23	S. Raymund of Peñafort	Semi Double		
24	S. Timothy	Double	S. Francis of Sales	Memorial
25	Conversion of S. Paul	Greater Double	Conversion of S. Paul	Feast
26	S. Polycarp	Double	Ss. Timothy and Titus	Memorial
27	S. John Chrysostom	Double	S. Angela dei Merici	Optional Memorial
28	S. Peter Nolasco	Double	S. Thomas Aquinas	Memorial
29	S. Francis of Sales	Double		
30	S. Martina	Semi Double		
31	S. John Bosco	Double	S. John Bosco	Memorial

FEBRUARY

Feb	Feast	Rank	Feast	Rank
1	S. Ignatius of Antioch	Double		
2	Purification of Our Lady	Double of 2nd Class	Presentation of the Lord	Feast
3	S. Blaise	Simple	S. Blaise S. Ansgar	Optional Memorial
4	S. Andrew Corsini	Double		
5	S. Agatha	Double	S. Agatha	Memorial
6	S. Titus	Double	Ss. Paul Miki and Companions	Memorial
7	S. Romuald	Double		
8	S. John of Matha	Double	S. Jerome Emiliani	Optional Memorial
9	S. Cyril of Alexandria	Double		
10	S. Scholastica	Double	S. Scholastica	Memorial
11	Apparition of the Immaculate Virgin Mary	Greater Double	Our Lady of Lourdes	Optional Memorial
12	Seven Holy Founders of the Servite Order	Double		
13				
14	S. Valentine	Simple	Ss. Cyril and Methodius	Memorial
15	Ss. Faustinus and Jovita	Simple		
16				
17			Seven Holy Founders of the Servite Order	Optional Memorial
18	S. Simeon	Simple		
19				
20				
21			S. Peter Damian	Optional Memorial
22	Chair of S. Peter at Antioch	Greater Double	Chair of S. Peter	Feast
23	S. Peter Damian	Double	S. Polycarp	Memorial

Feb	Feast	Rank	Feast	Rank
24	S. Matthew	Double of the 2nd class		
25				
26				
27	S. Gabriel of the Sorrowing Virgin	Double		
28				

Mar	Feast	Rank	Feast	Rank
1				
2				
3				
4	S. Casimir	Semi Double	S. Casimir	Optional Memorial
5				
6	Ss. Perpetua and Felicity	Double		
7	S. Thomas Aquinas	Double	Ss. Perpetua and Felicity	Memorial
8	S. John of God	Double	S. John of God	Optional Memorial
9	S. Frances of Rome	Double	S. Frances of Rome	Optional Memorial
10	Forty Martyrs of Sebaste	Semi Double		
11				
12	S. Gregory, Pope	Double		
13				
14				
15				
16				
17	S. Patrick	Double	S. Patrick	Optional Memorial
18	S. Cyril of Jerusalem	Double	S. Cyril of Jerusalem	Optional Memorial
19	S. Joseph	Double of 1st class	S. Joseph	Solemnity
20				
21	S. Benedict	Greater Double		
22				
23			S. Turibius	Optional Memorial
24	S. Gabriel	Greater Double		

Mar	Feast	Rank	Feast	Rank
25	Annunciation of the Virgin Mary	Double of 1st class	Annunciation of the Lord	Solemnity
26				
27	S. John of Damascus	Double		
28	S. John of Capistrano	Semi Double		
29				
30				
31				

Apr	Feast	Rank	Feast	Rank
1				
2	S. Francis of Paola	Double	S. Francis of Paola	Optional Memorial
3				
4	S. Isidore	Double	S. Isidore	Optional Memorial
5	S. Vincent Ferrer	Double	S. Vincent Ferrer	Optional Memorial
6				
7			S. John Baptist de la Salle	Memorial
8				
9				
10				
11	S. Leo I	Double	S. Stanislas	Optional Memorial
12				
13	S. Hermingild	Semi Double	S. Martin I	Optional Memorial
14	S. Justin	Double		
15				
16				
17	S. Anicetus	Simple		
18				
19				
20				
21	S. Anselm	Double	S. Anselm	Optional Memorial
22	Ss. Soter and Caius	Semi Double		
23	S. George	Semi Double	S. George	Optional Memorial
24	S. Fidelis of Sigmaringen	Double	S. Fidelis of Sigmaringen	Optional Memorial

Apr	Feast	Rank	Feast	Rank
25	S. Mark	Double of 2nd class	S. Mark	Feast
26	Ss. Cletus and Marcellinus	Semi Double		
27	S. Peter Canisius	Double		
28	S. Paul of the Cross	Double	S. Peter Chanel	Optional Memorial
29	S. Peter Martyr	Double	S. Catherine of Siena	Memorial
30	S. Catherine of Siena	Double	S. Pius V	Optional Memorial

May	Feast	Rank	Feast	Rank
1	Ss. Philip and James	Double of 2nd class	S. Joseph the Worker	Optional Memorial
2	S. Athanasius	Double	S. Athanasius	Memorial
3	Finding of the Holy Cross	Double of 2nd Class	Ss. Philip and James	Feast
4	S. Monica	Double		
5	S. Pius V	Double		
6	S. John before the Latin Gate	Greater Double		
7	S. Stanislas	Double		
8	Apparition of S. Michael	Greater Double		
9	S. Gregory Nazianzen	Double		
10	S. Antonine	Double		
11				
12	S. Nereus et al.	Semi Double	Ss. Nereus and Achilles S. Pancras	Optional Memorial
13	S. Robert Bellarmine	Double		
14	S. Boniface	Simple	S. Matthew	Feast
15	S. John Baptist de la Salle	Double		
16	S. Ubald	Semi Double		
17	S. Paschal Baylon	Double		
18	S. Venantius	Double	S. John I	Optional Memorial
19	S. Peter Celestine	Double		
20	S. Bernardine of Siena	Semi Double	S. Bernardine of Siena	Optional Memorial
21				
22				
23				
24				

May	Feast	Rank	Feast	Rank
25	S. Gregory VII	Double	S. Bede S. Gregory VII	Optional Memorial
26	S. Philip Neri	Double	S. Philip Neri	Memorial
27	S. Bede	Double	S. Augustine of Canterbury	Optional Memorial
28	S. Augustine of Canterbury	Double		
29	S. Mary Magdalene dei Pazzi	Semi Double		
30	S. Felix I	Simple		
31	S. Angela dei Merici	Double	The Visitation of B.V. Mary	Feast

Jun	Feast	Rank	Feast	Rank
1			S. Justin	Memorial
2	Ss. Marcellinus, Peter and Erasmus	Simple	Ss. Marcellinus and Peter	Optional Memorial
3			Ss. Charles Lwanga and Companions	Memorial
4	S. Francis Caracciolo	Double		
5	S. Boniface	Double	S. Boniface	Memorial
6	S. Norbert	Double	S. Norbert	Optional Memorial
7				
8				
9	Ss. Primus and Felician	Simple	S. Ephraem	Optional Memorial
10	S. Margaret	Semi Double		
11	S. Barnabas	Greater Double	S. Barnabas	Memorial
12	S. John of Sahagún	Double		
13	S. Anthony of Padua	Double	S. Anthony of Padua	Memorial
14	S. Basil	Double		
15	Ss. Vitus, Modestus and Crescentia	Simple		
16				
17				
18	S. Ephraem	Double		
19	S. Juliana Falconieri	Double	S. Romuald	Optional Memorial
20	S. Silverius	Simple		
21	S. Aloysius	Double	S. Aloysius	Memorial
22	S. Paulinus	Double	S. Paulinus Ss. John Fisher and Thomas More	Optional Memorial
23	Vigil of S. John the Baptist			

Jun	Feast	Rank	Feast	Rank
24	Birthday of S. John the Baptist	Double of 1st class with Octave	Birthday of S. John the Baptist	Solemnity
25	S. William	Double		
26	Ss. John and Paul	Double		
27	Of the Octave	Semi Double	S. Cyril of Alexandria	Optional Memorial
28	S. Irenaeus	Double	S. Irenaeus	Memorial
29	Ss. Peter and Paul	Double of 1st class with Octave	Ss. Peter and Paul	Solemnity
30	Commemoration of S. Paul	Greater Double	Protomartyrs of the Roman Church	Optional Memorial

Jul	Feast	Rank	Feast	Rank
1	The Precious Blood	Double of 1st class		
2	The Visitation of Our Lady	Double of 2nd class		
3	S. Leo II	Semi Double	S. Thomas	Feast
4	Of the Octave	Semi Double	S. Elisabeth of Portugal	Optional Memorial
5	S. Anthony Mary Zaccaria	Double	S. Anthony Mary Zaccaria	Optional Memorial
6	Octave of Ss. Peter and Paul	Greater Double	S. Maria Goretti	Optional Memorial
7	Ss. Cyril and Methodius	Double		
8	S. Elisabeth of Portugal	Semi Double		
9				
10	Seven Holy Brothers	Semi Double		
11	S. Pius I	Simple	S. Benedict	Memorial
12	S. John Gualbert	Double		
13	S. Anacletus	Semi Double	S. Henry	Optional Memorial
14	S. Bonaventure	Double	S. Camillus de Lellis	Optional Memorial
15	S. Henry	Semi Double	S. Bonaventure	Memorial
16	Our Lady of Mount Carmel	Great Double	Our Lady of Mount Carmel	Optional Memorial
17	S. Alexius	Semi Double		
18	S. Camillus de Lellis	Double		
19	S. Vincent de Paul	Double		
20	S. Jerome Emiliani	Double		
21	S. Praxede	Simple	S. Laurence of Brindisi	Optional Memorial
22	S. Mary Magdelene	Double	S. Mary Magdelene	Memorial
23	S. Apollinaris	Double	S. Birgitta	Optional Memorial

Jul	Feast	Rank	Feast	Rank
24	Vigil of S. James			
25	S. James	Double of 2nd class	S. James	Feast
26	S. Anne	Double of 2nd class	Ss. Joachim and Anne	Memorial
27	S. Pantaleon	Simple		
28	Ss. Nazarius et al.	Semi Double		
29	S. Martha	Semi Double	S. Martha	Feast
30	Ss. Abdon and Sennen	Simple	S. Peter Chrysologus	Optional Memorial
31	S. Ignatius Loyola	Greater Double	S. Ignatius Loyola	Memorial

Aug	Feast	Rank	Feast	Rank
1	S. Peter in Chains	Greater Double	S. Alphonsus de' Liguori	Memorial
2	S. Alphonsus de' Liguori	Double	S. Eusebius of Vercelli	Optional Memorial
3	The Finding of S. Stephen	Semi Double		
4	S. Dominic	Greater Double	S. John Vianney	Memorial
5	Dedication of the Church of Our Lady of the Snow	Greater Double	Dedication of the Basilica of Santa Maria Maggiore	Optional Memorial
6	The Transfiguration	Double of 2nd class	The Transfiguration	Feast
7	S. Cajetan	Double	Ss. Xystus II and Companions S. Cajetan	Optional Memorial
8	Ss. Cyriac et al.	Semi Double	S. Dominic	Memorial
9	S. John Vianney	Double		
10	S. Laurence	Double of 2nd class with Octave	S. Laurence	Feast
11	Ss. Tiburtius and Susanna	Simple	S. Clare	Memorial
12	S. Clare	Double		
13	Ss. Hippoloytus and Cassian	Simple	Ss. Pontianus and Hippolytus	Optional Memorial
14	Vigil of the Assumption			
15	The Assumption	Double of 1st class with Octave	The Assumption	Feast
16	S. Joachim	Double of 2nd class	S. Stephen of Hungary	Optional Memorial
17	S. Hyacinth	Double		
18	Of the Octave	Semi Double		
19	S. John Eudes	Double	S. John Eudes	Optional Memorial
20	S. Bernard	Double	S. Bernard	Double

Aug	Feast	Rank	Feast	Rank
21	S. Jane Frances de Chantal	Double	S. Pius X	Memorial
22	Immaculate Heart of Mary	Double of 2nd class	The Queenship of Mary	Feast
23	S. Philip Benizi	Double	S. Rose of Lima	Optional Memorial
24	S. Bartholemew	Double of 2nd class	S. Bartholemew	Feast
25	S. Louis	Semi Double	S. Louis S. Joseph Calasanz	Optional Memorial
26	S. Zephyrinus	Simple		
27	S. Joseph Calasanz	Double	S. Monica	Memorial
28	S. Augustine	Double	S. Augustine	Memorial
29	The Beheading of S. John the Baptist	Greater Double	The Passion of S. John the Baptist	Memorial
30	S. Rose of Lima	Double		
31	S. Raymund Nonnatus	Double		

Sep	Feast	Rank	Feast	Rank
1	S. Giles	Simple		
2	S. Stephen	Semi Double		
3			S. Gregory I	Memorial
4				
5	S. Laurence Giustiniani	Semi Double		
6				
7				
8	The Birthday of Our Lady	Double of 2nd class	The Birthday of Our Lady	Feast
9	S. Gorgonius	Simple		
10	S. Nicholas of Tolentino	Double		
11	Ss. Protus and Hyacinth	Simple		
12	The Holy Name of Mary	Greater Double		
13			S. John Chrysostom	Memorial
14	Exaltation of the Holy Cross	Greater Double	Exaltation of the Holy Cross	Feast
15	Seven Sorrows of Our Lady	Double of 2nd class	Our Lady of Sorrows	Memorial
16	Ss. Cornelius and Cyprian	Semi Double	Ss. Cornelius and Cyprian	Memorial
17	The Stigmata of S. Francis	Double	S. Robert Bellarmine	Optional Memorial
18	S. Joseph of Cupertino	Double		
19	Ss. Januarius and Companions	Double	S. Januarius	Optional Memorial
20	Ss. Eustace and Companions	Double		
21	S. Matthew	Double of 2nd class	S. Matthew	Feast
22	S. Thomas of Villanova	Double		

Sep	Feast	Rank	Feast	Rank
23	S. Linus	Semi Double		
24	Our Lady of Ransom	Greater Double		
25				
26	Ss. Cyprian and Justina	Simple	Ss. Cosmas and Damian	Optional Memorial
27	Ss. Cosmas and Damian	Semi Double	S. Vincent de Paul	Memorial
28	S. Wenceslas	Semi Double	S. Wenceslas	Optional Memorial
29	Dedication of S. Michael	Double of 1st class	Ss. Michael, Gabriel and Raphael	Feast
30	S. Jerome	Double	S. Jerome	Memorial

Oct	Feast	Rank	Feast	Rank
1	S. Remy	Simple	S. Teresa of Lisieux	Memorial
2	Guardian Angels	Greater Double	Guardian Angels	Memorial
3	S. Teresa	Double		
4	S. Francis of Assisi	Greater Double	S. Francis of Assisi	Memorial
5	S. Placid and Companions	Simple		
6	S. Bruno	Double	S. Bruno	Optional Memorial
7	The Holy Rosary	Double of 2nd class	Our Lady of the Rosary	Memorial
8	S. Bridget	Double		
9	S. John Leonard	Double	Ss. Denis and Companions S. John Leonard	Optional Memorial
10	S. Francis Borgia	Semi Double		
11	The Motherhood of Our Lady	Double of 2nd class		
12				
13	S. Edward	Semi Double		
14	S. Callistus I	Double	S. Callistus I	Optional Memorial
15	S. Teresa of Avila	Double	S. Teresa of Avila	Memorial
16	S. Hedwig	Semi Double	S. Hedwig S. Margaret Mary Alacocque	Optional Memorial
17	S. Margaret Mary Alacocque	Double	S. Ignatius of Antioch	Memorial
18	S. Luke	Double of 2nd class	S. Luke	Feast
19	S. Peter of Alcántara	Double	Ss. John de Brébeuf and Companions S. Paul of the Cross	Optional Memorial
20	S. John of Kanti	Double		
21	S. Hilarion	Simple		
22				

Oct	Feast	Rank	Feast	Rank
23			S. John of Capistrano	Optional Memorial
24	S. Raphael	Greater Double	S. Anthony Mary Claret	Optional Memorial
25	Ss. Chrysanthus and Daria	Simple		
26	S. Evaristus	Simple		
27	Vigil of Ss. Simon and Jude			
28	Ss. Simon and Jude	Double of 2nd class	Ss. Simon and Jude	Feast
29				
30				
31				

Nov	Feast	Rank	Feast	Rank
1	All Saints	Double of 1st class with Octave	All Saints	Solemnity
2	All Souls	Double	All Souls	Solemnity
3	Of the Octave	Semi Double	S. Martin de Porres	Optional Memorial
4	S. Charles Borromeo	Double	S. Charles Borromeo	Memorial
5	Of the Octave	Semi Double		
6	Of the Octave	Semi Double		
7	Of the Octave	Semi Double		
8	Octave of all Saints	Greater Double		
9	Dedication of Archbasilica of Our Saviour	Double of 2nd Class	Dedication of the Lateran Basilica	Feast
10	S. Andrew Avellino	Double	S. Leo	Memorial
11	S. Martin	Double	S. Martin	Memorial
12	S. Martin I	Semi Double	S. Josaphat	Memorial
13	S. Didacus	Semi Double		
14	S. Josaphat	Double		
15	S. Albert	Double	S. Albert	Optional Memorial
16	S. Gertrude	Double	S. Margaret of Scotland S. Gertrude	Optional Memorial
17	S. Gregory the Wonder-Worker	Semi Double	S. Elisabeth of Hungary	Memorial
18	Dedication of the Basilicas of Ss. Peter and Paul	Greater Double	Dedication of the Basilicas of Ss. Peter and Paul	Optional Memorial
19	S. Elisabeth of Hungary	Double		
20	S. Felix of Valois	Double		
21	Presentation of Our Lady	Greater Double	Presentation of Our Lady	Optional Memorial
22	S. Cecilia	Double	S. Cecilia	Memorial

Nov	Feast	Rank	Feast	Rank
23	S. Clement I	Double	S. Clement I S. Columba	Optional Memorial
24	S. John of the Cross	Double		
25	S. Catherine	Double		
26	S. Silvester	Double		
27				
28				
29	Vigil of S. Andrew			
30	S. Andrew	Double of 2nd class	S. Andrew	Feast

Dec	Feast	Rank	Feast	Rank
1				
2	S. Bibiana	Semi Double		
3	S. Francis Xavier	Greater Double	S. Francis Xavier	Memorial
4	S. Peter Chrysologus	Double	S. John Damascene	Optional Memorial
5	S. Sabbas	Commem- oration		
6	S. Nicholas	Double	S. Nicholas	Optional Memorial
7	S. Ambrose	Double	S. Ambrose	Memorial
8	The Immaculate Conception	Double of 1st class with Octave	The Immaculate Conception	Solemnity
9	Of the Octave	Semi Double		
10	Of the Octave	Semi Double		
11	S. Damasus I	Semi Double	S. Damasus I	Optional Memorial
12	Of the Octave	Semi Double	S. Jane Frances de Chantal	Optional Memorial
13	S. Lucy	Double		
14	Of the Octave	Semi Double	S. John of the Cross	Memorial
15	Octave of the Immaculate Conception	Greater Double		
16	S. Eusebius	Semi Double		
17				
18				
19				
20	Vigil of S. Thomas			
21	S. Thomas	Double of 2nd Class	S. Peter Canisius	Optional Memorial
22				
23			S. John of Kanti	Optional Memorial

Dec	Feast	Rank	Feast	Rank
24	Vigil of the Nativity			
25	The Nativity	Double of 1st class with privileged Octave	The Nativity	Solemnity
26	S. Stephen the First Martyr	Double of 2nd class with Octave	S. Stephen the First Martyr	Feast
27	S. John	Double of 2nd class with Octave	S. John	Feast
28	Holy Innocents	Double of 2nd class with Octave	Holy Innocents	Feast
29	S. Thomas Becket	Double	S. Thomas Becket	Optional Memorial
30	Of the Octave	Semi Double		
31	S. Silvester I	Double	S. Silvester I	Optional Memorial

TABLE 2

Date	Pre 1970	Post 1970
Wednesday after third Sunday of Advent	Ember Day	
Friday after third Sunday of Advent	Ember Day	
Saturday after third Sunday of Advent	Ember Day	
Sunday within the Octave of Christmas (or otherwise 30 December)		Holy Family
Sunday between the Circumcision and the Epiphany	Holy Name of Jesus	
Sunday with the Octave of the Epiphany	Holy Family	The Baptism of the Lord
Three Sundays before the first Sunday of Lent	Septuagesima	
Two Sundays before the first Sunday of Lent	Sexagesima	
Sunday before the first Sunday in Lent	Quinquagesima	
Wednesday after first Sunday in Lent	Ember Day	
Friday after first Sunday in Lent	Ember Day	
Saturday after first Sunday in Lent	Ember Day	
Fifth Sunday in Lent	Passion Sunday (followed by Passion Week)	
Friday in Passion Week	Seven Sorrows of Our Lady	
Sunday before Easter	Palm Sunday	
	Easter	Easter
Wednesday after second Sunday after Easter	Solemnity of S. Joseph, Patron of the Universal Church	
Monday before Ascension	Rogation Day	
Tuesday before Ascension	Rogation Day	
Wednesday before Ascension	Rogation Day	

Date	Pre 1970	Post 1970
Forty days after Easter	Ascension Thursday	Ascension Thursday
Fifty days after Easter	Pentecost	Pentecost
Wednesday after Pentecost	Ember Day	
Friday after Pentecost	Ember Day	
Saturday after Pentecost	Ember Day	
Sunday after Pentecost	Trinity Sunday	Trinity Sunday
Thursday after Trinity Sunday	Corpus Christi	Corpus Christi
Friday after the Octave of Corpus Christi	The Sacred Heart of Jesus	The Sacred Heart of Jesus
Saturday after the second Sunday after Pentecost		The Immaculate Heart of Our Lady
Wednesday after Exaltation of the Cross (14 September)	Ember Day	
Friday after Exaltation of the Cross (14 September)	Ember Day	
Saturday after Exaltation of the Cross (14 September)	Ember Day	
Last Sunday in October	Kingship of Christ	
Last Sunday of the liturgical year		Jesus Christ, the Universal King

BIBLIOGRAPHY

Angelis, Seraphinus de, *De Fidelium Associationibus*. Naples: M. d'Auria, 1959.

Aubert, Roger, *The Christian Centuries, Volume Five: The Church in a Secularised Society*. London: Darton, Longman and Todd, 1978.

Begg, Ean, *The Cult of the Black Virgin*. London: Arkana, 1985.

Beringer, Fr., *Les Indulgences: Leur Nature et leur Usage*. Paris: P. Liethielleux, 1925.

Bhardwaj, S.M. and Rinschede, G. (eds.), *Pilgrimage in World Religions* (Geographia Religionum 4). Berlin: Dietrich Reimer, 1988.

Bowie, Fiona (ed.), *Beguine Spirituality: An Anthology*. London: SPCK, 1989.

Burke, Peter, "How to be a Counter-Reformation Saint", in *The Historical Anthropology of Early Modern Italy*. Cambridge: Cambridge University Press, 1987.

Cabassut, A., "La Dévotion au Nom de Jésus dans l'Église d'Occident", in *La Vie Spirituelle*, no. 369 (January, 1952), pp. 46- 69.

Carroll, Michael P., *Catholic Cults & Devotions, a Psychological Inquiry*. Kingston: McGill-Queen's University Press, 1989.

————, *The Cult of the Virgin Mary: Psychological Origins*. Princeton, NJ: Princeton University Press, 1986.

The Catholic Encyclopedia. London: Caxton, 1907-1914.

Catholicisme: Hier, Aujourd'hui, Demain. Paris: Letouzey et Ané, 1948-.

Christian Jr, William A., *Apparitions in Late Medieval and Renaissance Spain*. Princeton, NJ: Princeton University Press, 1989.

————, *Moving Crucifixes in Modern Spain*. Princeton, NJ: Princeton University Press, 1992.

Clayton, Mary, *The Cult of the Virgin Mary in Anglo-Saxon England* (Cambridge Studies in Anglo-Saxon England 2). Cambridge: Cambridge University Press, 1990.

Code of Canon Law in English Translation. London: Collins, 1983.

Connelly, Joseph, *Hymns of the Roman Liturgy*. London: Longmans, 1957.

Coriden, James *et al.* (eds.), *The Code of Canon Law: Text and Commentary.* London: Geoffrey Chapman, 1985.

Cross, F.L. and Livingstone, E.A. (eds.), *The Oxford Dictionary of the Christian Church.* London: Oxford University Press, 1974.

Davies, J.G., *Pilgrimage Yesterday and Today.* London: SCM Press, 1988.

De Flores, Stefano and Meo, Salvatore (eds.), *Nuovo Dizionario di Mariologia.* Milan: Edizione Paoline, 1986.

Delooz, Pierre, *Sociologie et Canonisations.* The Hague: Martinus Nijhoff, 1969.

Dictionnaire d'Archéologie Chrétienne et de Liturgie. Paris: Letouzey et Ané, 1907-53.

Dictionnaire de Spiritualité. Paris: Beauchesne, 1937-.

Dictionnaire d'Histoire et de Géographie Ecclésiastique. Paris: Letouzey et Ané, 1912-.

Du Manoir, Hubert (ed.), *Maria: Études sur la Sainte Vierge.* Paris: Beauchesne, 1949-71.

Duffy, Eamon, *The Stripping of the Altars.* London: Yale University Press, 1992.

Farmer, David Hugh, *The Oxford Dictionary of Saints.* Oxford: Oxford University Press, 1987.

Fassler, Margot, "The Feast of Fools and *Danielis ludus*" in Kelly, Thomas Forrest (ed.), *Plainsong in the Age of Polyphony.* Cambridge: Cambridge University Press, 1992, pp. 65-99.

Filas, Francis L., *Joseph: The Man Closest to Jesus.* Boston, MA: St Paul's Editions, 1962.

Finucane, Ronald C, *Miracles and Pilgrims: Popular Beliefs in Medieval England.* London: J.M. Dent, 1977.

Garrido, Manuel, *Curso de Liturgia Romana.* Madrid: Biblioteca de Autores Cristianos, 1961.

Geary, Patrick J., *Furta Sacra: Theft of Relics in the Central Middle Ages.* Princeton, NJ: Princeton University Press, 1978.

Gillet, H.M., *The Story of the Relics of the Passion.* Oxford: Basil Blackwell, 1935.

Gougaud, Louis, *Devotional and Ascetic Practices in the Middle Ages.* London: Burns, Oates and Washbourne, 1927.

Graef, Hilda, *Mary: A History of Doctrine and Devotion.* London and New York: Sheed and Ward, vol. 1, 1963; vol. 2, 1965.

Jackson, Bernard, *Places of Pilgrimage.* London: Geoffrey Chapman, 1981.

Jacobs, Michael, *The Road to Santiago de Compostela.* London: Viking, 1991.

Jounel, Pierre, "Le Culte des Reliques", in *Notitiae*, 270-271 (1989), pp. 212-22.

Jounel, Pierre, "Problèmes relatifs au Culte des Saintes Reliques", in *Notitiae*, 270-271 (1989), pp. 222-6.

Jungmann, Joseph A., *The Mass of the Roman Rite*. London: Burns & Oates; New York: Benziger, 1951 and 1955 (2 vols).

Jungmann, Joseph A., *Pastoral Liturgy*. London(?): Challoner Publications, 1962.

Kantorowicz, Ernst H., *Laudes Regiae: A Study in Liturgical Acclamations and Mediaeval Ruler Worship*. Berkeley: University of California Press, 1946.

King, Archdale A., *Holy Water*. London: Burns, Oates and Washbourne, 1926.

Koch, Ludwig, *Jesuiten Lexikon*. Louvain: Verlag der Bibliothek S.J., 1962 (a reprint of the 1932 edition).

Lanzani, Vittorio, "I Patroni", in *Notitiae*, 270-271 (1989), pp. 226-33.

Lapidge, Michael (ed.) *Anglo-Saxon Litanies of the Saints*. London: Henry Bradshaw Society, 1991.

Le Goff, Jacques, *The Birth of Purgatory*. London: Scolar Press, 1984.

Lossky, Nicholas *et al.* (eds.), *Dictionary of the Ecumenical Movement*. Geneva: WCC Publications; London: Council of Churches for Britain and Ireland, 1991.

Laurentin, René, *The Apparitions of the Blessed Virgin Mary Today*. Dublin: Veritas, 1990.

Madden, Daniel M., *A Religious Guide to Europe*. London: Collier Macmillan, 1975.

Maës, Bruno, *Notre Dame de Liesse*. Paris: O.E.I.L., 1991.

Maindron, Gabriel, *Les Apparitions de Kibeho*. Paris: O.E.I.L., 1984.

Maraval, Pierre, *Lieux saints et pèlerinages d'Orient*. Paris: Cerf, 1985.

Martimort, Aimé Georges (ed.), *The Church at Prayer, Volume IV: The Liturgy and Time*. London: Geoffrey Chapman, 1986.

Mocchegiani, Petrus, *Collectio Indulgentiarum Theologice, Canonice ac Historice Digesta*. Quaracchi: Typographi Collegii S. Bonaventurae, 1897.

The New Catholic Encyclopedia. New York: McGraw Hill, 1967 (with later supplementary volumes).

Nolan, Mary Lee and Nolan, Sidney, *Christian Pilgrimage in Modern Western Europe*. Chapel Hill: University of North Carolina Press, 1989.

Orsi, Robert A., "'He keeps me going': Women's Devotion to Saint Jude Thaddeus and the Dialectics of Gender in American Catholicism, 1929-1965", in Kselman, Thomas (ed.), *Belief in History: Innovative Approaches to European and American Religion*. Notre Dame: University of Notre Dame Press, 1991, pp. 137-69.

The Oxford Dictionary of Byzantium. New York: Oxford University Press, 1991.

Poschmann, Bernhard, *Penance and the Anointing of the Sick.* New York: Herder & Herder, 1964.

Power, David and Collins, Mary, *Blessing and Power* (Concilium 178). Edinburgh: T.& T. Clark, 1985.

Radó, Polycarpus, *Enchiridion Liturgicum.* Rome, Herder, 1961.

Raitt, Jill (ed), *Christian Spirituality II: High Middle Ages and Reformation.* London: Routledge and Kegan Paul, 1987.

Richardson, Alan and Bowden, John (eds.), *A New Dictionary of Christian Theology.* London: SCM Press, 1983.

Rinschede, G. and Bhardway, S.M. (eds.), *Pilgrimage in the United States* (Geographia Religionum 5). Berlin: Dietrich Reimer, 1990.

Rollason, David, *Saints and Relics in Anglo-Saxon England.* Oxford: Basil Blackwell, 1989.

Rooney, Lucy and Faricy, Robert, *Medjugorje Journal.* Great Wakering: McCrimmon, 1987.

Rubin, Miri, *Corpus Christi: The Eucharist in Late Medieval Culture.* Cambridge: Cambridge University Press, 1991.

Sánchez-Ventura y Pascual, F., *The Apparitions of Garabandal.* Detroit: San Miguel Publishing, 1966.

Southern, R.W., *Western Society and the Church in the Middle Ages.* Harmondsworth: Penguin Books, 1970.

Sox, David, *Relics and Shrines.* London: George Allen and Unwin, 1985.

Sumption, Jonathan, *Pilgrimage: An Image of Mediaeval Religion.* London: Faber and Faber, 1975.

Talley, Thomas J., *The Origins of the Liturgical Year.* Collegeville, MN: Liturgical Press, 1991.

Tanner, Norman P. (ed.), *Decrees of the Ecumenical Councils.* London: Sheed and Ward; Washington, DC: Georgetown University Press, 1990.

Taves, Ann, *The Household of Faith: Roman Catholic Devotions in Mid-Nineteenth-Century America.* Notre Dame: University of Notre Dame Press, 1986.

Thurston, Herbert J. and Attwater, Donald, *Butler's Lives of the Saints.* London: Burns & Oates, 1981.

Thurston, Herbert J., *Familiar Prayers: Their Origin and History.* London: Burns & Oates, 1953.

———, *Holy Year of Jubilee.* London: Sands, 1900.

———, *Lent and Holy Week: Chapters on Catholic Observance and Ritual.*

London: Longmans, Green & Co., 1904.

———, *The Physical Phenomena of Mysticism*. London: Burns & Oates, 1952.

———, *The Stations of the Cross*. London: Burns & Oates, 1906.

Vauchez, André, "The Saint", in Le Goff, Jacques (ed.), *The Medieval World*. London: Collins and Brown, 1990.

Walsh, Michael (ed.), *Butler's Lives of the Patron Saints*. Tunbridge Wells: Burns & Oates, 1987.

Wilmart, André, *Le "Jubilus" dit de Saint Bernard*. Rome: Edizioni di Storia e Letteratura, 1944.

Wilson, Ian, *The Bleeding Mind*. London: Weidenfeld and Nicolson, 1988.

Woodward, Kenneth L., *Making Saints*. London: Chatto and Windus, 1991.

Zimdars-Swartz, Sandra L., *Encountering Mary*. Princeton, NJ: Princeton University Press, 1991.

INDEX

Entries in **bold** type in the Index are entries in the body of this *Dictionary*, as are "see" and "see also" references.